A COURSE IN ATTIC GREEK, II

1. The Soros, or burial mound, for the 192 Athenians who died at the Battle of Marathon, in 490 BC.

A COURSE IN ATTIC GREEK, II

James K. Finn
and
Frank J. Groten, Jr.

Revised & Expanded by
Patrick G. Lake

3rd Edition

The Hill School
Pottstown, Pennsylvania
2012

THIRD EDITION
ISBN: 978-1-300-05323-1
PRINTED IN THE UNITED STATES OF AMERICA

CONTENTS

PREFACE

This book is a revision of the second half of *A Basic Course for Reading Attic Greek*, a text first conceived of and written in the summer of 1978 by Frank J. Groten, Jr. and my former colleague James K. Finn, to be used in The Hill School's beginning and intermediate Greek courses. Like its companion text, *A Course in Attic Greek* I, this text has preserved the order of presentation of its original, but offers major revisions in terms of grammatical explanations, paradigm charts, appendices, and figures and illustrations. This newly revised text also features additional drill work and places a heavier emphasis on the explanation of euphonic change than its predecessor. All other principles governing the composition of this text are covered in some detail in the first volume.

Once more, thanks are owed to my colleague Henry V. Bender for his encouragement in the pursuit of this project and Headmaster David Dougherty for his support of the Classics generally at The Hill School. The energy and enthusiasm that many professionals in the field showed for this project, among them Charles Cave, Joe Jablonski, and Mark Ciabaton, have certainly guided this text towards its completion. As always, I owe a great debt to my students, who serve as the de facto editors of the text, as they have patiently endured the imperfections of its earlier editions.

The Hill School   Patrick G. Lake, Ph. D.
Pottstown, Pennsylvania
August, 2012

Lesson 31

τίς (τις). εἶς (οὐδείς). πᾶς
Genitive and Dative of Time

<u>τίς, τί</u>

The interrogative pronoun τίς (*who?*), τί (*what?*) is declined as follows:

	<u>singular</u>		<u>plural</u>	
	<u>masculine-feminine</u>	<u>neuter</u>	<u>masculine-feminine</u>	<u>neuter</u>
Nom.	τίς	τί	τίνες	τίνα
Gen.	τίνος (τοῦ)	τίνος (τοῦ)	τίνων	τίνων
Dat.	τίνι (τῷ)	τίνι (τῷ)	τίσι(ν)	τίσι(ν)
Acc.	τίνα	τί	τίνας	τίνα

<u>Notes</u>: The forms in parentheses above are alternate forms, which happen to look identical to the corresponding forms of the definite article in Greek.

The acute accent of τίς, τί <u>never</u> changes to a grave even when its monosyllabic forms precede other Greek words; this provides a crucial means whereby the interrogative (see below) can be differentiated from the indefinite in Greek.

τίς, τί may also be used as an interrogative adjective meaning "<u>which?</u>", "<u>what?</u>". Example:

τίνα δῶρα ἐδέξατο;
Which gifts did he receive?

The form τί (accusative singular) is often used as an interrogative adverb to mean "<u>why?</u>" as well as "<u>what?</u>". Example:

τί φεύγεις;
Why are you fleeing?

<u>τις, τι</u>

The <u>enclitic</u> forms τις, τι are used as indefinite pronouns and adjectives meaning "a," "a certain," "certain" (pl.), "some," "any," "someone," "anyone," "something," "anything." When used as an adjective, τις, τι typically follows the word it modifies. Examples:

δικασταί τινες νόμοις τισὶν οὐ πείθονται.
Certain judges do not obey certain/any/some laws.

ἔλεξέ τι, ἀλλ᾽ οὐκ ἤκουσα.
He said something/anything/a certain thing, but I did not hear him.

εἷς (οὐδείς)

a. The cardinal number εἷς, μία, ἕν (*one*) is declined as follows:

singular

	masculine	feminine	neuter
Nom.	εἷς	μία	ἕν
Gen.	ἑνός	μιᾶς	ἑνός
Dat.	ἑνί	μιᾷ	ἑνί
Acc.	ἕνα	μίαν	ἕν

b. οὐδείς (μηδείς), "no one," a compound of οὐδέ + εἷς, is declined like εἷς, μία, ἕν. The neuter οὐδέν (μηδέν) means "nothing."

οὐδείς (μηδείς), οὐδεμία (μηδέν) may also be used as an adjective meaning "no." Example:

περὶ τούτων οὐδεμίαν γνώμην ἔχει.
He has no (i.e. not one) opinion about these things.

πᾶς

The adjective πᾶς, πᾶσα, πᾶν ("every," "all") is declined like the <u>first aorist active participle</u> (see Lesson 28) as follows:

singular

	masculine	feminine	neuter
Nom.	πᾶς	πᾶσα	πᾶν
Gen.	παντός	πάσης	παντός
Dat.	παντί	πάσῃ	παντί
Acc.	πάντα	πᾶσαν	πᾶν

<u>plural</u>

	masculine	feminine	neuter
Nom.	πάντες	πᾶσαι	πάντα
Gen.	πάντων	πασῶν	πάντων
Dat.	πᾶσι(ν)	πάσαις	πᾶσι(ν)
Acc.	πάντας	πάσας	πάντα

<u>Notes</u>: When modifying a noun, πᾶς <u>usually</u> stands in the predicate position and means "all." Example:

πάντες οἱ ἄνθρωποι σοφοί εἰσιν.
All the men (individually) *are wise.*

When modifying a noun and in the <u>attributive</u> position, πᾶς denotes a (collective) whole. Examples:

οἱ πάντες ἄνθρωποι σοφοί εἰσιν.
(Absolutely) *all the men* (as a group) *are wise.*

ἡ πᾶσα ὁδὸς φυλάττεται.
The whole road is being guarded.

<u>Without the article</u>, πᾶς means "every" or "all" (i. e. "all conceivable"). Examples:

πάντες ἄνθρωποι ἀποθνήσκουσιν.
All men (everywhere) *die.*

πᾶς ἄνθρωπος ἀποθνήσκει.
Every man dies.

πάντες ἀποθνήσκουσιν.
Everyone dies. (lit., *All die*).

πάντα ὁρᾷ.
He sees everything (lit., all things).

Genitive of Time

The genitive case is used in Greek without a preposition to indicate the period of time within (during) which an action takes place. Example:

τᾶυτα μιᾶς ἡμέρας ἐγένετο.
These things happened during (within) one day.

Dative of Time

The dative case is used in Greek without a preposition to denote a <u>definite point of time when</u> an action takes place. Example:

τῇ πρώτῃ ἡμέρᾳ τῇ τοῦ ἔτους ἀπέθανεν.
On the first day of the year he died.

Vocabulary

τίς *who?*

τί *what?, why?*

τις *a, a certain, someone, anyone*

τινες, τινα *certain, some, any*

τι *a, a certain, something, anything*

εἷς, μία ἕν *one*

οὐδείς (μηδείς), οὐδεμία
   (μηδεμία), οὐδέν
   (μηδέν) *no*

οὐδείς (μηδείς) *no one*

οὐδέν (μηδέν) *nothing;*
   (adverb) *in no way, not at all*

οὐδέ (μηδέ) *and not (and ... not),*
   not even, not ... either

πᾶς, πᾶσα, πᾶν *every, all*

ἀγαθός, -ή, -όν *good, brave*

νύξ, νυκτός, ἡ *night*

φύλαξ, φύλακος, ὁ *guard*

Drill A

Give the following forms:

    1. τίς to agree with: φύλακος, πολεμίοις, ἔτος, νυκτί
    2. πᾶς to agree with: ὀνόματα, ἄλλων, πόλιν, δικασταῖς
    3. οὐδείς to agree with: μητρί, νεανίαν, δῶρον, τέλους

Drill B

Translate:

    1. Why did you lead me into danger?
    2. Some citizens are good rulers.

Drill B (continued)

3. Certain gifts were sent during the night.
4. Whom have they honored?
5. Whose (= of whom) body did I see?
6. I provided wine for certain friends.
7. What have you acquired during this year?
8. All the citizens will not forget you.

Drill C

Supply the appropriate form of the interrogative or indefinite adjective in Greek to agree with the noun provided. Translate the pair:

1. γέροντι (a certain)   4. (what) πραγμάτων
2. (what) τέλους   5. (a) φόνον
3. (what) γῇ   6. φύλακας (some)

Exercise A

Translate:

1. ἐγὼ μὲν διδάσκω οὐδένα· εἰ δέ τίς μου λέγοντος ἐθέλει ἀκούειν, οὐδὲν κωλύω αὐτόν, οὐδὲ χρήματα λαμβάνω.
2. οὐδ' εἴ τις ἐπειράσατο ἡμᾶς πάντας παύειν, ἐπαυσάμεθα ἂν λέγοντες περὶ ἀρετῆς.
3. τί πάντα μιᾶς νυκτὸς λαβόντες ὑμᾶς ἔλαθον;
4. τίς ἀνδρῶν ἦν ὁ τολμήσας τάδε;
5. οὐδεὶς γὰρ πᾶσαν ἀρετὴν ἀγαθός.

Exercise B

Translate (using participles wherever possible):

1. The brave guard was pleased because no one blamed (him).
2. What has been written by the Greeks about the soul?
3. Someone has fled after burying that body contrary to the law.
4. If no one had prevented (them), on the same day the enemy would have proceeded through the plain to the river.
5. You have all heard me teaching, and I have advised you well.

Lesson 32

φημί. Indirect Statement

φημί

The irregular verb φημί ("say") is conjugated as follows:

Present Active Indicative

singular	person	plural
φημί	1	φαμέν
φής	2	φατέ
φησί(ν)	3	φασί(ν)

Infinitive   φάναι

Imperfect Active Indicative

singular	person	plural
ἔφην	1	ἔφαμεν
ἔφησθα (ἔφης)	2	ἔφατε
ἔφη	3	ἔφασαν

Notes: All forms of the present indicative except φής are enclitic (compare εἰμί, see Lesson 14).

The first aorist of φημί seldom occurs in Attic prose. The imperfect frequently has the force of an aorist.

οὔ φημι is used to mean "deny," "refuse," "say ... not."

Indirect Statement

An indirect statement is a subordinate clause in which the words, thoughts, perceptions, or feelings of a speaker are reported indirectly. When the main verb of a sentence is one of mental activity or perception, typically the indirect statement takes the form of a subject accusative and an infinitive verb (see Lesson 34 for exceptions). In this construction, the infinitive is negated by οὐ. Example:

Direct Statement: ἡμεῖς θύομεν τοῖς θεοῖς.
We are sacrificing to the gods.

Indirect Statement: τοῖς θεοῖς φημι ἡμᾶς θύειν.
                           I say that we are sacrificing to the gods.

The accusative subject of an indirect statement <u>is omitted</u> in Greek if it is
the same as the subject of the main verb. Any modifiers of the omitted subject are
placed in the nominative case. Examples:

τοῖς θεοῖς φασι θύειν.
They say that they are sacrificing to the gods.

δίκαιοι εἶναί φασιν.
They say that they are just.

Tense of the Infinitive in Indirect Statement

a. The <u>present</u> infinitive represents an action which occurs at the <u>same</u>
time as that of the main verb (time simultaneous). Example:

τοῖς θεοῖς ἔφην αὐτοὺς θύειν.
I said that they were sacrificing to the gods.

<u>Note</u>: Here the present infinitive corresponds to an <u>imperfect indicative</u> in the
direct statement.

b. The <u>aorist</u> infinitive represents an action which occurs <u>before</u> the time
of the main verb (time prior) and corresponds to an <u>aorist indicative</u> in the indirect
statement. <u>Only in indirect statement</u> does the aorist infinitive have time value
(rather than simply expressing aspect). Examples:

τοῖς θεοῖς φασιν ἐκεῖνον θῦσαι.
They say that he / that man sacrificed to the gods.

ἔφη βιβλίον γράψαι.
He said that he wrote (had written) a book.

c. The <u>perfect</u> infinitive is used to indicate <u>prior</u> time when it corresponds
to a perfect or pluperfect indicative in the direct statement. Examples:

βιβλίον φησὶ γεγραφέναι.
He says that he has written a book.

βιβλίον ἔφη γεγραφέναι.
He said that he had written a book.

d. The <u>future</u> infinitive represents an action which occurs <u>after</u> the time of the main verb (time subsequent). Examples:

ἡμᾶς φησι εὖ πράξειν.
He says that we shall fare well.

ἔφη ἀποθανεῖσθαι.
He said that he would be killed.

Vocabulary

δοκέω, δόξω, ἔδοξα, ____, δέδογμαι, ____ *think, imagine; seem, be thought;* (impers.) *it seems best* (dogma)

ἐλπίζω, ____, ἤλπισα, ____, ____, ____ *hope, hope for, expect*

ἡγέομαι, ἡγήσομαι, ἡγησάμην, ____, ἥγημαι, ____ *lead; be leader of* (+ gen.), *be leader for* (+ dat.); *think, consider* (hegemony)

νομίζω, νομιῶ, ἐνόμισα, νενόμικα, νενόμισμαι, ἐνομίσθην *regard as a custom; think, consider; believe in, believe*

οἴομαι (οἶμαι), οἰήσομαι, ____, ____, ____, ᾠήθην *think, suppose*

φημί, φήσω, ἔφησα *say*

ἄγγελος, -ου, ὁ *messenger* (angel)

μάχη, -ης, ἡ *battle, fight*

ἄκων, -ουσα, -ον *unwilling* (often translated as adverb)

ἑκών, -οῦσα, -όν *willing* (often translated as adverb)

Drill A

Give the following forms:

1. aorist active infinitive of:
   μένω, λαμβάνω, ἀθροίζω, ἄγω

2. future middle infinitive of:
   φαίνω, ἡγέομαι, ἀφικνέομαι, δέχομαι

3. perfect active infinitive of:
   πλέω, εὑρίσκω, ἀποθνῄσκω, πάσχω

4. aorist passive infinitive of:
   ἄγω, θάπτω, κρίνω, ὁράω

Drill B

Translate:

1. ὑμᾶς ἔφασαν τῆς νυκτὸς ἀφίξεσθαι.
2. ἔδοξεν οὐκ ὀφθῆναι.
3. ἡγησάμην αὐτὸν τὸν ἄδικον τρόπον αἱρεῖσθαι.
4. οἴει παρασκευαζόμενός τινα λήσειν;

Drill C

Translate:

1. He says that I am good.
2. I say that I am good.
3. They say that I am not wise.
4. We were hoping that the city would be saved.

Exercise A

Translate:

1. ὁ Σωκράτης τῷ ὄντι ἐνόμισεν οὐδένα ἑκόντα ἀδικεῖν ὥστε βλάπτειν ἄλλους.
2. τέλος δὲ οἱ Ἀθηναῖοι τοῦ Σωκράτους κατηγόρουν ὡς διαφθείροντος τοὺς νέους οὐδὲ τοὺς νομίζοντος.
3. ὁ ἄγγελος ἔφη βουλήσεσθαι τοῖς στρατιώταις ἡγεῖσθαι μᾶλλον ἢ ἕπεσθαι.
4. τίς οἴεται πάντας περὶ μοίρας ἔχειν τὰς αὐτὰς γνώμας;
5. ἄλλοις μὲν πολλοῖς ἔδοξεν οὗτος ὁ ἀνὴρ εἶναι σοφός, ἐμοὶ δ᾽ οὔ.

Note: οὔ is accented when it stands at the end of a sentence or clause.

Exercise B

Translate:

1. The stranger says that he is a god, but the ruler thinks that he is lying.

Exercise B (continued)

     2.   To whom does it seem best to possess (= have acquired) much money in order to enjoy life?

     3. Certain heralds said that we were five stades away from the ships of the king.

     4. Some think that men do wrong unwillingly, others deny (it).

     5. They hope that Darius himself will be present to see the battle and the victory.

2. ἡ Ἀτταλικὴ στοά. The Stoa of Attalus, Athens, originally erected c. 150 BC.

Lesson 33

Imperative Mood (Active Voice)
The Vocative Case

Imperative Mood (Active Voice)

The imperative mood expresses a direct command. Greek imperatives are conjugated in the second and third persons, singular and plural, and have the following forms in the present and aorist active:

a. Present Active

Regular ω-verb, παιδεύω:

	singular	plural
2nd person	παίδευε *educate*	παιδεύετε *educate*
3rd person	παιδευέτω *let him educate*	παιδευόντων *let them educate*

ε-contract, ποιέω:

	singular	plural
2nd person	ποίει (ποίεε)	ποιεῖτε (ποιέετε)
3rd person	ποιείτω (ποιεέτω)	ποιούντων (ποιεόντων)

α-contract, τιμάω:

	singular	plural
2nd person	τίμα (τίμαε)	τιμᾶτε (τιμάετε)
3rd person	τιμάτω (τιμαέτω)	τιμώντων (τιμαόντων)

εἰμί:

	singular	plural
2nd person	ἴσθι	ἔστε
3rd person	ἔστω	ἔστων

φημί:

	singular	plural
2nd person	φαθί (φάθι)	φάτε
3rd person	φάτω	φάντων

b. First Aorist Active

Like the infinitive (see Lesson 8), the aorist imperative, formed from the third (active and middle) and sixth (passive) principal parts (for the middle and passive forms, see Lesson 35), has <u>no temporal augment</u> and thus expresses a type of action with a simply aspect with no time value.

Regular first aorist, παιδεύω:

	singular	plural
2nd person	παίδευσον *educate*	παιδεύσατε *educate*
3rd person	παιδευσάτω *let him educate*	παιδευσάντων *let them educate*

Liquid aorist, φαίνω:

	singular	plural
2nd person	φῆνον	φήνατε
3rd person	φηνάτω	φηνάντων

c. Second Aorist Active

The forms of the <u>second</u> aorist active imperative take the same endings as the present active imperative above.

λείπω:

	singular	plural
2nd person	λίπε	λίπετε
3rd person	λιπέτω	λιπόντων

<u>Note</u>: The second aorist active imperatives of ἔρχομαι, λαμβάνω, ὁράω, and εὑρίσκω are accented on the <u>ultima</u> in the second person singular and on the <u>penult</u> in the second person plural in the following manner:

	singular	plural
2ⁿᵈ person	ἐλθέ	ἐλθέτε
2ⁿᵈ person	λαβέ	λαβέτε
2ⁿᵈ person	ἰδέ	ἰδέτε
2ⁿᵈ person	εὑρέ	εὑρέτε

Prohibitions (Negative Imperatives)

A prohibition in the second or third person is expressed by μή and the present (rarely the aorist) imperative. Examples:

μὴ λάμβανε τὰ χρήματα.
Don't take the money.

μὴ λαμβανέτω τὰ χρήματα.
Let him not take the money.

The Vocative Case

The vocative case is used to express direct address. The vocative in modern texts is typically set off by commas. The article ὦ typically precedes the vocative in Greek in ordinary conversation, exclamations, and public speeches.

The vocative plural is always identical in form to the nominative plural. Example:

λέγετε τὴν ἀλήθειαν, ὦ ξένοι.
Tell the truth, strangers.

The vocative singular is formed in accordance with the following rules:

a. The First Declension

1. Category I & II nouns (ending in –η, -ᾱ, or -ᾰ) have a vocative singular identical to the nominative singular. Examples:

Nominative singular		Vocative singular
ἡ γῆ	→	ὦ γῆ
ἡ μοῖρα	→	ὦ μοῖρα

2. Category III nouns (ending is -ης or –ας) have a vocative singular ending in -α. Examples:

Nominative singular   Vocative singular
   ὁ νεανίας   →   ὦ νεανία
   ὁ πολίτης   →   ὦ πολῖτα
   ὁ/ἡ Πέρσης   →   ὦ Πέρσα

b. The Second Declension

The -ος ending of the nominative singular is replaced by -ε (except for
θεός, which remains unchanged). Neuter nouns are identical in the nominative
and vocative cases. Examples:

Nominative singular   Vocative singular
   ὁ στρατηγός   →   ὦ στρατηγέ
   ὁ φίλος   →   ὦ φίλε
   τὸ παιδίον   →   ὦ παιδίον

c. The Third Declension

     1. The vocative singular of neuter nouns and of masculine and
feminine nouns with <u>stems</u> ending in a labial (π, β, φ) or a palatal (κ, γ, χ) is
<u>usually</u> the same as the nominative singular. Examples:

Nominative singular   Vocative singular
   τὸ γένος   →   ὦ γένος
   ὁ κλώψ (κλώπ-)   →   ὦ κλώψ
   ὁ φύλαξ (φύλακ-)   →   ὦ φύλαξ

     2. The formation of the vocative singular of all other nouns of
the third declension nouns can be somewhat irregular, but abides by the following
general rules:
         a. if the nominative singular ends in a long vowel, that
     vowel is shortened in the vocative singular. Examples:

Nominative singular   Vocative singular
   ὁ Σώκρατης   →   ὦ Σώκρατες
   ὁ ῥήτωρ   →   ὦ ῥῆτορ

         b. if the final vowel of the nominative singular cannot
     be shortened, the final consonant is dropped in the vocative.
     Examples:

Nominative singular   Vocative singular
   ὁ βασιλεύς   →   ὦ βασιλεῦ
   ἡ πόλις   →   ὦ πόλι

Vocabulary

ἐάω (imperf. εἴων), ἐάσω, εἴασα, εἴακα, εἴαμαι, εἰάθην *allow; let go*

μάχομαι, μαχοῦμαι, ἐμαχεσάμην, ____, μεμάχημαι, ____ (+ dat.) *fight (with)*

οἰκέω, οἰκήσω, ᾤκησα, ᾤκηκα, ᾤκημαι, ᾠκήθην *live (in), inhabit*

πυνθάνομαι, πεύσομαι, ἐπυθόμην, ____, πέπυσμαι, ____ (+ gen. of person, acc. of thing) *learn* (by hearsay or inquiry), *inquire*

Ἀπόλλων, Ἀπόλλωνος, ὁ (voc. Ἄπολλον) *Apollo*

βάρβαρος, -ον *foreign* (not Greek); (as a plural noun) οἱ βάρβαροι *the barbarians*

Ζεύς, Διός, Διί, Δία, ὁ (voc. Ζεῦ) *Zeus*

οὖν (postpositive adverb) *therefore, now, well, then*

πρῶτον (adverb) *first, at first, for the first time*

ὦ (with vocatives) *O, oh*

Drill A

Give the following forms:

1. present active imperative, 2ⁿᵈ singular and plural of:
   σῴζω, νικάω, αἱρέω, πλέω, εἰμί, φημί

2. aorist active imperative, 2ⁿᵈ singular and plural of:
   πέμπω, ὁράω, αἱρέω, ἄρχω, ἔρχομαι

3. present active imperative, 3ʳᵈ singular and plural of:
   λύω, ζητέω, τολμάω, εἰμί, κρίνω

Drill B

Give the vocative singular of:

1. ξένος	6. χάρις
2. κέρδος	7. μοῖρα
3. θεός	8. ἰατρός
4. δικαστής	9. τριήρης
5. ῥήτωρ	10. παῖς

Exercise A: Reading

Coes makes a suggestion

Δαρεῖος δὲ ἐπεὶ ἀφίκετο καὶ ἡ στρατιὰ σὺν αὐτῷ ἐπὶ τὸν
Ἴστρον, ἐνταῦθα διαβάντων πάντων Δαρεῖος ἐκέλευσε τούς τε
Ἴωνας τὴν γέφυραν λύσαντες ἕπεσθαι κατὰ γῆν καὶ τὴν ἐκ τῶν
νεῶν στρατιάν. μελλόντων δὲ τῶν Ἰώνων τὴν γέφυραν λύσειν
5   καὶ ποιήσειν τὰ κελευόμενα Κώης ὁ Ἐρξάνδρου, στρατηγὸς
ὢν Μυτιληναίων, ἔλεξε Δαρείῳ τάδε, πυθόμενος πρῶτον εἰ
ἐκεῖνος ἐθέλει γνώμην ἀποδέχεσθαι παρὰ τοῦ βουλομένου
ἀποφαίνειν.
        Ὦ βασιλεῦ, ἐπὶ γῆν γὰρ μέλλεις πορεύσεσθαι οὐδὲ
10   οἰκουμένας πόλεις ἔχουσαν. σὺ οὖν ταύτην τὴν γέφυραν ἔα
κατὰ χώραν μένειν φύλακας λιπὼν τοὺς αὐτὴν ποιήσαντας. καὶ
ἡμῖν κατὰ γνώμην εὖ πράξασι καὶ εὑροῦσι Σκύθας ἐστὶ ἄφοδος,
ἀλλὰ ἡμῖν καὶ μὴ ἔχουσιν αὐτοὺς εὑρεῖν ἐστι ἄφοδος. οὐ γὰρ
ἔδοξα ἡμᾶς νικηθήσεσθαι ὑπὸ Σκυθῶν μάχῃ, ἀλλὰ μᾶλλον οὐκ
15   ἔχοντας τούτους εὑρεῖν πείσεσθαί τι. καὶ τάδε λέγειν φήσει τίς
με καταμενοῦντα· ἐγὼ δὲ αὐτὸς ἕψομαί σοι οὐ βουλόμενος
λειφθῆναι.

Adapted from Herodotus, *Histories* 4.97

2   Ἴστρον from Ἴστρος, -ου, ὁ *the Ister* (Danube river)
       διαβάντων gen. pl. aor. participle from διαβαίνω *cross*
3   Ἴωνας from Ἴωνες, -ων, οἱ *the Ionians*
5   Κώης, -ου, ὁ *Coes* (general of the soldiers from Mytilene)
       Ἐρξάνδρου from Ἐρξάνδρος, -ου, ὁ *Erxander* (father of Coes)
6   Μυτιληναίων from Μυτιληναῖοι, οἱ *the Mytilenians* (soldiers from
           Mytilene)
11   κατὰ χώραν (idiomatically) *in place*
12   ἄφοδος, -ου, ἡ *way back* (from ἀπό + ὁδός)

3. Οἱ Σκύθαι.

Exercise B

Translate:

1. First ask, O child, and you will receive; seek and you will find.
2. The wise man left his country for ten years in order to see other inhabited cities and learn about the customs of foreigners.
3. O master, in the name of Zeus let her bury her brother, who fought against (πρός) his fatherland.
4. Why, therefore, didn't the king allow the old men to honor and praise the foreign god?
5. Hear me, Apollo: let a terrible disease destroy those who have seized my daughter.

4. ὁ Πέρσης μάχεται τῷ Σκύθῃ,
as depicted on the tondo of a 5th c. red figure kylix.

Lesson 34

οἶδα. Indirect Statement (continued)

οἶδα

The irregular verb οἶδα ("know"), a second perfect with present meaning, is conjugated as follows:

Perfect Active Indicative			Pluperfect Active Indicative		
singular	person	plural	singular	person	plural
οἶδα *I know*	1	ἴσμεν *We know*	ἤδη (ἤδειν) *I knew*	1	ἦσμεν (ἤδεμεν) *We knew*
οἶσθα *You know*	2	ἴστε *You know*	ἤδησθα (ἤδεις) *You knew*	2	ἦστε (ἤδετε) *You knew*
οἶδε(ν) *He knows*	3	ἴσασι(ν) *They know*	ἤδει(ν) *He knew*	3	ἦσαν (ἤδεσαν) *They knew*

Infinitive
εἰδέναι
To know

Participle
εἰδώς, εἰδυῖα, εἰδός
(gen. εἰδότος, εἰδυίας, εἰδότος)

Imperative			Future Active Indicative		
singular	person	plural	singular	person	plural
ἴσθι *Know*	2	ἴστε *Know*	εἴσομαι *I will know*	1	εἰσόμεθα *We will know*
ἴστω *Let him know*	3	ἴστων *Let them know*	εἴσει (-η) *You will know*	2	εἴσεσθε *You will know*
			εἴσεται *He will know*	3	εἴσονται *They will know*

Notes: The form ἴσθι is ambiguous. It may be either the 2nd person singular imperative of οἶδα (as above) or the corresponding imperative form of εἰμί.

Be careful to distinguish the future forms of οἶδα from those of εἰμί (ἔσομαι, ἔσει (-η), ἔσται, ἐσόμεθα, ἔσεσθε, ἔσονται).

Indirect Statement (continued)

a. Participles in Indirect Statement

After certain verbs of <u>perception</u> (see, hear) and certain verbs of <u>mental activity</u> (know, remember), a supplementary participle is used instead of an infinitive in indirect statement. The tense of the participle is determined in accordance with the rules for the tense of the infinitive (see Lesson 32). As with the infinitive, the subject of the participle stands in the <u>accusative</u> case and is omitted if it is the same as the subject of the main verb. In the latter instance the participle stands in the <u>nominative</u> case. Examples.

ᾔσμεν ἐκεῖνον ὄντα τὸν κλῶπα.
We knew that he was the thief.

ᾔσαν αἱρεθέντες.
They knew that they had been chosen.

b. Finite Verbs in Indirect Statement

Certain verbs of <u>saying</u> govern an indirect statement which consists of a finite verb introduced by ὅτι ("that") or ὡς ("that"). The tense rule for infinitives and participles applies here also. Example:

εἶπεν ὡς ἥδεται.
He said that he was pleased. (direct statement: I am pleased.)

List of Verbs and Constructions in Indirect Statement

a. Verbs governing an infinitive:
δοκέω, ἐλπίζω, ἡγέομαι, κρίνω, λέγω (passive only), νομίζω, οἴομαι, φημί, κρίνω

b. Verbs governing a participle:
ἐπιλανθάνομαι, εὑρίσκω, μανθάνω, μέμνημαι, οἶδα, ὁράω

c. Verbs governing ὅτι (ὡς):
ἀποκρίνομαι, διδάσκω, εἶπον, λέγω, οἶδα, ὁράω

d. Verbs governing an infinitive or participle: ἀγγέλλω, πυνθάνομαι

e. Verbs governing an infinitive, participle, or ὅτι (ὡς):
     αἰσθάνομαι (usually a participle), ἀκούω (usually a participle),
     θαυμάζω.

Vocabulary

αἰσθάνομαι, αἰσθήσομαι, ᾐσθόμην, ____, ᾔσθημαι, ____ (+ gen. of
    person, acc. of thing) *perceive, learn* (by perception), *hear* (aesthetic)

ἀποκρίνομαι, ἀποκρινοῦμαι, ἀπεκρινάμην, ____, ἀποκέκριμαι,
    ____ *answer, reply*

____, ἐρῶ, εἶπον (imperat. εἰπέ), εἴρηκα, εἴρημαι, ἐρρήθην *say, tell,
    speak*

θαυμάζω, θαυμάσομαι, ἐθαύμασα, τεθαύμακα, τεθαύμασμαι,
    ἐθαυμάσθην *admire, wonder (at), be amazed* (thaumaturgy)

μανθάνω, μαθήσομαι, ἔμαθον, μεμάθηκα, ____, ____ *learn* (by study);
    understand (mathematics)

μέμνημαι (perf. with pres. meaning), μεμνήσομαι (μνησθήσομαι),
    ἐμνήσθην (+ gen.) *remember* (mnemonic)

οἶδα (perf. with pres. meaning), εἴσομαι *know* (by reflection)

ὅτι *that* (+ indirect statement); *because*

ὡς (+ indirect statement) *that*

Drill A

Supply the forms of οἶδα requested and translate:

1. perf. act. indic., 2ⁿᵈ sing   4. perf. act. part., fem. acc. sing.
2. fut. depon. indic., 1ˢᵗ pl.   5. perf. act. indic., 3ʳᵈ pl.
3. pluperf. act. indic., 3ʳᵈ pl.   6. perf. act. infin.

Drill B

Translate:

1. ᾖσμεν ὄντες σοφοί.
2. εἶπεν ὡς Δία τε καὶ Ἀπόλλωνα νομίζει.
3. τίς ἐπιλανθάνεσθαι τῶν καλῶν κἀγαθῶν οἷός
τ' ἐστιν;
4. οὐκ ἔφη ἀδικῆσαι.

Drill C

Change the direct statements (underlined) below to indirect statements;
translate the result:

1. νομίζομεν, σὺ τὸν πατέρα καὶ τὴν ματέρα ἀεὶ
τιμήσεις.
2. εἶπεν, ἐκεῖνος δικαστὴς τοὺς ἀδίκους κατηγόρους
μισεῖ.
3. οἴονται, αὐτὸς τοὺς τῷ βασιλεῖ μαχομένους ἐμίσησε.
4. πρῶτον, ἐπύθοντο, ἡμεῖς εἱλόμεθα ἄλλην ὁδὸν διὰ
τοῦ πεδίου. (use participle)

Drill D

Translate:

1. I understand that jealousy corrupts men.
2. Some think that Apollo is the sun.
3. Let the jurors admire honor and virtue.
4. He learned that the enemy was coming.

Exercise A

Translate:

1. οὐ μὲν ἑώρακε τὸν ἰατρόν, ᾔσθηται δ᾽ ἐν Ἀθήναις
αὐτόν.
2. εἰ μὴ ᾔδειν, ὦ ἄνδρες δικασταί, τοὺς κατηγόρους
βουλομένους ἐμὲ παντὶ τρόπῳ βλάπτειν, πολλὴν ἂν αὐτοῖς
χάριν εἶχον διὰ ταύτην τὴν κατηγορίαν.
3. παρὰ τοὺς λόγους τοὺς τῶν ἐχθρῶν δεόμεθα ὑμῶν
ἡμᾶς μὲν τιμᾶν, ἐκείνους δὲ ἡγεῖσθαι κακοὺς εἶναι.
4. ἐμάθομεν δὲ καὶ ὑμᾶς ταύτῃ τῇ γνώμῃ χρωμένους.
5. ἐγὼ γὰρ πρῶτον, χρημάτων μοι πολλῶν λειφθέντων
διὰ τὸν τοῦ πατρὸς πλοῦτον, ἐθαύμαζον οὐδένα μοι
ἐπιβουλεύοντα.

<u>Exercise B</u>

Translate:

     1.   First, then, announce that you will remember their favors.

     2.   After enjoying the wine, the old man forgot that he (i.e. himself) was dying.

     3.   Mother, who do you think is planning the murder?

     4.   When the herald said that the triremes were present, the general replied that he would fight and not flee.

     5.   Many have come to me, being amazed that I am prosecuting Socrates.

5. ἡ τριήρης, from a fragment of a 5th c. black figure column krater.

Lesson 35

Imperative Mood (Middle and Passive Voices)
Relative Pronoun

Imperative Mood (Middle and Passive Voices)

Greek middle and passive imperatives are conjugated as follows:

a. Present Middle-Passive

Regular ω-verb, παιδεύω:

	singular	plural
2nd person	παιδεύου *educate (for) yourself* *be educated*	παιδεύεσθε *educate (for) yourself* (mid.) *be educated* (pass.)
3rd person	παιδευέσθω *let him/her/it educate (for)* *him-/her-/itself* *let him/her/it be educated*	παιδευέσθων *let them educate (for) themselves* (mid.) *let them be educated* (pass.)

ε-contract, ποιέω:

	singular	plural
2nd person	ποιοῦ (ποιέου)	ποιεῖσθε (ποιέεσθε)
3rd person	ποιείσθω (ποιεέσθω)	ποιείσθων (ποιεέσθων)

α-contract, τιμάω:

	singular	plural
2nd person	τιμῶ (τιμάου)	τιμᾶσθε (τιμάεσθε)
3rd person	τιμάσθω (τιμαέσθω)	τιμάσθων (τιμαέσθων)

b. First Aorist Middle

Regular first aorist, παιδεύω:

	singular	plural
2nd person	παίδευσαι *educate (for) yourself*	παιδεύσασθε *educate (for) yourselves*

3rd person	παιδευσάσθω	~~παιδευσάσθων~~ *[handwritten: Παιδ ευ 6 α 6 θων]*
	let him/her/it educate (for) him-/her-/itself	*let them educate (for) themselves*

Liquid aorist, φαίνω:

	singular	plural
2nd person	φῆναι	φήνασθε
3rd person	φηνάσθω	φηνάσθων

c. Second Aorist Middle

λείπω:

	singular	plural
2nd person	λιποῦ	λίπεσθε
3rd person	λιπέσθω	λιπέσθων

d. Aorist Passive

Regular first aorist passive, παιδεύω:

	singular	plural
2nd person	παιδεύθητι	παιδεύθητε
3rd person	παιδευθήτω	παιδευθέντων

Second aorist passive, φαίνω:

	singular	plural
2nd person	φάνηθι	φάνητε
3rd person	φανήτω	φανέντων

Declension of the Relative Pronoun

In Greek the relative pronoun, ὅς, ἥ, ὅ ("who," "which," "that"), is declined as follows:

singular

masculine	feminine	neuter
ὅς *who*	ἥ *who*	ὅ *which*
οὗ *whose*	ἧς *whose*	οὗ *of which*
ᾧ *to whom*	ᾗ *to whom*	ᾧ *to which*
ὅν *whom*	ἥν *whom*	ὅ *which*

<u>plural</u>

οἵ *who*	αἵ *who*	ἅ *which*
ὧν *whose*	ὧν *whose*	ὧν *of which*
οἷς *to whom*	αἷς *to whom*	οἷς *to which*
οὕς *whom*	ἅς *whom*	ἅ *which*

<u>Agreement of the Relative Pronoun</u>

a. The relative pronoun agrees in gender and number with the word (or phrase) to which it is referring, i.e. its antecedent. The <u>case</u> of the relative pronoun, however, is determined by its <u>use in its own clause</u>. Example:

ἡ γυνὴ ἣν εἶδές ἐστι ἡ μήτηρ ἐμοῦ.
The woman whom you saw is my mother.

In this example the phrase "whom you saw," is the relative clause. It describes its antecedent, "the woman." Since "woman" is feminine and singular, the relative pronoun ἣν is feminine and singular. Since ἣν serves as the direct object of its own clause – "you saw (the woman)" – it is placed in the accusative case.

b. A relative pronoun in the <u>accusative</u> case, however, is sometimes attracted to the case of an antecedent which stands in the <u>genitive</u> or <u>dative</u>, especially when the antecedent and relative pronoun are right next to each other. This phenomenon is typically referred to as "attraction." Example:

ἐπελάθου τῶν χρημάτων ὧν ἤθροισας.
You forgot the money which you collected.

In this example, the relative pronoun *should* be ἅ – a neuter plural form to agree with τῶν χρημάτων – rather than ὧν, but the relative has been "attracted" to the genitive case of τῶν χρημάτων and hence mirrors it.

<u>Note</u>: The relative pronoun, which is sometimes omitted in English, must <u>always</u> be expressed in Greek. Example:

τὴν γυναῖκα ἣν εἶδον ἐν τῇ ἀγορᾷ οὐ φιλῶ.
I do not love the woman (whom) I saw in the market-place.

<u>Vocabulary</u>

ἀπολογέομαι, ἀπολογήσομαι, ἀπελογησάμην, ____,
      ἀπολελόγημαι, ____ *defend oneself, make a defense* (apology)

ἐπιμελέομαι, ἐπιμελήσομαι, ἐπεμελησάμην, ____, ἐπιμεμέλημαι,
ἐπιμελήθην (+ gen.) *take care (of), care for*

μισέω, ____, ἐμίσησα, μεμίσηκα, μεμίσημαι, ἐμισήθην *hate*
(misanthrope)

φιλέω, φιλήσω, ἐφίλησα, πεφίληκα, πεφίλημαι, ἐφιλήθην *love*

ἔργον, -ου, τό *work, deed* (energy)   ἔτι (adverb) *still*

ἕκαστος, -η, -ον *each*   πολλάκις (adverb) *often, many times*

ὅς, ἥ, ὅ *who, which, that*   οὔτε (μήτε) ... οὔτε (μήτε)

ἀεί (adverb) *always*   *neither ... nor*

Drill A

Conjugate:

1. aorist middle imperative of: δέχομαι, γίγνομαι
2. present middle imperative of: φιλέω, πειράομαι
3. aorist passive imperative of: φαίνω, ἥδομαι

Drill B

Locate the following forms:

1. ἀφικοῦ   6. ἰδέ
2. ἀφίκου   7. ἐλελύκει
3. ἀποκρινάσθων   8. ᾠήθητε
4. ηὕρομεν   9. βουλήθητε
5. δόκει   10. τιμάσθω

Drill C

Supply the appropriate form of the relative pronoun (the antecedent will
be underlined); translate the completed phrase:

    1. τὴν πόλιν _____ τοὺς βαρβάρους πολλοὺς ἔχει ἔτι
οἰκοῦμεν.
    2. τοῦ ἀνθρώπου _____ ὧν ἐν τῇ ἀγορᾷ ἔτυχε δέονται.
    3. ὁ τῶν κακῶν φόνος ἐστὶ ἔργον _____ οἱ θεοὶ
τιμωρήσονται.
    4. εὑρισκέτω τὰ χρήματα _____ βούλεται.
    5. δεῖ τοὺς ἀνθρώπους _____ οἱ πολλοὶ μίσουσι
πολλάκις ἀπολογεῖσθαι.

Exercise A

Translate:

1. οὐ μὲν εἴδομεν τὴν τοῦ γέροντος γυναῖκα, ᾐσθόμεθα
δ᾽ ἔτι οὖσαν αὐτήν.
2. τοὺς φίλους ἀδικεῖς οὓς ἐκ τῆς πόλεως ἐκβέβληκας.
3. ἀκήκοας τῶν λόγων ὧν Ζεὺς εἶπε πρὸς σοῦ
φαινόμενος.
4. εἶπεν ὅτι οὐδενὶ τρόπῳ οἷόν τ᾽ ἐστιν αὐτοὺς
ἐπαινεῖν.
5. ἔπραξε γὰρ οὗτος ταῦτα τὰ ἔργα, δι᾽ ἃ οὔτε πρὸς
τῶν φίλων φιλεῖται οὔτε πρὸς τῶν ἐχθρῶν μισεῖται.

Exercise B

Translate:

1. Let each answer and defend himself according to the laws of
our fatherland.
2. Always take care of the children whose fathers have died in
the war.
3. Soldiers, use your shields and fight the barbarians.
4. Socrates often said that each ought to care for his soul.
5. O Apollo, save those who have been wronged by the judges.

6. The Temple of Apollo, Delphi 4th c. BC.

Lesson 36

Review

<u>Drill A</u>

Give the following forms:

    1. τις to agree with: μάχης, βάρβαρον, νυκτί, νῆες
    2. οὐδείς to agree with: κέρδος, πόλιν, τριήρει, φύλακος
    3. πᾶς to agree with: ἔργα, χάριν, γένος, νεανίας (acc.)

<u>Drill B</u>

Conjugate:

    1. pluperfect indicative of: οἶδα
    2. present indicative of: φημί
    3. aorist middle imperative of: ἀποκρίνομαι

<u>Drill C</u>

Change the verbs to the voice indicated in parentheses, retaining the original tense, mood, person, and number; translate the result:

    1. φίλησαι (active)   5. ἐλπιζομένους (active)
    2. θαυμάζετε (passive)   6. μισηθέντων (active)
    3. εἰρηκέναι (passive)   7. λανθανέτω (passive)
    4. ἔα (middle)   8. πλεύσον (middle)

<u>Exercise A: Reading</u>

Darius accepts Coes' suggestion.

    Ἥσθη τῇ γνώμῃ Δαρεῖος καὶ ἐκείνῳ ἀπεκρίνατο τάδε·
    Ξένε, σωθέντος ἐμοῦ εἰς τὴν οἰκίαν φάνηθί μοι, καί σε
εὖ συμβουλεύσαντα ἔργοις ἀξίοις τιμήσω.
    Ταῦτα εἰπὼν καὶ ἀφάψας ἄμματα ἑξήκοντα ἐν ἱμάντι,
κελέσας εἰς λόγους τοὺς Ἰώνων δεσπότας ἔλεγε τάδε·
    Ἄνδρες Ἴωνες, ἡ μὲν γνώμη ῥηθεῖσα πρὸς τὴν γέφυραν
ἐάσθω, ἔχοντες δὲ τὸν ἱμάντα τόνδε ποιεῖτε τάδε· ἐμὲ ἰδόντες

5

πορευόμενον ἐπὶ Σκύθας, ἀπὸ τούτου ἀρξάμενοι τοῦ χρόνου
λύετε ἄμμα ἓν ἑκάστης ἡμέρας· ἐμοῦ δὲ ἐν τούτῳ τῷ χρόνῳ μὴ
10   παρόντος ἀλλὰ διεξελθουσῶν ὑμῖν τῶν ἡμερῶν, ἀποπλεῖτε εἰς
τὰς τῆς πατρίδος πόλεις. μέχρι δὲ τούτου, ἐπειδὴ οὕτως ὑμῖν
ἔδοξε, φυλάττετε τὴν γέφυραν, πᾶσαν προθυμίαν σωτηρίας
παρεχόμενοι. ταῦτα δὲ ποιοῦντες ἐμοὶ χάριν μεγάλην πράξετε.
Δαρεῖος μὲν ταῦτα εἰπὼν τῇ ἄλλῃ στρατιᾷ ἡγεῖτο.

Adapted from Herodotus, *Histories* 4.97-98

4   ἀφάψας ἄμματα ἑξήκοντα ἐν ἱμάντι *having tied sixty knots in a string*
11 μέχρι (+ gen.) *up to, during*
12 προθυμίαν σωτηρίας lit., *zeal of safety*, i.e. *zeal to save it*

7. ὁ Δαρεῖος, as depicted on his tomb at Naqsh-e Rustam,
northwest of Persepolis in modern day Iran.

Exercise B

Translate:

1. O earth, receive the souls of the dead.
2. In addition to these things, he hated many whose names were
worthy of note.
3. O herald, first announce to each soldier that the barbarians
will fight us within five days.
4. On the first day of the year he made his defense against
(πρός) all his accusers.
5. Who does not believe that certain words often conquer
deeds?

Lesson 37

Subjunctive Mood (Active Voice). Dependent Uses

Subjunctive Mood (Active Voice)

The subjunctive mood is a <u>primary mood</u> used only to express present or future actions. As a primary mood, when the subjunctive is used in a subordinate clause, it may <u>only</u> follow a main verb that is in a primary tense: the present, future, or the perfect. For secondary tenses, i.e. tenses that receive a temporal augment in the indicative mood, namely the imperfect, aorist, and pluperfect, the optative mood is used in Greek (see Lesson 39).

The most common tenses of the subjunctive are the present and aorist. The difference in sense between these two tenses in the subjunctive is not one of time, but rather of aspect. The present subjunctive will be used to express an action in the present or future with a progressive aspect. The aorist subjunctive will be used to express an action in the present or future with a simple aspect.

All forms of the subjunctive feature a lengthening of the thematic vowels ε and ο to η or ω respectively. This is even the case for first aorists, despite the fact that these forms do not feature a thematic vowel in the indicative mood.

a. <u>Present Active</u>

The present active subjunctive, formed from the first principal part, is conjugated as follows:

Regular ω-verb, παιδεύω:

singular	person	plural
παιδεύω	1	παιδεύωμεν
παιδεύῃς	2	παιδεύητε
παιδεύῃ	3	παιδεύωσι(ν)

ε-contract, ποιέω:

singular	person	plural
ποιῶ (ποιέω)	1	ποιῶμεν (ποιέωμεν)
ποιῇς (ποιέῃς)	2	ποιῆτε (ποιέητε)
ποιῇ (ποιέῃ)	3	ποιῶσι(ν) (ποιέωσι)

α-contract, τιμάω:

singular	person	plural
τιμῶ (τιμάω)	1	τιμῶμεν (τιμάωμεν)
τιμᾷς (τιμάῃς)	2	τιμᾶτε (τιμάητε)
τιμᾷ (τιμάῃ)	3	τιμῶσι(ν) (τιμάωσι)

εἰμί:

singular	person	plural
ὦ	1	ὦμεν
ἦς	2	ἦτε
ἦ	3	ὦσι(ν)

φημί:

singular	person	plural
φῶ	1	φῶμεν
φῇς	2	φῆτε
φῇ	3	φῶσι(ν)

οἶδα:

singular	person	plural
εἰδῶ	1	εἰδῶμεν
εἰδῇς	2	εἰδῆτε
εἰδῇ	3	εἰδῶσι(ν)

b. First Aorist Active

The first aorist active subjunctive, formed from the third principal part (minus the temporal augment), is conjugated as follows:

Regular first aorist, παιδεύω:

singular	person	plural
παιδεύσω	1	παιδεύσωμεν
παιδεύσῃς	2	παιδεύσητε
παιδεύσῃ	3	παιδεύσωσι(ν)

Liquid aorist, φαίνω:

singular	person	plural
φήνω	1	φήνωμεν
φήνῃς	2	φήνητε
φήνῃ	3	φήνωσι(ν)

c. Second Aorist Active

The second aorist active subjunctive, formed from the third principal part (minus the temporal augment), is conjugated as follows:

λείπω:

singular	person	plural
λίπω	1	λίπωμεν
λίπῃς	2	λίπητε
λίπῃ	3	λίπωσι(ν)

Conditions (continued)

a. Particular Conditions

These conditions <u>refer to a particular event</u> in either present or past time and imply nothing as to their fulfillment. They take the indicative mood in both the protasis and apodosis, as follows:

	<u>Protasis</u> (negated by μή)	<u>Apodosis</u> (negated by οὐ)
<u>Present Particular</u>:	εἰ + pres. indicative	pres. indicative
	If ... am	*am*

εἰ πείθεσθε τοῖς πολεμίοις, τοὺς συμμάχους βλάπτετε.
If you are (now/ in fact) obeying the enemy, you are harming your allies.

	<u>Protasis</u> (negated by μή)	<u>Apodosis</u> (negated by οὐ)
<u>Past Particular</u>:	εἰ + past indicative	past indicative
	If ... was	*was*

εἰ τὸν κλῶπα εἶδεν, ἡμῖν οὐκ εἶπεν.
If he (in fact) saw the thief, he did not tell us.

b. Present General Conditions

These conditions express actions of a <u>general nature</u> which are customary or repeated in present time. The <u>protasis</u> uses the <u>subjunctive</u> (present or aorist) introduced by ἐάν (ἤν, ἄν); the <u>apodosis</u> uses the <u>present indicative</u>, as follows:

	<u>Protasis</u> (negated by μή)	<u>Apodosis</u> (negated by οὐ)
<u>Present General</u>:	ἐάν (ἤν, ἄν) + pres./aor. subj.	pres. indicative
	If (ever) ... am	*am*

ἐάν τις βλάπτῃ τοὺς φίλους, ἀδικεῖ.
If anyone (ever) harms his friends, he does wrong.

c. Future More Vivid Conditions

In these future conditions, the <u>protasis</u> uses the <u>subjunctive</u> (present or aorist) introduced by ἐάν (ἤν, ἄν); the <u>apodosis</u> uses the <u>future indicative,</u> as follows:

<u>Protasis</u> (negated by μή)   <u>Apodosis</u> (neg. by οὐ)

<u>Future More Vivid:</u> ἐάν (ἤν, ἄν) + pres./aor. subj.   fut. indicative

If . . . am   *will*

ἐὰν μὴ τὰ χρήματα παράσχῃς, ἐπ᾽ Ἀθήνας οὐ πλεύσομαι.

If you do not provide the money, I will not sail to Athens.

Purpose Clauses

The subjunctive (present or aorist) is used after a primary tense (present, perfect, future) to express purpose. The purpose clause is introduced by the conjunctions ἵνα, ὡς or ὅπως. The negative is μή, which always follows the conjunction. Example:

ἔρχεται ἵνα τὰ χρήματα κλέψῃ.

He is coming in order that he may steal the money.

or

He is coming to steal the money.

Fear Clauses

Verbs of fearing govern noun clauses which take the subjunctive (present or aorist) after a primary tense, if the fear refers to a future event. For contemporary or past events, Greek uses the indicative mood . Affirmative fear clause are introduced by μή (*that*) and negative clauses by μὴ οὐ (*that . . . not*). Examples:

φοβοῦμαι μὴ ἡμᾶς ἴδῃ. (subjunctive)

I am afraid that he may see us.

φοβοῦμαι μὴ ἡμᾶς εἶδεν. (indicative)

I am afraid that he saw us.

δέδιμεν μὴ οὐ πέντε ἡμερῶν ἔλθῃ. (subjunctive).

We are afraid <u>that</u> he may <u>not</u> come within five days.

<u>Vocabulary</u>

φοβέομαι, φοβήσομαι, ____, ____, πεφόβημαι, ἐφοβήθην *fear, be afraid*
(phobia)

____, ____ ἔδεισα, δέδοικα (δέδια) *fear, be afraid (of)*

συμφορά, -ᾶς, ἡ *misfortune, chance*   ἵνα (ὡς, ὅπως) *in order that*

νῦν (adverb) *now, at this time*   ὡς (+ indicative) *as, since, when*

ἐάν (ἄν, ἤν) *if*

<u>Note</u>: The perfect δέδοικα has a <u>present</u> meaning, and the pluperfect
ἐδεδοίκη has the sense of an <u>imperfect</u>. The conjugation of the perfect
system follows. The forms placed in parentheses are rare.

<u>Perfect Active Indicative</u>

singular	person	plural
δέδοικα (δέδια)	1	δέδιμεν (δεδοίκαμεν)
δέδοικας (δέδιας)	2	δέδιτε (δεδοίκατε)
δέδοικε (δέδιε(ν))	3	δεδίασι(ν) (δεδοίκασι(ν))

<u>Infinitive</u>   δεδιέναι (δεδοικέναι)

<u>Participle</u>

δεδιώς (δεδοικώς), δεδιυῖα (δεδοικυῖα), δεδιός (δεδοικός)

<u>Pluperfect Active Indicative</u>

singular	person	plural
ἐδεδοίκη (ἐδεδίη)	1	ἐδέδιμεν
ἐδεδοίκης (ἐδεδίης)	2	ἐδέδιτε
ἐδεδοίκει(ν) (ἐδεδίει(ν))	3	ἐδέδισαν (ἐδεδοίκεσαν)

<u>Drill A</u>

Conjugate:

1. present active subjunctive of:
      τιμωρέω, τολμάω, εἰμί, οἶδα

2. aorist active subjunctive of:
      αἱρέω, θαυμάζω, τυγχάνω

Drill B

Give the following forms:

       1. aorist active subjunctive, 2nd plural of:
          ἔρχομαι, δοκέω, εὑρίσκω

       2. present active subjunctive, 3rd singular of:
          φιλέω, νικάω, φημί

Drill C

Identify the type of condition type found in the sentences below. Indicate the tense and mood that would be used in Greek to express the verb in the protasis and the apodosis of each condition:

       1. If Milo wins, they will celebrate in Croton.
       2. If ever Milo wins, they celebrate in Croton.
       3. If Milo won, they celebrated in Croton.
       4. If Milo were winning, they would be celebrating in Croton.
       5. If the trireme had failed to reach Mytiline, the Athenians would have regretted their rashness.
       6. If you ever go into battle, return with your shield or on it.
       7. Oedipus caused the plague, if he killed his father.
       8. We would be fortunate, if we were honoring the gods.

Drill D

Transform the underlined clauses, which currently use ὡς + a future participle to express purpose, into purpose clauses using the subjunctive mood; translate the new sentences into English:

       1. τὸν Ὅμηρον εἰς τὴν νῆσον πέμψομεν <u>ὡς μὴ παιδεύσοντα τὰ παιδία</u>.
       2. οἱ πολλοὶ τοῖς θεοῖς ἐν ταῖς ὁδοῖς θύσουσι(ν) <u>ὡς τὸν πόλεμον παύσοντες</u>.
       3. ἀγγέλους πέμπουσιν ἐξ ἀγορᾶς οἱ βάρβαροι <u>ὡς λύσοντες τὴν εἰρήνην</u>.

Exercise A

Translate:

       1. ἐὰν ἐπὶ τῇ διαβολῇ οἱ ῥήτορές μου κατηγορῶσι, ἀπολογήσομαι πρὸς δικαστῶν.

Exercise A (continued)

2. εἰ μὲν ἐκεῖνος Διὸς παῖς ἦν, οὐκ ἦν ἄδικος· εἰ δ᾽
ἄδικος, οὐκ ἦν Διὸς παῖς.
3. δέδοικας μή σ᾽ οὗτος ἀποκτεῖναι ἐθέλῃ;
4. ἀλλ᾽, ὦ Σώκρατες, ἔτι καὶ νῦν ἐμοὶ πεῖσαι καὶ
σώθητι, ὡς ἐμοί, ἢν σὺ ἀποθάνῃς, οὐ μία συμφορὰ ἔσται, ἀλλὰ
πολλαί.
5. ταύτης τῆς συμφορᾶς σοι γεγονυίας, μὴ φοβοῦ μὴ
οὐκ οἷός τ᾽ ὦ τῆς τε γυναικός σου καὶ τῶν παιδίων
ἐπιμελεῖσθαι.

Exercise B

Translate:

1. Stay here, young man, in order that we may judge with regard
to the injustice of the murder.
2. Each man will fight well if he fears that he will die.
3. If we have money, we shall have friends.
4. He collects money secretly from all the cities in order to fight
his brother.
5. Either I do not corrupt those present, or, if I (ever) happen to
corrupt them, I corrupt them unwillingly.

8. ὁ Οἰδίπους καὶ ἡ Σφίγξ, from a tondo of a red figure kylix, c. 470 BC.

Lesson 38

Adjectives of the Third Declension. Dative with Adjectives
Reflexive Pronouns

Adjectives of the Third Declension

a. The following adjectives of the third declension have <u>two</u> terminations, one for the masculine and feminine genders, the other for the neuter gender.

<u>singular</u>

	<u>masculine-feminine</u>	<u>neuter</u>
Nom.	εὐδαίμων	εὔδαιμον
Gen.	εὐδαίμονος	εὐδαίμονος
Dat.	εὐδαίμονι	εὐδαίμονι
Acc.	εὐδαίμονα	εὔδαιμον

<u>plural</u>

	masculine-feminine	neuter
Nom.	εὐδαίμονες	εὐδαίμονα
Gen.	εὐδαιμόνων	εὐδαιμόνων
Dat.	εὐδαίμοσι(ν)	εὐδαίμοσι(ν)
Acc.	εὐδαίμονας	εὐδαίμονα

Note: The masculine and feminine forms of εὐδαίμων decline like a nasal stem third declension (see χειμών, Lesson 21)

<u>singular</u>

	<u>masculine-feminine</u>	<u>neuter</u>
Nom.	ἀληθής	ἀληθές
Gen.	ἀληθοῦς	ἀληθοῦς
Dat.	ἀληθεῖ	ἀληθεῖ
Acc.	ἀληθῆ	ἀληθές

<u>plural</u>

Nom.	ἀληθεῖς	ἀληθῆ
Gen.	ἀληθῶν	ἀληθῶν
Dat.	ἀληθέσι(ν)	ἀληθέσι(ν)
Acc.	ἀληθεῖς	ἀληθῆ

<u>Note</u>: The masculine and feminine forms of ἀληθής decline like the sibilant stem τριήρης; the neuter forms behave like the neuter sibilant stem κέρδος (see Lesson 21).

b. Certain adjectives of the third declension have three terminations. Adjectives of this type have third declension endings in the <u>masculine</u> and <u>neuter</u> forms, but their <u>feminine</u> forms are declined like a category Ib first declension noun (see μοῖρα, Lesson 18).

<u>singular</u>

	masculine	feminine	neuter
Nom.	ἡδύς	ἡδεῖα	ἡδύ
Gen.	ἡδέος	ἡδείας	ἡδέος
Dat.	ἡδεῖ (ἡδέϊ)	ἡδείᾳ	ἡδεῖ (ἡδέϊ)
Acc.	ἡδύν	ἡδεῖαν	ἡδύ

<u>plural</u>

	masculine	feminine	neuter
Nom.	ἡδεῖς (ἡδέες)	ἡδεῖαι	ἡδέα
Gen.	ἡδέων	ἡδειῶν	ἡδέων
Dat.	ἡδέσι(ν)	ἡδείαις	ἡδέσι(ν)
Acc.	ἡδεῖς	ἡδείας	ἡδέα

<u>Dative with Adjectives</u>

The dative case is used with certain adjectives meaning friendly (to), faithful (to), dear (to), like (to), similar (to), equal (to), evident (to), and common (to) (and with their opposites). A partial list follows:

δῆλος,-η, -ον *evident*

ἐχθρός, -ά, -όν *hostile*

ἐναντίος, -α, -ον *opposite*

ἴσος, -η, -ον *equal*

κοινός, -ή, -όν *common*

ὅμοιος, -α, -ον *like*

πιστός, -ή, -όν *faithful*

πολέμιος, -α, -ον *hostile*

φίλος, -η, -ον *dear*

φίλιος, -α, -ον *friendly*

Example: ὁ υἱὸς τῷ πατρὶ ὁμοῖός ἐστιν.
The son is like his father.

Reflexive Pronouns

The reflexive pronouns are formed by combining the personal pronouns with the proper case forms of αὐτός. Only in the plural of the first and second persons are they written as two words, both of which are declined. Since each reflexive refers to the subject of the clause in which it stands, it has no nominative forms. The reflexive pronouns are declined as follows:

a. First Person

	singular	plural
	masculine, feminine	masculine, feminine
Gen.	ἐμαυτοῦ, -ῆς *of myself*	ἡμῶν αὐτῶν *of ourselves*
Dat.	ἐμαυτῷ, -ῇ *to/for myself*	ἡμῖν αὐτοῖς, -αῖς *to/for ourselves*
Acc.	ἐμαυτόν, -ήν *myself*	ἡμᾶς αὐτούς, -άς *ourselves*

b. Second Person

	singular	plural
	masculine, feminine	masculine, feminine
Gen.	σεαυτοῦ, -ῆς (σαυτοῦ, -ῆς) *of yourself*	ὑμῶν αὐτῶν *of yourselves*
Dat.	σεαυτῷ, -ῇ (σαυτῷ, -ῇ) *to/for yourself*	ὑμῖν αὐτοῖς, -αῖς *to/for yourselves*
Acc.	σεαυτόν, -ήν (σαυτόν, -ήν) *yourself*	ὑμᾶς αὐτούς, -άς *yourselves*

c. Third Person

singular

	masculine, feminine, neuter	alternate masc., fem., neut.
Gen.	ἑαυτοῦ, -ῆς, -οῦ *of himself, herself, itself*	(αὑτοῦ, -ῆς, -οῦ) *of himself, herself, itself*
Dat.	ἑαυτῷ, -ῇ, -ῷ *to/for himself, herself, itself*	(αὑτῷ, -ῇ, -ῷ) *to/for himself, herself, itself*
Acc.	ἑαυτόν, -ήν, -ό *himself, herself, itself*	(αὑτόν, -ήν, -ό) *himself, herself, itself*

plural

	masculine, feminine, neuter	alternate masc., fem., neut.
Gen.	ἑαυτῶν *of themselves*	(αὑτῶν) *of themselves*
Dat.	ἑαυτοῖς, -αῖς, -οῖς *to/for themselves*	(αὑτοῖς, -αῖς, -οῖς) *to/for themselves*
Acc.	ἑαυτούς, -άς, -ά *themselves*	(αὑτούς, -άς, -ά) *themselves*

Notes: The alternative forms of the reflexive pronoun in the third person are distinguished from the forms of αὐτός (see Lesson 16) only by a rough breathing. Example:

ὁ βασιλεὺς <u>αὑτὸν</u> ἀπέκτεινεν.
The king killed <u>himself</u>. (reflexive)

ὁ βασιλεὺς <u>αὐτὸν</u> ἀπέκτεινεν.
The king killed <u>him</u>. (personal)

When used to indicate possession in the genitive case, a reflexive stands in attributive position. This is in contrast to the personal pronoun, which is placed in predicate position when it is used to indicate possession in the genitive case. In the sentence below, ἑαυτοῦ is reflexive; αὐτῆς is personal:

ὁ βασιλεὺς ἔθυσε τὴν ἑαυτοῦ θυγατέρα καὶ τὸν παῖδα αὐτῆς.
The king sacrificed his (own) daughter and her child.

Indirect Reflexive

An <u>indirect reflexive</u> is a reflexive pronoun which stands in a subordinate clause and refers to the subject of the <u>main</u> clause. Example:

ἡμᾶς ἔφη αὑτοῦ φείσασθαι.
He said that we had spared him. (i.e. the subject "he.")

Vocabulary

εὐδαίμων, -ον *fortunate, prosperous, happy*   δῆλος, -η, -ον *evident, clear*

ἀληθής, -ές *true*   ἐναντίος, -α, -ον *opposite*

ἀσφαλής, -ές *safe, secure* (asphalt)   πιστός, -ή, -όν *faithful*

ἡδύς, -εῖα, -ύ *sweet, pleasant*   φίλιος, -α, -ον *friendly*

ταχύς, -εῖα, -ύ *swift, fast* (tachometer)   φίλος, -η, -ον *dear*

Drill A

Give the following forms:

1. εὐδαίμων to agree with:
   γένος, γυναιξί, κέρδη, βασιλέα, μοίρᾳ
2. ταχύς to agree with:
   τριήρη, ναῦς (acc.), θάνατον, παιδίον, χρόνου
3. ἀσφαλής to agree with:
   γέφυραν, ὁδοῖς, πράγματα, νόμου, γνώμας

Drill B

Select the form of the adjective in parentheses that agrees with the noun supplied; translate the adjective/noun pair:

1. βασιλέα (ἑκών ἑκόντα ἑκόντες)
2. τέλος (εὔδαιμον εὐδαίμονος εὐδαίμων)
3. φύλαξ (πιστόν πιστῶν πιστός)
4. νίκαῖς (ἡδύς ἡδείας ἡδείαις)
5. ἵππου (ταχέος ταχέων ταχύ)
6. δικασταί (ἀληθεῖ ἀληθεῖς ἀληθές)
7. γυναῖκος (φίλος φίλου φίλης)

Drill B (continued)

8. ἔτους (ἕκαστος ἑκάστου ἑκάστους)
9. νῆσος (ἀσφαλής ἀσφαλοῦς ἀσφαλεῖς)
10. σώματα (πάντα πᾶσι πᾶσα)
11. θυγάτηρ (οὐδείς οὐδεμία οὐδέν)
12. πόλει (φίλιαν φιλίαις φίλιᾳ)

Drill C

Translate:

1. I was honoring myself.
2. He himself will avenge his father's murder.
3. I suppose a thief is not faithful even to himself.
4. He had known them well.
5. Always take care of yourself.
6. No one praises a man who talks about himself.
7. We escaped the notice of the guards themselves.
8. Having left the marketplace, we spoke among ourselves.

Exercise A: Reading

The Scythians make an offer.

Οἱ Σκύθαι πρῶτοι ἐπὶ τὴν γέφυραν ἀφίκοντο. μαθόντες
δὲ τοὺς Πέρσας οὔπω ἀφιγμένους ἔλεγον πρὸς τοὺς Ἴωνας
ὄντας ἐν ταῖς ναυσί·
    Ἄνδρες Ἴωνες, αἵ τε ἡμέραι τοῦ ἀριθμοῦ παρεληλύθασι
5   καὶ οὐ ποιεῖτε δίκαια ἔτι παραμένοντες· ἀλλ' ἐπεὶ πρότερον
φοβούμενοι ἐμένετε, νῦν λύσαντες τὴν γέφυραν ἀπελθέτε καὶ
ὑμᾶς αὐτοὺς σώσατε εἰς Ἰωνίαν, θεοῖς τε καὶ Σκύθαις εἰδότες
χάριν. τὸν δὲ πρότερον ὄντα ὑμῶν δεσπότην τιμωρησόμεθα
ὥστε μηκέτι ἐπὶ ἀνθρώπους αὐτὸν πορευθῆναι.
10   Πρὸς ταῦτα Ἴωνες ἐβουλεύοντο.

Adapted from Herodotus, *Histories* 4.136

2   οὔπω *not yet*
4   ἀριθμοῦ from ἀριθμός, ὁ *number, numbering, reckoning*
5   πρότερον *formerly, before*
7-8   εἰδότες χάριν = ἔχοντες χάριν
9   μηκέτι *no longer, no more*

Exercise B

Translate:

     1. The virtue of a judge is to judge whether (εἰ) an orator speaks just things or not, but the virtue of an orator is to speak true and clear things.

     2. It is pleasant to have prosperous and friendly allies who are faithful to you.

     3. The swift triremes were now stationed ten stades from the plain and opposite the island.

     4. In this war I hope that we will be able to save everything dear to ourselves.

     5. Unless they intend to harm themselves, they will choose the safe road in order that they may avoid danger.

9. Funerary Krater, from the Dipylon Cemetery, Athens,
from the late Geometric period, c. 750 BC.

Lesson 39

Optative Mood (Active Voice). Dependent Uses
Genitive of the Whole (Partitive Genitive)

<u>Optative Mood (Active Voice)</u>

The dependent uses of the optative mood are similar to those of the subjunctive. While the subjunctive is a primary mood, and thus is used in certain subordinate clauses following a main verb in a primary tense (i.e. the present, future, or perfect), the optative is a <u>secondary mood</u>, and thus follows secondary tenses (i.e. <u>augmented tenses</u>: the imperfect, aorist, and pluperfect).

Like the subjunctive, the optative mood has a present and aorist tense. The future optative (see Lesson 49) is used rarely in Greek.

The aorist optative has no temporal augment. Thus, as is the case in nearly all moods but the indicative in Greek, the aorist optative expresses <u>aspect</u> only (see Lesson 8). Thus, the present optative expresses an action with a progressive aspect, and the aorist optative expresses an action with a simple aspect.

Note that in the optative final -οι and -αι are considered <u>long</u> for purposes of accentuation.

a. <u>Present Active</u>

Regular ω-verb, παιδεύω:

<u>singular</u>	<u>person</u>	<u>plural</u>
παιδεύοιμι	1	παιδεύοιμεν
παιδεύοις	2	παιδεύοιτε
παιδεύοι	3	παιδεύοιεν

ε-contract, ποιέω:

<u>singular</u>	<u>person</u>	<u>plural</u>
ποιοίην (ποιεοίην)	1	ποιοῖμεν (ποιέοιμεν)
ποιοίης (ποιεοίης)	2	ποιοῖτε (ποιέοιτε)
ποιοίη (ποιεοίη)	3	ποιοῖεν (ποιέοιεν)

α-contract, τιμάω:

<u>singular</u>	<u>person</u>	<u>plural</u>
τιμῴην (τιμαοίην)	1	τιμῷμεν (τιμάοιμεν)
τιμῴης (τιμαοίης)	2	τιμῷτε (τιμάοιτε)
τιμῴη (τιμαοίη)	3	τιμῷεν (τιμάοιεν)

εἰμί:

singular	person	plural
εἴην	1	εἶμεν
εἴης	2	εἶτε
εἴη	3	εἶεν

φημί:

singular	person	plural
φαίην	1	φαῖμεν
φαίης	2	φαίητε
φαίη	3	φαῖεν

οἶδα:

singular	person	plural
εἰδείην	1	εἰδεῖμεν
εἰδείης	2	εἰδεῖτε
εἰδείη	3	εἰδεῖεν

b. First Aorist Active

Regular first aorist, παιδεύω:

singular	person	plural
παιδεύσαιμι	1	παιδεύσαιμεν
παιδεύσειας (παιδευσαις)	2	παιδεύσαιτε
παιδεύσειε(ν) (παιδεύσαι)	3	παιδεύσειαν (παιδεύσαιεν)

Liquid aorist, φαίνω:

singular	person	plural
φήναιμι	1	φήναιμεν
φήνειας (φήναις)	2	φήναιτε
φήνειε(ν) (φήναι)	3	φήνειαν (φήναιεν)

c. Second Aorist Active

λείπω:

singular	person	plural
λίποιμι	1	λίποιμεν
λίποις	2	λίποιτε
λίποι	3	λίποιεν

Conditions (continued)

a. Past General Conditions

These conditions express actions of a general nature which are customary or repeated in past time (compare present general conditions, see Lesson 37). The protasis uses the optative (in the present or aorist tense) introduced by εἰ, and the apodosis employs a past indicative, usually the imperfect indicative, as follows:

	Protasis (negated by μή)	Apodosis (negated by οὐ)
Past General:	εἰ + pres./aor. optative	imperfect indicative
	If (ever) … was	*was*

εἴ τις βλάπτοι τοὺς φίλους, ἠδίκει.
If anyone (ever) harmed his friends, he did wrong.

b. Future Less Vivid Conditions

These conditions use the optative (present or aorist) in both clauses to indicate that the fulfillment of a future action is possible but less likely to occur than in future more vivid conditions. The protasis is introduced by εἰ, and the apodosis always contains the post-positive adverb ἄν, formed as follows:

	Protasis (negated by μή)	Apodosis (negated by οὐ)
Future Less Vivid:	εἰ + pres./aor. optative	pres./aor. optative + ἄν
	If … were to/should	*would*

εἰ μὴ τὰ χρήματα πέμψειας, ἐπ᾽ Ἀθήνας οὐκ ἂν ἔλθοιμι.
If you were not to (should not) send the money, I would not come to Athens.

Purpose Clauses (continued; see Lesson 37)

The optative (present or aorist) is used after a secondary tense (aorist, imperfect, pluperfect) to express purpose. Example:

ἔφυγον ὅπως μὴ ἀποθάνοιεν.
They fled in order that they might not be killed.

Fear Clauses (continued; see Lesson 37)

The optative (present or aorist) is used after a verb of fearing in a secondary tense. Examples:

ἐφοβούμεθα μὴ ἡμᾶς ἴδοι.
We were afraid that he might see us.

ἔφυγε, δείσας μὴ αὐτῷ ἐπιβουλεύσαιμεν.
He fled, fearing that we might plot against him,

Genitive of the Whole (Partitive Genitive)

The genitive case is used to express the whole of which a part is mentioned. Examples:

μέγα μέρος <u>τῆς στρατιᾶς</u> ἐνικήθη.
A large part <u>of the army</u> was conquered.

ὀλίγος <u>στρατιώτων</u> ἐπὶ τοῦ πολέμου ἀπέθανε.
Few <u>of the soldiers</u> died in (the time of) the war.

Vocabulary

πίπτω, πεσοῦμαι, ἔπεσον, πέπτωκα, ____, ____ *fall; fall out, turn out*

ἡδονή, -ῆς, ἡ *pleasure, enjoyment*
(hedonist)

μέρος, μέρους, τό *part, portion*

νέμεσις, νεμέσεως, ἡ *retribution, vengeance*

παράδειγμα, παραδείγματος, τό
example, precedent (paradigm)

τύραννος, -ου, ὁ *tyrant*

ἴσος, -η, -ον *equal* (isosceles)

κοινός, -ή, -όν *common* (coin)

ὅμοιος, -α, -ον *like, similar*
(homogeneous)

ὀλίγος, -η, -ον *(a) little*; (pl.) *few*
(oligarchy)

ὀλίγου (adv.) *almost*

Drill A

Conjugate:

1. aorist active optative of:
    πίπτω, πράττω, ἀθροίζω

Drill A (continued)

2. present active optative of:
   πλέω, ὁράω, φημί, ἀγγέλλω, οἶδα

3. aorist active subjunctive of:
   μανθάνω, ἔρχομαι, ἀποκτείνω

Drill B

Locate the following forms:

1. κελεῦσαι   6. εἰδῇ
2. κελεύσαι   7. ἴδῃ
3. κέλευσαι   8. σφάξειαν
4. ἐπεμελοῦντο   9. ᾖ
5. πεπτωκυίᾳ   10. φιλοίη

Drill C

Choose the appropriate form of the verb in parentheses to complete the purpose/fearing clause; translate the sentence:

1. διὰ τοῦ πεδίου πεμφθήσεσθε ὅπως μὴ (λύσωσιν / λύσειαν) οἱ ξένοι τὴν εἰρήνην.

2. φοβεῖ μὴ (ἔχῃς / ἔχοις) ὀλίγα χρήματα;

3. εἰς τὴν νῆσον ἦλθες ἵνα τὰ φίλα παιδία (φυλάττῃς / φυλάττοις).

4. ἐδέδιτε μὴ ὁ ῥήτωρ ἡμᾶς (πείθῃ / πείθοι).

5. τῶν στρατιωτῶν πέντε παρὰ τὴν θάλατταν τάξει ὅπως τὴν νέμεσιν ἐπὶ τοὺς πολεμίους (ἀγάγωσιν / ἀγάγοιεν).

6. ὁ τύραννος ἐφοβήθη μὴ ὁ χειμών (ᾖ / εἴη) μέγας.

Exercise A

Translate:

1. θαυμάζοιμ' ἂν εἰ οἷός τ' εἴην ἐγὼ ὑμῶν ταύτην τὴν διαβολὴν ἐξελέσθαι ἐν οὕτως ὀλίγῳ χρόνῳ οὕτω πολλὴν γεγονυῖαν.

Exercise A (continued)

2. εὖ γὰρ ἴστε, ἐάν με ἀποκτείνητε, οὐκ ἐμὲ μᾶλλον βλάψετε ἢ ὑμᾶς αὐτούς.

3. εἴη ἂν δεινὸν παράδειγμα ἀδικίας, εἰ λύσαιτε τοὺς κλέψαντας.

4. θάψομεν τοὺς ἐν τῷ πολέμῳ πεπτωκότας ὡς αὐτοῖς ἴσον μέρος τιμῆς παρέχωμεν

5. ἐν ταῖς Ἀθήναις, εἰ γυνὴ τὸν ἄνδρα ἀποκτείνειεν, τὸν υἱὸν ἔδει κατὰ τὸν νεμέσεως νόμον τιμωρήσασθαι καίπερ τὴν μητέρα οὖσαν.

Exercise B

Translate:

1. If we really believe that all men are brothers, enemies will become friends, and wars will cease.

2. We were afraid that we might suffer something like death at the hands of the tyrant.

3. We happen to think that wine is a pleasure common to almost all men.

4. He was so afraid of falling that he actually fell.

5. The tyrant collected equal portions of money from his friends in order to plot against his fatherland.

10. ἡ Ἀθηνᾶ.

Lesson 40

Review

Drill A

Give the following forms:

1. dative singular of:
ἡ ἀσφαλὴς ὁδός, ὁ εὐδαίμων Ἀθηναῖος,
ὁ ταχὺς νεανίας, ἡ ἡδεῖα νίκη

2. accusative plural of:
τὸ μέγα γένος, πᾶς τις, ὁ πιστὸς δικαστής,
ὁ ἀληθὴς κίνδυνος

3. dative plural of:
τὸ ἴσον μέρος, ὁ ἐχθρὸς γέρων, ἡ δήλη νύξ,
πολίτης ἑκών

Drill B

Give the following forms:

1. aorist active optative, 3rd plural of: πίπτω, ἐλπίζω, κρίνω
2. aorist active subjunctive, 1st plural of: μισέω, εὑρίσκω
3. present active subjunctive, 3rd singular of: εἰμί, δοκέω,
ἐάω, φημί, νομίζω
4. present active optative, 2nd singular of: οἰκέω, μένω,
ὁράω, εἰμί

Exercise A: Reading

The Scythian offer is rejected. The Ionians plan a strategy.

Μιλτιάδου μὲν τοῦ Ἀθηναίου, στρατηγοῦ ὄντος καὶ
τυραννεύοντος Χερσονησιτῶν τῶν ἐν Ἑλλησπόντῳ, ἦν γνώμη
πείθεσθαι Σκύθαις καὶ σώζειν Ἰωνίαν, Ἱστιαίου δὲ τοῦ
Μιλησίου ἐναντία ταύτῃ, λέγοντος ὡς νῦν μὲν διὰ Δαρεῖον
5   ἕκαστος αὐτῶν τυραννεύει πόλεως, τῆς Δαρείου δὲ στρατιᾶς
καθαιρεθείσης οὔτε αὐτὸς Μιλησίων οἷός τ' ἔσται ἄρχειν οὔτε
ἄλλος οὐδεὶς οὐδένων· βουλήσεσθαι γὰρ ἔφη ἑκάστην τῶν

πόλεων δημοκρατεῖσθαι μᾶλλον ἢ τυραννεύεσθαι. Ἱστιαίου δὲ
τὴν γνώμην ταύτην ἀποφαίνοντος, πάντες τετραμμένοι ἦσαν
10   πρὸς ταύτην τὴν γνώμην, πρότερον τὴν Μιλτιάδου αἱρούμενοι.
οὗτοι οὖν ἐπειδὴ τὴν Ἱστιαίου ἡροῦντο γνώμην, ἔδοξε αὐτοῖς
πρὸς ταύτῃ τῇ γνώμῃ μέρος τι τῆς γεφύρας λύειν τὸ κατὰ τοὺς
Σκύθας ὄν, ἵνα καὶ ποιεῖν τι δοκοῖεν ποιοῦντες μηδὲν καὶ οἱ
Σκύθαι μὴ τολμῷεν διαβῆναι κατὰ τὴν γέφυραν. πρὸς δὲ
15   τούτοις εἶπον ὡς λύοντες τῆς γεφύρας τὸ μέρος τὸ κατὰ τοὺς
Σκύθας ὄν πάντα ποιήσουσι ἃ Σκύθαις ἐστὶ ἐν ἡδονῇ.

Adapted from Herodotus, *Histories* 4.137 and 139

1   Μιλτιάδου from Μιλτιάδης, ὁ *Miltiades*, Athenian tyrant of the
Thracian Chersonese since c. 524 BC; depends on γνώμη (2)

2   Χερσονησιτῶν from Χερσονησῖται, οἱ *inhabitants of the Chersonese*, the
Thracian peninsula, known as the Gallipoli peninsula today
Ἑλλησπόντῳ dat. sg. of Ἑλλήσποντος, ὁ *the Hellespont*, the narrow
strait dividing Europe from Asia

3   Ἱστιαίου from Ἱστίαιος, ὁ *Histiaeus*, tyrant of Miletus; depends on
γνώμη to be supplied with ἐναντία (4)

4   Μιλησίου from Μιλήσιος, ὁ *Milesian, citizen of Miletus*

7   οὐδένων gen. pl. of οὐδείς; depends on ἄρχειν; translate as *anyone*

10   πρότερον *formerly, before*

14   διαβῆναι aorist active infinitive of διαβαίνω, *cross*

<u>Exercise B</u>

Translate:

1. My enemies spoke in such a way that I almost forgot myself.
2. If any of us is faithful to his friends, he is both happy and
dear to the gods.
3. For a long time the prosperous ruler was afraid that swift
Nemesis would strike (hit) him and that he would fall into misfortune.
4. If anyone honored Zeus, he gained peace and a secure life.
5. Let them consult Apollo in order that they may not harm
themselves unwillingly.

11. ὁ Μιλτιάδης.

Lesson 41

Comparison of Adjectives. Genitive of Comparison
ὡς (ὅτι) with a Superlative

Comparison of Adjectives

a. In Greek the comparative degree of the majority of adjectives is
formed by adding -τερος, -α,-ον to the stem of the positive, the superlative
degree by adding -τατος, -η, -ον to the same stem. If the penult of an adjective
in -ος is long, the vowel preceding -τερος or -τατος is ο. On the other hand, if
the penult is short, the ο is lengthened to ω. A penult is long either by nature (long
vowel or diphthong) or by position (when a short vowel precedes two consonants
or a double consonant: ζ, ξ, ψ).

Long penult:

Positive	Comparative	Superlative
δεινός, -ή, -όν	δεινότερος, -α, -ον	δεινότατος, -η, -ον
δίκαιος, -α, -ον	δικαιότερος, -α, -ον	δικαιότατος, -η, -ον
πιστός, -ή, -όν	πιστότερος, -α, -ον	πιστότατος, -η, -ον
μακρός, -ά, -όν	μακρότερος, -α, -ον	μακρότατος, -η, -ον
μικρός, -ά, -όν	μικρότερος, -α, -ον	μικρότατος, -η, -ον

Short penult:

Positive	Comparative	Superlative
σοφός, -ή, -όν	σοφώτερος, -α, -ον	σοφώτατος, -η, -ον
ἄξοις, -α, -ον	ἀξιώτερος, -α, -ον	ἀξιώτατος, -η, -ον
φίλος, -η, -ον	φιλώτερος, -α, -ον	φιλώτατος, -η, -ον

b. Adjectives ending in -ης add -τερος, -α, -ον and -τατος, -η, -ον to
the stem of the positive. Examples:

Positive	Comparative	Superlative
ἀληθής, -ές (stem: ἀληθεσ-)	ἀληθέστερος, -α, -ον	ἀληθέστατος, -η, -ον
ἀσφαλής, -ές (stem: ἀσφαλεσ-)	ἀσφαλέστερος, -α, -ον	ἀσφαλέστατος, -η, -ον

Note: Most adjectives ending in -ων are compared similarly. Example:

Positive	Comparative	Superlative
εὐδαίμων, -όν	εὐδαιμονέστερος, -α, -ον	εὐδαιμονέστατος, -η, -ον

    c. Certain other adjectives, especially those ending in -ρος and -υς, use -ιων, -ιον for the comparative and -ιστος, -η, -ον for the superlative. The comparative, declined in full below, follows the pattern of εὐδαίμων, -ον (see Lesson 38).

Positive	Comparative	Superlative
ἐχθρός, -ά, -όν	ἐχθίων, -ιον	ἔχθιστος, -η, -ον
ἡδύς, -εῖα, -ύ	ἡδίων, -ιον	ἥδιστος, -η, -ον

Declension of the comparative ending in -ιων, -ιον

singular

masculine-feminine	neuter
ἡδίων	ἥδιον
ἡδίονος	ἡδίονος
ἡδίονι	ἡδίονι
ἡδίονα (ἡδίω)	ἥδιον

plural

ἡδίονες (ἡδίους)	ἡδίονα (ἡδίω)
ἡδιόνων	ἡδιόνων
ἡδίοσι(ν)	ἡδίοσι(ν)
ἡδίονας (ἡδίους)	ἡδίονα (ἡδίω)

Irregular Comparisons

Positive	Comparative	Superlative
ἀγαθός, -ή, -όν *good*	ἀμείνων, -ον *better, braver*	ἄριστος, -η, -ον *best, bravest*
	βελτίων, -ιον *(morally) better*	βέλτιστος, -η, -ον *(morally) best*
	κρείττων, -ον *better, stronger*	κράτιστος, -η, -ον *best, strongest*

κακός, -ή, -όν	κακίων, -ιον	κάκιστος, -η, -ον
bad	*worse*	*worst*
	χείρων, -ον	χείριστος, -η, -ον
	worse	*worst*
καλός, -ή, -όν	καλλίων, -ιον	κάλλιστος, -η, -ον
beautiful	*more beautiful*	*most beautiful*
μέγας, μεγάλη, μέγα	μείζων, -ον	μέγιστος, -η, -ον
large	*larger*	*largest*
πολύς, πολλή, πολύ	πλείων, -ον	πλεῖστος, -η, -ον
much	*more*	*most*
ῥᾴδιος, -α, -ον	ῥᾴων, -ον	ῥᾷστος, -η, -ον
easy	*easier*	*easiest*
ταχύς, -εῖα, -ύ	θάττων, -ον	τάχιστος, -η, -ον
swift	*swifter*	*swiftest*

Expressions of Comparison

The Greek word for "than" is ἤ. When ἤ is used with a comparative, the second element of the comparison always appears in the same case as the first. Example:

οἶνον ἡδίω ἤ τοῦτον οὔποτε εὑρήσω.
I shall never find a wine sweeter than this.

Genitive of Comparison

If ἤ is omitted, the second element of the comparison is placed in the genitive case. Example:

οἶνον ἡδίονα τούτου οὔποτε εὑρήσω.
I shall never find a wine sweeter than this.

ὡς (ὅτι) with a Superlative

When ὡς (ὅτι) is used with a superlative, it means "as . . . as possible."
Example:

ὁ γέρων ἦν ὡς (ὅτι) εὐδαιμονέστατος.
The old man was as happy as possible.

Vocabulary

ἁμαρτάνω, ἁμαρτήσομαι, ἥμαρτον, ἡμάρτηκα, ἡμάρτημαι,
ἡμαρτήθην *miss* (+gen.); *err*

διέξοδος, -ου, ἡ *way out, escape, escape route, passage* (exodus)

δοῦλος, -ου, ὁ *slave*

χρησμός, -οῦ, ὁ *oracle, oracular
response*

αἴτιος, -α, -ον (+ gen.) *responsible
(for)* (aetiology)

δειλός, -ή, -όν *cowardly, miserable*

μακρός, -ά, -όν *long* (macron)

μικρός, -ά, -όν *small, little, short*
    (microscope)

ῥᾴδιος, -α, -ον *easy*

μόγις (adverb) *hardly, scarcely, with
difficulty*

ὡς (ὅτι) (+ superl.) *as . . . as possible*

Drill A

Give the following forms:

1. ἡδίων to agree with:
    χρησμῷ, λόγοις, βίον (2 forms),
    κέρδος, ἡδονάς (2 forms)

2. βέλτιστος to agree with:
    δεσπότῃ, ψυχῇ, γένη, νεανίαν, ἄνδρας

3. θάττων to agree with:
    νεώς, τριήρη (2 forms), νεμέσει, ἄγγελοι,
    φυλάκων

Drill B

Supply the the comparative and superlative forms of the following
unfamiliar adjectives:

      1. πονηρός, ά, -όν
      2. σαφής, -ές
      3. μόνος, -η, -ον

Exercise A

Translate:

      1. πολλοὺς μὲν γέροντας καὶ εὐδαίμονας πολλάκις
ἑόρακα, εὐδαιμονέστερον δὲ σοῦ ἑόρακα οὐδένα.
      2. τί ἐστι ἥδιον ἢ ἰδεῖν κλῶπα δειλὸν συμφορὰν
πάσχοντα;
      3. βελτίονα μὲν οἶδα καὶ ἐπαινῶ χείρονα δὲ ποιῶ.
      4. οἱ γὰρ Ἕλληνές φασι τὰς αὑτῶν τριήρεις εἶναι
μακροτέρας καὶ θάττους ἢ τὰς τῶν πολεμίων ναῦς τὰς μικράς.
      5. ἡ δὴ οἰκία ἦν οὕτω μεγάλη ὥστε τὴν διέξοδον μόγις
εὕρομεν.

Exercise B

Translate:

      1. The oracle of Apollo said that no one was wiser than
Socrates.
      2. Nothing is better than the pleasures of wine and as many
women as possible.
      3. I accused him and brought him into court on the grounds
that he was responsible for the murder of his wife.
      4. Socrates sent a faithful slave to consult the oracle of Zeus.
      5. It is easier to err and do wrong than to obey the laws and be
an example of virtue.

Lesson 42

Subjunctive Mood (Middle and Passive Voices). Independent Uses

Subjunctive Mood (Middle and Passive Voices)
In the middle and passive voices, as in the active voice, the subjunctive is formed by lengthening to thematic vowels ο and ε to ω and η respectively. As a primary mood, the subjunctive takes primary middle-passive endings (i.e. -μαι, -σαι, -ται, etc.) throughout all of its tenses.

a. Present Middle-Passive

The present middle-passive subjunctive, formed from the first principal part, is conjugated as follows:

Regular ω-verb, παιδεύω:

singular	person	plural
παιδεύωμαι	1	παιδευώμεθα
παιδεύῃ	2	παιδεύησθε
παιδεύηται	3	παιδεύωνται

ε-contract, ποιέω:

singular	person	plural
ποιῶμαι (ποιέωμαι)	1	ποιώμεθα (ποιεώμεθα)
ποιῇ (ποιέῃ)	2	ποιῆσθε (ποιέησθε)
ποιῆται (ποιέηται)	3	ποιῶνται (ποιέωνται)

α-contract, τιμάω:

singular	person	plural
τιμῶμαι (τιμάωμαι)	1	τιμώμεθα (τιμαώμεθα)
τιμᾷ (τιμάῃ)	2	τιμᾶσθε (τιμάησθε)
τιμᾶται (τιμάηται)	3	τιμῶνται (τιμάωνται)

b. First Aorist Middle

The aorist middle subjunctive, formed from the third principal part (minus the temporal augment), is conjugated as follows:

Regular first aorist, παιδεύω:

singular	person	plural
παιδεύσωμαι	1	παιδευσώμεθα
παιδεύσῃ	2	παιδεύσησθε
παιδεύσηται	3	παιδεύσωνται

Liquid aorist, φαίνω:

singular	person	plural
φήνωμαι	1	φηνώμεθα
φήνῃ	2	φήνησθε
φήνηται	3	φήνωνται

c. Second Aorist Middle

λείπω:

singular	person	plural
λίπωμαι	1	λιπώμεθα
λίπῃ	2	λίπησθε
λίπηται	3	λίπωνται

d. Aorist Passive

The aorist passive, formed from the sixth principal part (minus the temporal augment), is conjugated as follows:

First aorist passive, παιδεύω:

singular	person	plural
παιδευθῶ	1	παιδευθῶμεν
παιδευθῇς	2	παιδευθῆτε
παιδευθῇ	3	παιδευθῶσι(ν)

Second aorist passive, φαίνω:

singular	person	plural
φανῶ	1	φανῶμεν
φανῇς	2	φανῆτε
φανῇ	3	φανῶσι(ν)

Hortatory Subjunctive

The hortatory subjunctive expresses a command in the first person and uses the present or aorist subjunctive. The negative is μή, which generally occurs first in the sentence. Examples:

ἑλώμεθα ἄρχοντα.
Let us choose a ruler.

τοῖς πολεμίοις μαχώμεθα.
Let us keep fighting the enemy.

μὴ πάθω τὴν συμφοράν.
Let me not suffer misfortune.

Prohibitions

A prohibition (negative imperative) is expressed by using μή with either the present imperative (see Lesson 33) or the aorist subjunctive in the second person. The third person of the aorist imperative is sometimes found in prohibitions. Examples:

μὴ ποίει τοῦτο. (imperative)
Do not keep on doing this.

μὴ ποιήσῃς τοῦτο. (subjunctive)
Don't do this.

μηδεὶς ποιησάτω τοῦτο. (imperative)
Let no one do this.

μὴ οἰηθῆτέ μ' ἀδικεῖν. (subjunctive)
Don't think that I am unjust.

Deliberative Subjunctive

The present or aorist subjunctive is used in questions where a possible course of action is being considered or deliberated. The negative is μή. Examples:

μείνω ἢ φύγω;
Am I to remain or flee?

μὴ τοῦτο ποιῶμεν;
Are we not to do this?

Vocabulary

ἀπορέω, ἀπορήσω, ἠπόρησα, ἠπόρηκα, ἠπόρημαι, ἠπορήθην
   be at a loss (aporetic)

ἐλέγχω, ἐλέγξω, ἤλεγξα, ____, ἐλήλεγμαι, ἠλέγχθην *refute, cross-examine*
   (elenchus)

τρέχω, δραμοῦμαι, ἔδραμον, -δεδράμηκα, -δεδράμημαι, ____ *run*
   (syndrome)

ὠφελέω, ὠφελήσω, ὠφέλησα, ὠφέληκα, ὠφέλημαι, ὠφελήθην *help, aid*

περὶ πολλοῦ (πλείονος, πλείστου) ποιεῖσθαι *to consider (more, most)*
   important

ἔχω (+ adv.) *be*

ἐλευθερία, -ας, ἡ *freedom*

κλέος, ____, τό (used only in
    nom. and acc. sg.) *fame, glory*

ἀσθενής, -ές *weak* (asthenic)

ἐλεύθερος, -α, -ον *free*

ἕτοιμος, -η, -ον *ready, prepared*

Note: A hyphen before the verb (i.e. -δεδράμηκα) indicates that the form occurs
only with a prefix.

Drill A

Locate the following forms:

1. ἁμάρτωμεν
2. αἰσθάνωνται
3. ὠφελήσειε
4. αἴσθωνται
5. πύθῃ

6. χρήσηται
7. λυθῆτε
8. πείθητε
9. ἐχρήσω
10. πεπτωκέναι

Drill B

Translate:

1. Are we to help or harm him?
2. Answer me, stranger!
3. Don't answer him, my slave!
4. Let us take care of ourselves.
5. He knows that he erred.
6. Seek in order that you may find.
7. Let those who have died be honored.
8. He happened to be at a loss.
9. I say that he is weak in body.
10. I am afraid that I may forget.
11. Some men are free, others are slaves.

Exercise A

Translate:

1. βασιλεὺς αἱρεῖται οὐχ ἵνα αὑτοῦ ἐπιμελῆται ἀλλ' ἵνα
οἱ ἑλόμενοι δι' αὐτὸν εὖ πράττωσιν.

2. οἱ νόμοι τοὺς νέους παιδεύειν οἷοί τ' εἰσι καὶ
βελτίους ποιοῦσιν; οὕτως ἔχει.

Exercise A (continued)

3. δέδοικα μὴ ἡ γυνὴ τὸν βασιλέα τιμωρήσηται ἅτε τὴν θυγατέρα θύσαντα.
4. τίνα οἰώμεθα εἶναι τὸν σοφώτατον τῶν ἀνδρῶν;
5. πρὸς δὲ θεῶν μὴ ἐπιβουλεύσητε τοῖς κρείττοσιν.

Exercise B

Translate:

1. Even if we err unwillingly, the gods will be ready to punish us.
2. What are we to say to those who accuse us?
3. The Greeks considered freedom more important than life itself.
4. Don't accuse Socrates, for he will refute you and acquire fame.
5. The swift herald ran for many stades in order to announce the victory to the Athenians.

12. οἱ δράμοντες, as depicted on a black figure amphora, c. 530 BC.

Lesson 43

Adverbs. Comparison of Adverbs
Dative of Degree of Difference

Formation of Adverbs

Adverbs of manner can be formed from many adjectives. These adverbs usually end is -ως and can be formed by removing ν from the genitive masculine plural of the adjective and adding ς. Examples:

Adjective (genitive plural)	Adverb
δικαίων *just*	δικαίως *justly*
καλῶν *fine*	καλῶς *well*
ταχέων *swift*	ταχέως *swiftly*
ἀσφαλῶν *safe*	ἀσφαλῶς *safely*

Comparison of Adverbs

The comparative of an adverb is identical to the accusative neuter singular of the comparative adjective. The superlative is identical to the accusative neuter plural of the superlative adjective. Examples:

δικαίως *justly*	δικαιότερον *more justly*	δικαιότατα *most justly*
σοφῶς *wisely*	σοφώτερον *more wisely*	σοφώτατα *most wisely*
ἡδέως *gladly*	ἥδιον *more gladly*	ἥδιστα *most gladly*
ταχέως *swiftly*	θᾶττον *more swiftly*	τάχιστα *most swiftly*
εὖ *well*	ἄμεινον, βέλτιον *better*	ἄριστα, βέλτιστα *best, very well*
κακῶς *badly*	κάκιον, χεῖρον *worse*	κάκιστα, χείριστα *worst*
μεγάλως, μέγα *greatly, loudly*	μεῖζον *more (greatly)*	μέγιστα, μέγιστον *most (greatly)*
ῥᾳδίως *easily*	ῥᾷον *more easily*	ῥᾷστα *most easily*

μάλα	μᾶλλον	μάλιστα
very	*more, rather*	*most, certainly, very much, especially*

μικρόν	ἧττον	ἥκιστα
little	*less*	*least, very little*

πολύ	πλεῖον, πλέον	πλεῖστα
much	*more*	*most, very much*

Dative of Degree of Difference

The dative case without a preposition is used to describe the degree of difference between two elements of a comparison. Example:

ἥδε ἡ ὁδός ἐστι πολλῷ (δέκα σταδίοις) μακροτέρα ἢ ἐκείνη.
This road is much (ten stades) longer than that.

Vocabulary

βοάω, βοήσομαι, ἐβόησα, ____, ____, ____ *shout, call out*

ἥκω, ἥξω ____, ____, ____, ____ *have come, come, arrive*

ῥίπτω, ῥίψω, ἔρριψα, ἔρριφα, ἔρριμμαι, ἐρρίφθην *throw, throw away*

ἀλλήλων, ἀλλήλοις (-αις), ἀλλήλους (-ας, -α) *each other, one another*

πύλαι, -ῶν, αἱ *gates; mountain pass* (Thermopylae)

φόβος, -ου, ὁ *fear*

ἐλάττων, -ον (comparative of μικρός or ὀλίγος) *smaller, less*

ἐλάχιστος, -η, -ον (superlative of μικρός or ὀλίγος) *smallest, least*

τότε (adverb) *then, at that time*

οἱ τότε . . . οἱ νῦν *men of old (of that time) . . . men of today*

πρό (+ gen.) *before; instead of, on behalf of* (progeny)

<u>Drill</u>

Choose the Greek word which best translates the underlined English word:

    1. The men <u>wisely</u> (σοφοί, σοφῶς, σοφώτερον) consulted the oracle before acting.

    2. A horse is <u>more swift</u> (θάττων, ταχύς, ὡς τάχιστος) than a man.

    3. Which Greek heroes are considered to be <u>the best</u> (χείριστοι, ἀμείνονες, ἄριστοι)?

    4. The Ionians conceived of a plan <u>as cowardly as possible</u> (δειλότατον, ὡς δειλότατον, ὅτι δειλότερον).

    5. <u>Scarcely</u> (μάλα, εὖ, μόγις) did they escape the fire with their lives.

    6. They cared <u>less</u> (πολύ, ἧττον, χείριστα) about truth than about winning the argument.

<u>Exercise A: Reading</u>

The Ionian strategy succeeds, but the Persians panic.

      Σκύθαι μὲν Ἴωσι πιστεύσαντες λέγειν ἀληθῆ ἐζήτουν
τοὺς Πέρσας καὶ ἡμάρτανον πάσης τῆς ἐκείνων διεξόδου.
αἴτιοι δὲ τούτου αὐτοὶ οἱ Σκύθαι ἐγένοντο, τὰς τῶν ἵππων
νομὰς διαφθείραντες. εἰ γὰρ ταῦτα μὴ ἐποίησαν, ἐξῆν ἂν
5   αὐτοῖς, εἰ ἐβούλοντο, ῥᾳδίως ἐξευρεῖν τοὺς Πέρσας. νῦν δὲ ἃ
αὐτοῖς ἐδόκει ἄριστα βεβουλεῦσθαι κακῶς ἔπεσεν. οἱ δὲ δὴ
Πέρσαι τὴν ὁδὸν καθ᾽ ἣν πρότερον ἀφιγμένοι ἦσαν φυλάττοντες
ἔφευγον καὶ οὕτω μόγις εὗρον τὴν διέξοδον. ἅτε δὲ νυκτός τε
ἀφικόμενοι καὶ λελυμένης τῆς γεφύρας τυχόντες εἰς πάντα
10   φόβον ἀφίκοντο μὴ αὐτοὺς οἱ Ἴωνες ἀπολελοιπότες εἶεν.

Adapted from Herodotus, *Histories* 4.140

4   νομάς from νομή, -ῆς, ἡ *pasturage*

Exercise B

Translate:

      1. Men of old treated each other much more justly than do men of today.

      2. Our messenger shouted as loudly as possible before the gates of the city because he was afraid that the enemy were coming to seize him.

      3. The old man willingly threw himself into the sea to escape those who were intending to harm him.

      4. In battle, don't throw away your shields, cowards, if you perceive that death is at hand (present).

      5. Men of old considered most important those thoughts which men of today consider least important.

13. Entrance to the Treasury of Atreus, a Bronze Age Tholos Tomb
in Mycenae, Greece, c. 1350 BC.

Lesson 44

Optative Mood (Middle and Passive Voices). Independent Uses

<u>Optative Mood (Middle and Passive Voices)</u>
As a secondary mood, the optative takes <u>secondary</u> middle-passive endings (i.e. -μην, -σο, -το, etc.) throughout all of its tenses.

a. Present Middle-Passive

The present middle-passive optative, formed from the first principal part, is conjugated as follows:

Regular ω-verb, παιδεύω:

singular	person	plural
παιδευοίμην	1	παιδευοίμεθα
παιδεύοιο	2	παιδεύοισθε
παιδεύοιτο	3	παιδεύοιντο

ε-contract, ποιέω:

singular	person	plural
ποιοίμην (ποιεοίμην)	1	ποιοίμεθα (ποιεοίμεθα)
ποιοῖο (ποιέοιο)	2	ποιοῖσθε (ποιέοισθε)
ποιοῖτο (ποιέοιτο)	3	ποιοῖντο (ποιέοιντο)

α-contract, τιμάω:

singular	person	plural
τιμῴμην (τιμαοίμην)	1	τιμῴμεθα (τιμαοίμεθα)
τιμῷο (τιμάοιο)	2	τιμῷσθε (τιμάοισθε)
τιμῷτο (τιμάοιτο)	3	τιμῷντο (τιμάοιντο)

b. First Aorist Middle

The aorist middle optative, formed from the third principal part (minus the temporal augment), is conjugated as follows:

Regular first aorist, παιδεύω: Liquid aorist, φαίνω:

singular	person	plural	singular	person	plural
παιδευσαίμην	1	παιδευσαίμεθα	φηναίμην	1	φηναίμεθα
παιδεύσαιο	2	παιδεύσαισθε	φήναιο	2	φήναισθε
παιδεύσαιτο	3	παιδεύσαιντο	φήναιτο	3	φήναιντο

c. Second Aorist Middle

λείπω:

singular	person	plural
λιποίμην	1	λιποίμεθα
λίποιο	2	λίποισθε
λίποιτο	3	λίποιντο

d. Aorist Passive

The aorist passive optative, formed from the sixth principal part (minus the temporal augment), is conjugated as follows:

First aorist passive, παιδεύω: Second aorist passive, φαίνω:

singular	person	plural	singular	person	plural
παιδευθείην	1	παιδευθεῖμεν	φανείην	1	φανεῖμεν
παιδευθείης	2	παιδευθεῖτε	φανείης	2	φανεῖτε
παιδευθείη	3	παιδευθεῖεν	φανείη	3	φανεῖεν

Wishes

Like conditions, wishes are of two types: those which can be fulfilled and those which are impossible to fulfill (contrary-to-fact).

a. Possible Wishes

These wishes refer to future action and use the present or aorist tense of the optative, depending upon whether the action is expressed with a progressive (present tense) or simple aspect (aorist tense). εἴθε or εἰ γάρ, while sometimes omitted, are usually used to introduce such wishes. The negative is μή. Examples:

(εἰ γὰρ) ὁ στρατηγὸς τοὺς βαρβάρους νικῴη.
May the general conquer the barbarians!
or
If only the general would conquer the barbarians!

(εἴθε) μὴ ἀπορρίψειε τὴν ἀσπίδα.
May he not throw away his shield!
or
If only he would not throw away his shield!

b. Impossible Wishes

Here the pattern established for contrary-to-fact conditions (see Lesson 13) is followed. In imitation of the protasis of a contrary-to-fact present condition, the imperfect indicative is used for wishes that are impossible to realize in present time. In imitation of the protasis of a contrary-to-fact past condition, the aorist indicative is used for wishes that are impossible to realize (as they refer to past events that can no longer be altered). These wishes must be introduced by εἴθε or εἰ γάρ. The negative is μή. Examples:

εἴθε μὴ τὰς Ἀθήνας ἔλειπον.
If only I were not leaving Athens!

εἰ γάρ, ὦ γῆ, τότε μ᾽ ἐδέξω.
O earth, if only you had received me then!

Potential Optative

The optative is used with ἄν to denote a possible or probable future action. This construction is comparable to the apodosis of a future less vivid condition (see Lesson 39). In English the auxiliary verbs may, might, should, would, can, or could are used to translate a potential optative. The negative is οὐ. Examples:

ἡδέως δ᾽ ἂν αὐτὸν χρήματα αἰτοίην.
I would like to ask him for money.

οὐκ ἂν δικαίως εἰς κακόν τι πέσοιμι.
I could not justly fall into any evil.

Vocabulary

τρέφω, θρέψω, ἔθρεψα, τέτροφα, τέθραμμαι, ἐτράφην *nourish, raise, support* (atrophy, autotroph)

φέρω, οἴσω, ἤνεγκα (aor. infin. ἐνεγκεῖν; aor. imper. 2nd sg. ἔνεγκε), ἐνήνοχα, ἐνήνεγμαι, ἠνέχθην *carry, bring, bear* (metaphor)

ἀρχή, -ῆς, ἡ *beginning; rule, government* (anarchy)

πάθος, πάθους, τό *experience, suffering*

πλῆθος, πλήθους, τό *largest part, multitude, majority, mob* (plethora)

ὕβρις, ὕβρεως, ἡ *insolence, arrogance* (hubris)

ἤδη (adverb) *already, now*

ἴσως (adverb) *equally; perhaps*

πάλαι (adverb) *long ago, for a long time* (palaeography)

ὑπέρ (+ gen.) *over, above, on behalf of* (hypercritical, hyperbole)
    (+ acc.) *beyond, in excess of*

εἰ γάρ *if only*

εἴθε *if only*

Drill A

Conjugate:

1. aorist passive optative of: γράφω, φέρω

2. present middle-passive optative of: φιλέω, χράομαι

3. aorist middle optative of: πείθω, αἰσθάνομαι

Drill B

Give the following forms:

1. present middle-passive optative, 3rd singular of:
    ἔρχομαι, φέρω, ἀπολογέομαι, ὁράω

2. aorist middle optative, 2nd singular of:
    πυνθάνομαι, χράομαι, γίγνομαι, ὑπισχνέομαι

3. aorist passive optative, 3rd plural of:
    λαμβάνω, φέρω, ὁράω, τρέφω

Exercise A

Translate:

1. εἴθ', ὦ παῖ, ἦσθα πατρὶ ὁμοῖος.

2. καίπερ τοῦ πλήθους κελεύοντος καὶ βοῶντος καὶ ἤδη
ἑτοίμου ὄντος ἀποκτεῖναί με, μετὰ τοῦ ἀρχῆς γενέσθαι καὶ
ἁμαρτάνειν.

3. ὕβρις ἥδε ἂν εἴη, εἴ τις κρείττων θεῶν εἶναι
βούλοιτο.

4. ὁ τύραννος ἂν μάλιστα ἡσθείη ἀκούων τοῦ πλήθους
τὸ αὑτοῦ ὄνομα βοῶντος.

5. ὁ γέρων παῖδά τινα εἰς τὴν οἰκίαν ἤνεγκεν ὡς ἡ
γυνὴ αὐτὸν τρέφοι.

Exercise B

Translate:

1. If only I had done many things worthy of honor on behalf of
my country!

2. Who would fear any experience more than death?

3. Someone of you might perhaps believe that insolence is the
beginning of all evils.

4. I would have been refuted long ago if I had not consulted
you.

5. May the gods bring you as much wealth and fame as possible
because of your honorable deeds.

14. Restored north entrance of the Bronze Age
Palace of King Minos, Knossos, Crete.

Lesson 45

Review

Drill A

Locate the following forms:

1. τραφείη
2. ἀποροίην
3. βοῆσαι
4. ῥιφθῶσι
5. κατηγορήσοντες

6. δράμοιεν
7. φοβηθῇ
8. ἀπολογήσαιο
9. θαυμάσονται
10. οἰκηθεῖεν

Drill B

Give the following forms:

1. μείζων to agree with:
   κλέος, ἐλευθερίᾳ, μερῶν, ἡδοναῖς

2. ῥᾷστος to agree with:
   διέξοδοι, ἔργου, ἄρχοντας, κέρδος

3. ταχύς to agree with:
   ἄνδρα, τριήρεσι, νεώς, μοῖραν

Drill C

Give the following forms:

1. accusative singular of:
   ἡ ἀσθενεστέρα γυνή, τὸ ἥδιστον κέρδος,
   ἡ χείρων ὕβρις

2. nominative plural of:
   ὁ ἕτοιμος στρατιώτης, τὸ ῥᾷον παράδειγμα,
   ὁ ἀσθενὴς δοῦλος

3. dative singular of:
   ἡ μεγίστη πόλις, ὁ κακίων χρησμός,
   ἡ καλλίων θυγάτηρ

Exercise A: Reading

The Persians are saved by the Ionians with the help of an Egyptian.

Ἦν δὲ περὶ Δαρεῖον ἀνὴρ Αἰγύπτιος βοῶν μέγιστον
ἀνθρώπων· τοῦτον τὸν ἄνδρα ταχθέντα ἐπὶ τοῦ χείλους τοῦ
Ἴστρου ἐκέλευε Δαρεῖος καλεῖν Ἱστιαῖον Μιλήσιον. ὁ μὲν δὴ
ἐποίει ταῦτα, Ἱστιαῖος δὲ ἀκούσας τάς τε ναῦς πάσας παρεῖχε
σώσων τὴν στρατιὰν καὶ τὴν γέφυραν ἔζευξε. Πέρσαι μὲν οὖν
οὕτω ἐξέφευγον, Σκύθαι δὲ διώκοντες ἥμαρτον τῶν Περσῶν,
καὶ τοῦτο μέν, ὡς ὄντας Ἴωνας ἐλευθέρους, χειρίστους καὶ
δειλοτάτους ἔκρινον εἶναι πάντων ἀνθρώπων, τοῦτο δέ, ὡς
ὄντας Ἴωνας δούλους, φιλοδεσπότους ἔφασαν εἶναι καὶ
ἀδράστους μάλιστα. ταῦτα δὴ Σκύθαις εἰς Ἴωνας ἀπέρριπται.

Adapted from Herodotus, *Histories* 4 141-142

1	Αἰγύπτιος, -α, -ον *Egyptian*
2	χείλους from χεῖλος, χείλυυς, τό *edge*
3	Ἴστρου from Ἴστρος, -ου, ὁ *the Ister* (Danube river)
5	ἔζευξε aorist active indicative, 3ʳᵈ singular of ζεύγνυμι *connect*
7	τοῦτο μέν . . . τοῦτο δέ (8) *on the one hand . . . on the other hand*
9	φιλοδεσπότους from φιλοδέσποτος, -ον *fond of masters*
10	ἀδράστους from ἄδραστος, -ον *not inclined to run away*

Exercise B

Translate:

1. O Zeus, may brothers not fight with each other; for instead of war let them choose peace.

2. Finally let us obey the law and spare him, for another like him will not quickly be found.

3. What, therefore, are we to consider more important than to make young men as good as possible?

4. Men of old threw stones which men of today would not be able to carry easily.

5. Don't think that the bravest man is more fortunate than the weakest god.

Lesson 46

Irregular Second Aorists (α and ο Root Aorists). Articular Infinitives

Irregular Second Aorists (α and ο Root Aorists)

Several Greek verbs have second aorists which are irregular because of euphonic changes that result when an α (as in βαίνω) or ο (as in γιγνώσκω) stem (or *root*) vowel interacts with the thematic vowel of the verb's ending:

a. α Root Aorist, βαίνω (*go*)

Indicative:			Subjunctive:		
singular	person	plural	singular	person	plural
ἔβην	1	ἔβημεν	βῶ	1	βῶμεν
ἔβης	2	ἔβητε	βῇς	2	βῆτε
ἔβη	3	ἔβησαν	βῇ	3	βῶσι(ν)

Optative:			Imperative:		
singular	person	plural	singular	person	plural
βαίην	1	βαῖμεν			
βαίης	2	βαῖτε	βῆθι	2	βῆτε
βαίη	3	βαῖεν	βήτω	3	βάντων

Infinitive:
βῆναι

Participle:
Nominative singular

βάς, βᾶσα, βάν

Genitive singular

βάντος, βάσης, βάντος

b. ο Root Aorist, γιγνώσκω (*know*)

Indicative:			Subjunctive:		
singular	person	plural	singular	person	plural
ἔγνων	1	ἔγνωμεν	γνῶ	1	γνῶμεν
ἔγνως	2	ἔγνωτε	γνῷς	2	γνῶτε
ἔγνω	3	ἔγνωσαν	γνῷ	3	γνῶσι(ν)

Optative:			Imperative:		
singular	person	plural	singular	person	plural
γνοίην	1	γνοῖμεν			
γνοίης	2	γνοῖτε	γνῶθι	2	γνῶτε
γνοίη	3	γνοῖεν	γνώτω	3	γνόντων

Infinitive:
γνῶναι

Participle:
Nominative singular

γνούς, γνοῦσα, γνόν

Genitive singular

γνόντος, γνούσης, γνόντος

Articular Infinitives

When preceded by a <u>neuter article</u>, the infinitive is used as a verbal noun (gerund) in Greek. As a noun, the articular infinitive is commonly used as a subject, direct object, or object of a preposition. As a verb, it has voice and tense and can govern any construction normally associated with a verb. The subject, if expressed, is placed in the <u>accusative</u> case. The negative is μή. Usually it is best to translate a Greek articular infinitive into English by using the "-ing" or "to" form of the verb, e.g. "running," "to run"; "talking," "to talk," etc., but certain constructions demand other idiomatic translations. Examples:

δικαστὴς αἱρεῖται ἐπὶ τῷ κατὰ τοὺς νόμους κρίνειν.
A judge is chosen for the purpose of judging according to the laws.
or
A judge is chosen to judge according to the laws.

τί ἐστι βέλτιον τοῦ τοῖς νόμοις πείθεσθαι;
What is better than obeying the laws?

διὰ τὸ ὑμᾶς ἡμαρτηκέναι κακῶς πράττομεν.
We are faring badly because you have erred. (lit., because of the fact that you have erred)

ἀνδρὸς τὸ πολέμειν.
To make war is characteristic of man.

Vocabulary

ἀκολουθέω, ἀκολουθήσω, ____, ____, ____, ____ (+dat.) *follow, accompany* (anacoluthon)

ἁλίσκομαι, ἁλώσομαι, ἑάλων, ἑάλωκα ____, ____ (used as passive of αἱρέω) *be taken, be caught, be captured, be convicted*

ἀναβαίνω, ἀναβήσομαι, ἀνέβην, ἀναβέβηκα ____, ____ *go up*

γιγνώσκω, γνώσομαι, ἔγνων, ἔγνωκα, ἔγνωσμαι, ἐγνώσθην *know* (by observation, as opposed to οἶδα, know by reflection), *perceive, recognize* (governs all three constructions in indirect statement) (agnostic)

ἀναγιγνώσκω *read*

μεταπέμπω (usually in middle) *summon, send for*

ἐπιστολή, -ῆς, ἡ *letter* (epistle)

Δελφοί, -ῶν, οἱ *Delphi* (site of Apollo's oracle)

Κῦρος, -ου, ὁ *Cyrus* (pretender to throne of Persia)

Ξενοφῶν, Ξενοφῶντος, ὁ *Xenophon* (author and soldier in Cyrus' expedition)

πορεία, -ας, ἡ *journey*

ἀρχαῖος, -α, -ον *old, ancient* (archaeology)

πρόθυμος, -ον *willing, eager*

μέντοι (postpositive adverb) *however; of course*

Drill A

Conjugate:

1. aorist active indicative of: ἀναβαίνω, ἁλίσκομαι
2. aorist active imperative of: γιγνώσκω, ἀναβαίνω
3. aorist active subjunctive of: ἁλίσκομαι, ἀναβαίνω

Drill B

Give the following forms:

1. aorist active indicative, 3rd plural of:
    φέρω, τρέχω, ἀναγιγνώσκω, τρέφω, λανθάνω

Drill B (continued)

2. aorist active optative, 3rd singular of:
   ἀναβαίνω, ἁλίσκομαι, γιγνώσκω, ὠφελέω,
   φέρω

3. aorist active infinitive of:
   ἁλίσκομαι, ἀναβαίνω, φέρω, ῥίπτω

Exercise C

Translate the English words in parentheses using the appropriate form of an articular infinitive in Greek; translate the completed sentence:

1. ἄξιός εἶ (of being avenged).
2. τοῦτό ἐστι (doing injustice), (to seek) πλέον τῶν ἄλλων ἔχειν.
3. τί ἐστι τὸ δίκαιον; τὸ δίκαιόν ἐστι τοὺς μὲν φίλους (helping), τοὺς δὲ ἐχθροὺς (harming).
4. παιδευόμεθα ἵνα ἕτοιμοι ὦσιν εἰς (speaking) τε καὶ (doing).
5. ὁ ἄνθρωπος διὰ (killing) ἀδελφὸν ὑπὸ τοῦ πατρὸς κατηγορήθη.

Exercise A: Reading

Born in Athens about 428/7 BC, Xenophon was raised during the Peloponnesian War, a demoralizing period of political and military decline for the Athenian democracy. As a young aristocrat and associate of the followers of Socrates, he found life in Athens politically difficult during a series of upheavals from 404 to 401 BC. As a result, he left home for Persia to join a Greek mercenary army in the pay of Cyrus, a Persian noble who aspired to the throne of his brother. When the expedition failed and thousands of Greek mercenaries found themselves abandoned in an unfriendly country, Xenophon led them to safety. After several subsequent military campaigns in Asia Minor and Greece, Xenophon resided in Sparta, where much of his literary career was spent. Among his best known works are the *Anabasis* (see below and Lesson 47), an account of the expedition with Cyrus, and the *Memorabilia* (see Lessons 55-60), an account of Socrates' character and conversations. For both the volume of his writings and the range of his subjects, Xenophon ranks as one of the most prolific authors of antiquity. Because of the simplicity of his language and style, he has traditionally been considered a representative of classical Attic prose at its finest.

Xenophon asks Socrates for advice.

Ἦν δέ τις ἐν τῇ στρατιᾷ Ξενοφῶν Ἀθηναῖος, ὅς οὔτε
στρατηγὸς οὔτε στρατιώτης ὢν συνηκολούθει, ἀλλὰ Πρόξενος
αὐτὸν μετεπέμψατο ἐξ Ἀθηνῶν ξένος ὢν ἀρχαῖος· ὑπισχνεῖτο δὲ
αὐτῷ τάδε·
5   Ἐὰν ἔλθῃς, φίλον σε Κύρῳ ποιήσω, ὃν αὐτὸς
φιλότερον ἐμαυτῷ νομίζω τῆς πατρίδος.
           Ὁ μέντοι Ξενοφῶν ἀναγνοὺς τὴν ἐπιστολὴν
συνεβουλεύσατο Σωκράτει τῷ Ἀθηναίῳ περὶ τῆς πορείας. καὶ ὁ
Σωκράτης δείσας μὴ Κύρῳ τὸ φίλον γενέσθαι εἴη αἴτιον
10   κατηγορίας τινὸς πρὸς πόλεως, ὅτι ἐδόκει ὁ Κῦρος προθύμως
τοῖς Λακεδαιμονίοις ἐπὶ τὰς Ἀθήνας συμμαχέσασθαι,
συνεβούλευσε τῷ Ξενοφῶντι ἐλθόντι εἰς Δελφοὺς χρήσασθαι τῷ
θεῷ περὶ τῆς πορείας.

Adapted from Xenophon, *Anabasis* 3.1.4-5

2   Πρόξενος, -ου, ὁ *Proxenus* (a Theban general and friend of Xenophon)
11   Λακεδαιμονίοις from Λακεδαιμόνιοι, -ων, οἱ *the Lacedaemonians*
       (another name for the Spartans)

Exercise B

Translate:

1. The Greeks always considered knowing themselves more
important than (knowing) others.
2. If I had known that you were at a loss, I would perhaps have
gone up to Delphi for the purpose of consulting Apollo about the
outcome.
3. After consulting Socrates, Xenophon eagerly accompanied
Cyrus with the avowed purpose of helping him with regard to the
expedition.
4. Summoning me by letter, the great king provided money in
order that I might make the long journey to his country.
5. Socrates, however, has already been convicted by the
Athenians on the grounds that he is friendly to the Lacedaemonians.

Lesson 47

εἶμι. Verbal Adjectives

εἶμι

The irregular verb εἶμι (*go*) is conjugated as follows:

<table>
<tr><td colspan="3">Present Indicative</td><td colspan="3">Present Subjunctive</td></tr>
<tr><td>singular</td><td>person</td><td>plural</td><td>singular</td><td>person</td><td>plural</td></tr>
<tr><td>εἶμι</td><td>1</td><td>ἴμεν</td><td>ἴω</td><td>1</td><td>ἴωμεν</td></tr>
<tr><td>εἶ</td><td>2</td><td>ἴτε</td><td>ἴῃς</td><td>2</td><td>ἴητε</td></tr>
<tr><td>εἶσι(ν)</td><td>3</td><td>ἴασι(ν)</td><td>ἴῃ</td><td>3</td><td>ἴωσι(ν)</td></tr>
</table>

<table>
<tr><td colspan="3">Present Optative</td><td colspan="3">Present Imperative</td></tr>
<tr><td>singular</td><td>person</td><td>plural</td><td>singular</td><td>person</td><td>plural</td></tr>
<tr><td>ἴοιμι (ἰοίην)</td><td>1</td><td>ἴοιμεν</td><td></td><td></td><td></td></tr>
<tr><td>ἴοις</td><td>2</td><td>ἴοιτε</td><td>ἴθι</td><td>2</td><td>ἴτε</td></tr>
<tr><td>ἴοι</td><td>3</td><td>ἴοιεν</td><td>ἴτω</td><td>3</td><td>ἰόντων</td></tr>
</table>

<table>
<tr><td>Present Infinitive</td><td>Present Participle</td></tr>
<tr><td>ἰέναι</td><td>Nominative singular
ἰών, ἰοῦσα, ἰόν</td></tr>
<tr><td></td><td>Genitive singular
ἰόντος, ἰούσης, ἰόντος</td></tr>
</table>

Imperfect Indicative

singular	person	plural
ἦα (ᾔειν)	1	ᾖμεν
ᾔεισθα (ᾔεις)	2	ᾖτε
ᾔειν (ᾔει)	3	ᾖσαν (ᾔεσαν)

Notes: The present indicative of εἶμι has a future meaning and is used instead of ἐλεύσομαι (the future of ἔρχομαι), which is seldom found in Attic prose.

Be careful to distinguish the various forms of εἶμι (*go*), εἰμί (*be*), especially in the present and imperfect tenses, and οἶδα (*know*) in the perfect and pluperfect tenses.

Formation of Verbal Adjectives

Verbal adjectives are formed by adding -τέος, -τέα, -τέον to the verb stem, usually found by dropping the temporal augment and -θην from the sixth principal part. A partial list follows:

a. Verbal adjectives formed from the sixth principal part:

First principal part	Sixth principal part	Verbal adjective
πείθω	ἐπείσθην	πειστέος
αἱρέω	ἡρέθην	αἱρετέος
πράττω	ἐπράχθην	πρακτέος
πέμπω	ἐπέμφθην	πεμπτέος
ὁράω	ὤφθην	ὀπτέος
κρίνω	ἐκρίθην	κριτέος
ποιέω	ἐποιήθην	ποιητέος
πειράομαι	ἐπειράθην	πειρατέος

Note: for verbs like ὁράω, πέμπω, πράττω, aspirated consonants remaining after dropping -θην from the sixth principal part must be unaspirated to find the verb stem, hence ὤφθην → ὀπτέος, ἐπέμφθην → πεμπτέος, and ἐπράχθην → πρακτέος.

b. Irregular Verbs

First principal part	Verbal adjective
διαβαίνω	διαβατέος
εἶμι	ἰτέος
οἶδα	ἰστέος
φέρω	οἰστέος
φημί	φατέος

Uses of Verbal Adjectives

a. When used personally, the verbal adjective is passive in sense, and denotes necessity or obligation. An appropriate form of εἰμί is expressed or understood. The dative of agent is used with this construction. Examples:

οὐ γὰρ πρὸ τῆς ἀληθείας τιμητέος (ἐστὶ) ἀνήρ.
For a man must not be (lit., is not to be) honored before the truth.

ὠφελητέα σοι ἡ πόλις ἐστίν.
The city must be (lit., is to be) helped by you.

ταῦτα ἡμῖν ποιητέον ἐστίν.
These things must be done by us.

b. When used impersonally, the verbal adjective (in the neuter singular or occasionally neuter plural) is best translated with the phrase "it is necessary" + the infinitive in English. Here also a form of εἰμί is expressed or understood, and the dative is again used for the agent. Examples:

ὑμῖν πειστέον ἐστὶ τοῖς τοῦ πατρὸς λόγοις.
It is necessary for you to obey your father's words.

ὑμῖν αὐτὸν πειστέον ἐστίν.
It is necessary for you to persuade him.

c. Compare these sentences expressed with δεῖ:

ὑμᾶς δεῖ τοῖς τοῦ πατρὸς λόγοις πείθευθαι.
It is necessary that you obey your father's words.

ὑμᾶς δεῖ αὐτὸν πεῖσαι.
It is necessary for you to persuade him.

Vocabulary

αἰτιάομαι, αἰτιάσομαι, ἠτιασάμην, ____, ἠτίαμαι, ____ *blame*

διαβαίνω, διαβήσομαι, διέβην, διαβέβηκα, ____, ____ *go across, cross*

εἶμι *go*

ἐπινοέω, ἐπινοήσω, ἐπενόησα, ____, ____, ____ *have in mind, intend*

ἔρομαι, ἐρήσομαι, ἠρόμην, ____, ____, ____ *ask*

ἐρωτάω, ἐρωτήσω, ἠρώτησα, ἠρώτηκα, ἠρώτημαι, ἠρωτήθην *ask*

εὔχομαι, εὔξομαι, ηὐξάμην, ____, ηὔγμαι, ____ *pray (for), vow, boast*
   (governs infinitive in indirect statement)

χρή (imperf. ἐχρῆν or χρῆν; impersonal verb, used with acc. and infin.) *it is necessary, must, ought*

ἐλπίς, ἐλπίδος, ἡ *hope*

χαλεπός, -ή, -όν *difficult*

πάλιν (adverb) *back, back again* (palindrome)

<u>Drill A</u>

Conjugate:

    1. imperfect active indicative of: εἶμι, εἰμί
    2. pluperfect active indicative of: οἶδα, ἐρωτάω
    3. present active indicative of: εἶμι, εἰμί
    4. perfect active indicative of: οἶδα, διαβαίνω

<u>Drill B</u>

Translate, indicating whether the following verbs are forms of εἰμί, εἶμι, or οἶδα. Some forms are ambiguous.

    1. ἦμεν   6. ἤεισθα
    2. εἶ   7. ἤδη
    3. εἰσί(ν)   8. ἴσασι(ν)
    4. ἦσθα   9. ἴασι(ν)
    5. ἴστε   10. ἦσμεν

<u>Drill C</u>

Supply the appropriate form of the verbal adjective to translate the English phrase in parentheses and, if necessary, to agree with the nominative subject supplied; translate the completed sentence:

    1. ὁ ποταμὸς ἡμῖν (must be crossed) ἐστί.
    2. ἡμῖν (it is necessary to persuade) ἐστί.
    3. (must be helped) σοι ἡ πόλις ἐστίν.
    4. ἄλλαι νῆες ἐκ τῶν συμμάχων (must be summoned)
εἰσίν.
    5. ἀλήθειάν γε περὶ πολλοῦ (it is necessary to consider).

Exercise A: Reading

a. The right answer to the wrong question

ἐλθὼν δ' ὁ Ξενοφῶν ἐπήρετο τὸν Ἀπόλλωνα τίνι ἂν
θεῶν θύων καὶ εὐχόμενος κάλλιστα καὶ ἄριστα ἔλθοι τὴν ὁδὸν
ἣν ἐπενόει καὶ καλῶς πράξας σωθείη. καὶ ἀνεῖλεν αὐτῷ ὁ
Ἀπόλλων οἷς ἔδει θύειν. ἐπεὶ δὲ πάλιν ἦλθε, ἔλεξε τὸν χρησμὸν
5   τῷ Σωκράτει. ὁ δ' ἀκούσας ᾐτιᾶτο αὐτὸν ὅτι οὐ τοῦτο πρῶτον
ἠρώτα, πότερον ἄμεινόν ἐστι αὐτῷ πορεύεσθαι ἢ μένειν, ἀλλ'
αὐτὸς κρίνας ἰτέον εἶναι τοῦτ' ἐπυνθάνετο, ὅπως ἂν κάλλιστα
πορευθείη.
       Ἐπεὶ μέντοι οὕτως ἤρου, ταῦτ', ἔφη, χρὴ ποιεῖν ἃ ὁ
10   θεὸς ἐκέλευσεν.
       Ὁ μὲν δὴ Ξενοφῶν οὕτω θυσάμενος οἷς ἀνεῖλεν ὁ θεὸς
ἐξέπλει.

Adapted from Xenophon, *Anabasis* 3.1.6-8

2   τὴν ὁδόν (used as an adverbial accusative) *on the journey*
3   ἀνεῖλεν from ἀναιρέω *answer, tell*
6   πότερον *whether*
7   ὅπως *how*
11   θυσάμενος The middle voice is used because Xenophon had a priest
     sacrifice for him.

15. Detail of Xenophon and Socrates
from Raphael's School of Athens, The Vatican, 1509.

b. To love or not to love?

χαλεπὸν τὸ μὴ φιλῆσαι·
χαλεπὸν δὲ καὶ φιλῆσαι·
χαλεπώτερον δὲ πάντων
ἀποτυγχάνειν φιλοῦντα.

From the *Anacreontea* 27B.1-4 (Bergk)

4   ἀποτυγχάνειν from ἀποτυγχάνω *fail*

Exercise B

Translate:

1. O stranger, if you are at a loss, you must go (use εἶμι) back to Delphi in order to pray to Apollo.
2. We had to cross the river and proceed as quickly as possible so as to reach the sea. (Express in two ways.)
3. What do you have in mind to do? Our hope is (use dative of possessor) to find Xenophon and ask him about his journey.
4. He often thought that guarding good things is more difficult than acquiring (them).
5. No one would blame her because she has erred unwillingly.

16. The Omphalos at Delphi, Greece.

Lesson 48

Questions. Object Clauses. Accusative Absolute. μέλει

Questions

Questions are of two types, those requiring an affirmative (*yes*) or negative (*no*) answer, and those introduced by interrogative words such as τίς (*who*), τί (*what, why*), etc.

a. Questions requiring an affirmative or negative answer but implying nothing as to which answer the speaker expects are indicated merely by a question mark. Occasionally these questions are introduced by ἆρα or ἦ. Example:

ἦ (ἆρα) τέθνηκε Σωκράτης;
Has Socrates died?

b. Questions expecting an affirmative answer are introduced by ἆρα οὐ (ἆρ᾽ οὐ), οὐ, οὐκοῦν, or ἄλλο τι ἤ. Example:

ἆρα οὐ (οὐκοῦν, ἄλλο τι ἤ, οὐ) τέθνηκε Σωκράτης;
Socrates has died, hasn't he?
or
Hasn't Socrates died?

c. Questions expecting a negative answer are introduced by ἆρα μή, μή, or μὴ οὖν (= μῶν). Example:

ἆρα μὴ (μή, μῶν) τέθνηκε Σωκράτης;
Socrates hasn't died, has he?

d. Double questions are introduced by πότερον (πότερα)...ἤ. πότερον (πότερα) may be omitted. Example:

πότερον (πότερα) τέθνηκε Σωκράτης ἢ οὔ;
Has Socrates died or not?

e. All other questions are introduced by interrogative words, such as τίς (*who*), τί (*what, why*), etc. (see Lesson 49).

Object Clauses

A noun clause, introduced by ὅπως (negative ὅπως μή) (rarely ὡς, scarcely ever ἵνα) is used with the future indicative in both primary and secondary sequence after verbs meaning "deliberate," "consider," "care for," "strive," "effect" (e.g. βουλεύομαι, ἐπιμελοῦμαι, παρασκευάζομαι, πράττω, φράζω). Occasionally the indicative is replaced by the subjunctive in primary sequence and by the optative in secondary sequence. Example:

καλὸν τὸ ἐπιμελεῖσθαι ὅπως ὡς βέλτισται
ἔσονται τῶν πολιτῶν αἱ ψυχαί.

It is a fine thing to take care that the souls of the citizens be as good as possible.

Accusative Absolute

Instead of the genitive absolute, the accusative absolute is used with neuter singular participles of impersonal verbs, with the participle of εἰμί (ὄν), and with such impersonal passive participles as: γεγραμμένον, δεδρογμένον, εἰρημένον, προστεταγμένον, προσταχθέν. Examples:

σὲ δ᾽ οὐκ ἐσώσαμεν οἷόν τε ὂν σῶσαι.

*We did not save you, although it was possible to save (*lit.*, it being possible to save) you.*

δόξαν ὑμῖν τοῦτο, εἵλεσθαι ἄνδρας δέκα.

*Since this seemed best (*lit.*, This seeming best) to you, you chose ten men.*

μέλει

With the impersonal verb μέλει (*it is a care*), the person feeling the emotion is expressed by the dative case, and the object of the emotion by the genitive case. Example:

ἐμοὶ μάχης οὐ μέλει.

*I don't care for battle (*lit. There is not a care for me for battle*).*

Vocabulary

μέλει, μελήσει, ἐμέλησε, μεμέληκε, _____, _____ *care (it is a care)*

σιγάω, σιγήσομαι, ἐσίγησα, σεσίγηκα, σεσίγημαι, ἐσιγήθην *be silent*

ἐκκλησία, -ας, ἡ *assembly*
(ecclesiastical)

τεκμήριον, -ου, τό *sign, proof,*
evidence

αἰσχρός, -ά, -όν *shameful, base,*
disgraceful

ἅπας, ἅπασα, ἅπαν *every, all*

ἱκανός, -ή, -όν *sufficient, enough,*
competent

μόνος, -η, -ον *alone, only*
(monologue)

πλήν (+ gen.) *except*

πῶς *how*

ὅπως (conjunction) *that; how*

καίτοι (conjunction) *and yet*

γε (enclitic) *at least; of course* (often
untranslatable; used to
emphasize previous word)

νυν (enclitic) *now* (as a connective;
inferential, without temporal
significance)

ἆρα (sign of a question)

ἦ (sign of a question)

ἄλλο τι ἤ (sign of a question,
expecting an affirmative answer)

οὐκοῦν (sign of a question,
expecting an affirmative answer)

μῶν (= μὴ οὖν) (sign of a question,
expecting a negative answer)

πότερον . . . ἤ (sign of a double
question)

Drill

Translate:

1. Do you love me or not, mother?
2. Isn't the sun many stades away from the earth?
3. Didn't the young men learn many things from Socrates?
4. Through(out) his long life, this citizen never cared (use μέλει) for shameful gain.
5. Take care that your fame be as great as possible and your arrogance as little (use ἐλάχιστος) as possible.
6. If only we were faring well and able to help our friends!

Exercise A: Reading

A member of a distinguished Athenian family, Plato aspired to a career in
statesmanship but, disenchanted by the deplorable spectacle of contemporary
Greek politics, concluded that statesmanship was a hopeless occupation until rulers
became philosophers or philosophers became rulers. After the execution of his
mentor Socrates in 399 B.C., Plato, an eyewitness at the trial, retired to Megara,
where other followers of Socrates had sought political refuge. After more than a
decade of travel including sojourns in Sicily, Italy, and Egypt, Plato again settled in
Athens about 386 BC to begin formal teaching at a place known as the Academy, a
park and gymnasium located outside the city wall. Here, with the intention of
training others for service to the state, he lectured almost without interruption for
the remaining forty years of his life. Most of Plato's voluminous writings, which
treat such critical issues as the role of the individual in society, the nature of the
soul and the purpose and means of a good education, reflect the pervasive
influence exerted over him by Socrates' life and death. Among his early works are
the *Apology* (see below and Lesson 49), his own rendition of Socrates' defense
speech against the charges of corrupting Athenian youth and rejecting the gods
recognized by the city, and the *Lysis* (see Lessons 51-54), a dialogue on friendship
in which Socrates is the principal conversationalist. One of the greatest
philosophical writers of all time, Plato is also distinguished by the endless variety of
his styles, which makes him an unrivalled exponent of the power, flexibility, and
beauty of Greek prose.

Socrates questions Meletus about his charge against him of corrupting the youth.

     Καί μοι, ὦ Μέλητε, εἰπέ· ἄλλο τι ἢ περὶ πλείστου ποιῇ
ὅπως ὡς βέλτιστοι οἱ νεώτεροι ἔσονται;
     Ἔγωγε.
     Ἴθι δή νυν εἰπὲ τούτοις τοῖς δικασταῖς, τίς αὐτοὺς

5   βελτίους ποιεῖ; δῆλον γάρ ἐστι ὅτι οἶσθα, μέλον γέ σοι. τὸν
μὲν γὰρ διαφθείροντα ἐξευρών, ὡς φῄς, ἐμὲ εἰσάγεις εἰς δίκην
καὶ κατηγορεῖς· τὸν δὲ δὴ βελτίους ποιοῦντα ἴθι εἰπὲ καὶ
μήνυσον αὐτοῖς τίς ἐστιν. ὁρᾷς, ὦ Μέλητε, ὅτι σιγᾷς καὶ οὐκ
ἔχεις εἰπεῖν; καίτοι οὐκ αἰσχρόν σοι δοκεῖ εἶναι καὶ ἱκανὸν

10   τεκμήριον οὗ δὴ ἐγὼ λέγω, ὅτι σοι οὐδὲν μεμέληκεν; ἀλλ᾿ εἰπέ,
ὠγαθέ, τίς αὐτοὺς ἀμείνους ποιεῖ;
     Οἱ νόμοι.
     Ἀλλ᾿ οὐ τοῦτο ἐρωτῶ, ὦ βέλτιστε, ἀλλὰ τίς ἄνθρωπος,
ὃς πρῶτον καὶ αὐτὸ τοῦτο οἶδε, τοὺς νόμους;

15   Οὗτοι, ὦ Σώκρατες, οἱ δικασταί.
     Πῶς λέγεις, ὦ Μέλητε; οἵδε τοὺς νέους παιδεύειν οἷοί
τέ εἰσι καὶ βελτίους ποιοῦσιν;
     Μάλιστα.

Πότερον ἅπαντες, ἢ οἱ μὲν αὐτῶν, οἱ δ' οὔ;
20 Ἅπαντες.
Εὖ γε λέγεις καὶ πλῆθος τῶν ὠφελούντων. τί δὲ δή; οἱ
δὲ ἀκούοντες βελτίους ποιοῦσιν ἢ οὔ;
Καὶ οὗτοι.
Τί δέ, οἱ βουλευταί;
25 Καὶ οἱ βουλευταί.
Ἀλλ' ἆρα, ὦ Μέλητε, μὴ οἱ ἐν τῇ ἐκκλησίᾳ, οἱ
ἐκκλησιασταί, διαφθείρουσι τοὺς νεωτέρους; ἢ κἀκεῖνοι
βελτίους ποιοῦσιν ἅπαντες;
Κἀκεῖνοι.
30 Πάντες, ὡς δοκεῖ, Ἀθηναῖοι καλοὺς κἀγαθοὺς ποιοῦσι
πλὴν ἐμοῦ, ἐγὼ δὲ μόνος διαφθείρω. οὕτω λέγεις;
Ταῦτά γε λέγω.

Adapted from Plato, *Apology* 24c-25a

1   Μέλητε from Μέλητος, -ου, ὁ *Meletus*, one of Socrates' three
     prosecutors
4   Ἴθι The imperative of εἶμι, in conjunction with another imperative,
     means "come."
8   μήνυσον aorist active imperative, 2nd singular of μηνύω *inform*
21   τί δὲ δή; *What about this?*
24   βουλευταί from βουλευτής, -οῦ, ὁ *senator*

Exercise B

Translate:

       1. Learning from him who speaks well in the assembly would
be most pleasant.
       2. No one will choose the greater evil when it is possible to
choose the lesser. (Use an accusative absolute.)
       3. There isn't sufficient evidence, is there, that everyone except
you dared to follow the barbarians?
       4. How could you be silent if you really hate him?
       5. The guard has in mind to raise our child without the
knowledge of the king.

Lesson 49

Future Optative. Indirect Questions
Infinitives and Interrogatives

Future Optative

a. Future Active

The future active optative, formed from the second principal
part, is conjugated as follows:

Regular ω-verb, παιδεύω:

singular	person	plural
παιδεύσοιμι	1	παιδεύσοιμεν
παιδεύσοις	2	παιδεύσοιτε
παιδεύσοι	3	παιδεύσοιεν

Liquid future, φαίνω:

singular	person	plural
φανοίην	1	φανοῖμεν
(φανεοίην)		(φανέοιμεν)
φανοίης	2	φανοῖτε
(φανεοίης)		(φανέοιτε)
φανοίη	3	φανοῖεν
(φανεοίη)		(φανέοιεν)

b. Future Middle

The future middle optative, formed from the second principal
part, is conjugated using secondary middle-passive endings (as in the
present middle-passive and aorist middle optative) as follows:

Regular ω-verb, παιδεύω:

singular	person	plural
παιδευσοίμην	1	παιδευσοίμεθα
παιδεύσοιο	2	παιδεύσοισθε
παιδεύσοιτο	3	παιδεύσοιντο

Liquid future, φαίνω:

singular	person	plural
φανοίμην	1	φανοίμεθα
(φανεοίμην)		(φανεοίμεθα)
φανοῖο	2	φανοῖσθε
(φανέοιο)		(φανέοισθε)
φανοῖτο	3	φανοῖντο
(φανέοιτο)		(φανέοιντο)

c. Future Passive

The future passive optative, formed from the sixth principal part (minus the temporal augment), is conjugated as follows:

First future passive, παιδεύω:

singular	person	plural
παιδευθησοίμην	1	παιδευθησοίμεθα
παιδευθήσοιο	2	παιδευθήσοισθε
παιδευθήσοιτο	3	παιδευθήσοιντο

Second future passive, φαίνω:

singular	person	plural
φανησοίμην	1	φανησοίμεθα
φανήσοιο	2	φανήσοισθε
φανήσοιτο	3	φανήσοιντο

Optative in Indirect Statement

In indirect statements, any tense of the optative may replace the corresponding tense of the indicative in secondary sequence. The future optative, therefore, is used as an alternative to the future indicative. Example:

ἔγνων ὅτι πέντε ἡμερῶν ἀποθανοῖτο.
I knew that he would die within five days.

Indirect Questions

An indirect question is a type of noun (object) clause introduced by an interrogative (i.e. a question word, like "who," "what," "how," etc.). It is used to report indirectly a question that was asked directly. In Greek, the indicative mood is used in an indirect question after a main verb that is in a primary tense (i.e. present, future, perfect); after a main verb in a secondary tense (imperfect, aorist, pluperfect), the optative mood often replaces the indicative in the indirect question. The tense of the verb in the indirect question is determined in accordance with the rules given already for indirect statement (see Lesson 32). The tense will correspond to the tense of the original question. ὅστις (see below) often replaces τίς to introduce an indirect question. πότερον, εἰ, or εἴτε (*whether*) is used to introduce double questions. Examples:

Direct Question:

τίς ἐστιν;
Who is he?

Indirect Question:

ἀλλήλους ἤροντο ὅστις εἴη (ἐστίν).
They asked each other who he was.

Direct Question:

πότερον ἡμᾶς αἰτιάσεται ἢ οὔ;
Will he blame us or not?

Indirect Question:

ἐθαυμάζομεν πότερον ἡμᾶς αὐτοὺς αἰτιάσοιτο ἢ οὔ (μή).
We wondered whether he would blame us or not.

Indefinite Relative Pronoun

The indefinite relative pronoun, ὅστις (*whoever, he who, anyone who, who*), ὅ τι (*whatever, what*), is formed and translated as a compound of the indefinite and relative pronouns in Greek. It is declined as follows:

	masculine	singular feminine	neuter
Nom.	ὅστις	ἥτις	ὅ τι
Gen.	οὗτινος (ὅτου)	ἧστινος	οὗτινος (ὅτου)
Dat.	ᾧτινι (ὅτῳ)	ᾗτινι	ᾧτινι (ὅτῳ)
Acc.	ὅντινα	ἥντινα	ὅ τι

	masculine	plural feminine	neuter
Nom.	οἵτινες	αἵτινες	ἅτινα (ἅττα)
Gen.	ὧντινα (ὅτων)	ὧντινα	ὧντινα (ὅτων)
Dat.	οἷστισι(ν) (ὅτοις)	αἷστισι(ν)	οἷστισι(ν) (ὅτοις)
Acc.	οὕστινας	ἅστινας	ἅτινα (ἅττα)

Example:

εὐδαίμων ἐσθ᾽ ὅστις πλοῦτόν τε καὶ κλέος ἔχει.
Happy is he who has both wealth and fame.

βουλεύομαι ὅπως εὐδαιμονία γενήσεται ᾧτινί μου μέλει.
I deliberate about how happiness may come to be for whomever it is I care about.

Note: The conjunction ὅτι (*that, because*) must be distinguished from the neuter nominative and accusative singular indefinite relative pronoun ὅ τι (*whatever*). The latter is usually written as two words to aid the reader in making such a distinction.

Indefinite and Interrogatives

Interrogatives (Direct or indirect question)	Interrogatives (Indirect question)	Indefinites (Enclitics)	Relative Adverbs
τίς *who*	ὅστις *who*	τις *anyone*	-------
ποῦ *where, in what place*	ὅπου *where*	που *somewhere, anywhere; perhaps, I suppose*	οὗ, ὅπου *where*
ποῖ *to where, to what place*	ὅποι *to where*	ποι *to somewhere*	οἷ, ὅποι *to where*
πόθεν *from where, from what place*	ὁπόθεν *from where*	ποθεν *from somewhere*	ὅθεν, ὁπόθεν *from where*
πῶς *how*	ὅπως *how*	πως *somehow*	ὡς, ὅπως *how*
πότε *when*	ὁπότε *when*	ποτε *at some (any) time, ever, once*	ὅτε, ὁπότε *when*

Notes: Interrogatives are <u>always</u> accented with an actute or a circumflex accent. In indirect questions, interrogatives *tend* to apply a ὁ- to the beginning of the form; compare column one and column two above. Indefinites are unaccented by nature. Relative adverbs differ from interrogatives by a loss of initial π. The sequence of interrogatives in English of "where," "whither," and "whence" – while the latter two are somewhat antiquated – nicely mirror the sequence of ποῦ, ποῖ, πόθεν in Greek.

Vocabulary

ἐργάζομαι, ἐργάσομαι, εἰργασάμην, ____, εἴργασμαι, εἰργάσθην *do*
   (something to someone; + two accusatives), *perform, make*

καταγιγνώσκω (+ gen. of person, acc. of thing) *condemn*

σύνειμι, συνέσομαι (+ dat.) *be with, associate with*

εὐδαιμονία, -ας, ἡ *good fortune, prosperity, happiness*

πονηρός, -ά, -όν *worthless, base, bad*   πάνυ (adverb) *very; by all means*

σαφής, -ές *clear, plain, distinct*   ὅστις, ἥτις, ὅ τι *whoever, he who,*

χρηστός, -ή, -όν *useful, good*   *anyone who, who, whatever, what*

ἀλλὰ γάρ *but in point of fact*   τίς ποτε *who in the world*

καί . . . καί *both . . . and*   τί ποτε *what in the world*

δῆτα (postpositive adverb) *surely,*   εἰ (indirect question) *whether*

   indeed   πότερον (indirect question) *whether*

Drill A

Translate the underlined English (words) into Greek using the correct form of the interrogative, indefinite, or relative adverb:

    1. <u>How</u> will the Athenians defeat the Persians at Marathon?
    2. <u>To whomever</u> (masc. pl.) the gods give honor, those men live a happy and secure life.
    3. I don't know <u>where</u> the oracle is located. _____
    4. <u>Who in the world</u> could question to judgment of a god?
    5. We'll find it <u>somewhere</u>, I suppose. _____
    6. <u>From where</u> did such an outstanding character derive?

Drill B

Translate:

    1. εὐδαίμων ἐσθ' ᾧτινι θεὸς μοῖραν καλῶν παρέχει.
    2. ποῖ τρέψωμαι; ποῖ πορευθῶ;
    3. ἦλθέ ποθεν τεκμήριον ὅτι ἡ πόλις σωθήσοιτο.
    4. πάλαι δ' ἠπόρουν τί ποτε λέγοι ὁ τοῦ Ἀπόλλωνος χρησμός.

5. πρῶτον μέν, ὦ δοῦλε, ἂν ποι βούλῃ ἰέναι, χρή σε
δεῖσθαι τοῦ δεσπότου.
    6. ὁμοίας φαμὲν ἁπάσας ἡδονὰς εἶναι καὶ τιμητέας ἐξ
ἴσου.
    7. τὴν ἐπιστολὴν ἀναγνοὺς ἤρετό με πόθεν λάβοιμι.

Exercise A: Reading

Further discussion on corrupting youth

            Πολλήν γέ μου κατέγνωκας συμφοράν. καί μοι
       ἀπόκριναι· ἦ καὶ περὶ ἵππους οὕτω σοι δοκεῖ ἔχειν; οἱ μὲν
       βελτίους ποιοῦντας αὐτοὺς πάντες ἄνθρωποι εἶναι, εἷς δέ τις ὁ
       διαφθείρωνι; ἢ τοὐναντίον τούτου πᾶν εἷς μέν τις ὁ βελτίους
5   οἷός τ᾽ ὢν ποιεῖν ἢ πάνυ ὀλίγοι, οἱ ἱππικοί, οἱ δὲ πολλοὶ ἐὰν
       συνῶσι καὶ χρῶνται ἵπποις, διαφθείρουσιν; οὐχ οὕτως ἔχει, ὦ
       Μέλητε, καὶ περὶ ἵππων καὶ τῶν ἄλλων ἁπάντων ζῴων;
       πάντως γε, ἐάντε σὺ καὶ Ἄνυτος οὐ φῆτε ἐάντε φῆτε· πολλὴ γὰρ
       ἄν τις εὐδαιμονία εἴη περὶ τοὺς νέους εἰ εἷς μὲν μόνος αὐτοὺς
10   διαφθείρει, οἱ δ᾽ ἄλλοι ὠφελοῦσιν. ἀλλὰ γάρ, ὦ Μέλητε,
       ἱκανῶς ἀποφαίνεις ὅτι οὔποτε ἐπεμελήσω τῶν νέων, καὶ σαφῶς
       ἀποφαίνεις τὴν σαυτοῦ ἀμέλειαν, ὅτι οὐδέν σοι μεμέληκεν περὶ
       ὧν ἐμὲ εἰσάγεις.
            Ἔτι δὲ ἡμῖν εἰπέ, ὦ πρὸς Διὸς Μέλητε, πότερόν ἐστιν
15   οἰκεῖν ἄμεινον ἐν πολίταις χρηστοῖς ἢ πονηροῖς; ὦ φίλε,
       ἀπόκριναι· οὐδὲν γάρ που χαλεπὸν ἐρωτῶ. οὐχ οἱ μὲν πονηροὶ
       κακόν τι ἐργάζονται τοὺς ἀεὶ αὐτοῖς συνόντας, οἱ δ᾽ ἀγαθοὶ
       ἀγαθόν τι;
            Πάνυ γε.
20   Ἔστιν οὖν ὅστις βούλεται ὑπὸ τῶν συνόντων
       βλάπτεσθαι μᾶλλον ἢ ὠφελεῖσθαι; ἀποκρίνου, ὦ ἀγαθέ· καὶ γὰρ
       ὁ νόμος κελεύει ἀποκρίνεσθαι. ἔσθ᾽ ὅστις βούλεται βλάπτεσθαι;
            Οὐ δῆτα.
            Φέρε δή, πότερον ἐμὲ εἰσάγεις εἰς δίκην ὡς
25   διαφθείροντα τοὺς νέους καὶ πονηροτέρους ποιοῦντα ἑκόντα ἢ
       ἄκοντα;
            Ἑκόντα ἔγωγε.

                Adapted from Plato, *Apology* 25a-d

5   ἱππικοί from ἱππικός, -οῦ, ὁ *horseman*
7   ζῴων from ζῷον, -ου, τό *animal*
8   ἐάντε . . . ἐάντε *whether . . . or*
     Ἄνυτος, -ου, ὁ Anytus, a wealthy Athenian leader of the democratic
     politicians. He was one of the three prosecutors of Socrates.
12   ἀμέλειαν from ἀμέλεια, -ας, ἡ. What must this noun mean if the
     alpha is privative?
24   Φέρε. In the imperative mood φέρω, as here, often means "come."

Exercise B

Translate:

1. You asked the assembly, I suppose, whether it would
condemn the worthless guard to death or not.
2. Is there anyone except you who clearly remembers where the
stranger is living or from where he has come?
3. Socrates once dared to ask whether anyone was wiser than he.
4. From where have you come, Xenophon, and to where are
you hastening?
5. What in the world did you have in mind to do to him when
he was cross-examining you about stealing the gold?

Lesson 50

Review

Drill

Locate the following forms:

1. καταγνοίη	8. ἡτιῶ	15. μεταπεμφθησοίμην
2. ἐρήσοιο	9. κρινοῖτε	16. βούληται
3. ᾖα	10. κρίνοιτε	17. ἀναγνωσθῆναι
4. ἑῷεν	11. ἑάλωσαν	18. οἴει
5. μέλῃ	12. ηὐχόμεθα	19. γενώμεθα
6. μέλλῃ	13. ἁλῶναι	20. ἔγνωμεν
7. ἰέναι	14. διαβάντος	21. ἐργάσοιντο

Exercise A

Translate:

1. τὸν ποταμὸν διαβάντες εἰς ἐλπίδα ἥκομεν τοῦ ἑλεῖν τὴν ἀρχαίαν πόλιν.

2. πότερον ἠρώτησας ὅ τι ἡμῖν ποιητέον εἴη ἢ οὔ;

3. ἐχρῆν που ἐπιμελεῖσθαι ὅπως ὡς ἐλάχιστα μὲν ὄψεσθε, ἐλάχιστα δ' ἀκούσεσθε, ἐλάχιστα δ' ἐρήσεσθε.

4. ἀλλ', ὦ φίλη παῖ, εἰ τὰ πλείω χρηστὰ τῶν κακῶν ἔχεις, ἄνθρωπος οὖσα, πάνυ γ' εὖ πράξειας ἄν.

5. ἆρα μὴ ὑμᾶς ἤρετο ὁ Κῦρος ὁπόθεν λήψοισθε τὸ χρυσίον καὶ ὅστις ὑμῶν ἔσοιτο ὁ κλώψ;

6. ὅντινα τιμῶσιν ἀθάνατοι, τούτῳ καὶ ἀνθρώπων κλέος ἕπεται.

7. οἱ βάρβαροι ἐθαύμαζον ὅποι ποτὲ τρέψοιντο οἱ Ἕλληνες καὶ τί βουλεύοιντο.

8. ἐμοὶ μὲν οὐδεὶς φίλος ἐστίν, ὅστις οὐχ ἱκανός ἐστιν ἴσα πάσχειν ἐμοί.

9. οὐκοῦν αἰτιᾷ τὸν κλέπτοντα, ὡς αἰσχρὸν ὂν τὸ κλέπτειν;

10. λέξω δὲ καὶ σοὶ τῆς ἐμαυτοῦ γνώμης ὁδόν· ἐπεί με συμφορά ποθεν ἔλαβεν, ἐπεμελούμην ὅπως κάλλιστ' ἐνέγκαιμ' αὐτήν.

11. ἆρ' οὖν οἶσθα, ὦ Σώκρατες, ὅτι οἱ πολλοὶ τῶν ἀνθρώπων ἐμοί τε καὶ σοὶ οὐ πείθονται, ἀλλὰ πολλούς φασι γιγνώσκοντας τὰ βέλτιστα οὐκ ἐθέλειν πράττειν, ἐξὸν αὐτοῖς, ἀλλὰ ἄλλα πράττειν;

Exercise A (continued)

12. πράξας μὲν γὰρ εὖ πᾶς ἀνὴρ ἀγαθός, κακὸς δ᾽ εἰ κακῶς.

13. ᾧτινι τῶν φίλων μέλει, τοῦτον ἐγὼ ἐπαινῶ καὶ φιλῶ.

14. τὸν ξένον πονηρὸν θαυμάζοντες οἱ δοῦλοι ἀλλήλους ἤροντο τίς ποτ᾽ εἴη καὶ πόθεν ἔλθοι.

15. ἦν γάρ ποτε χρόνος ὅτε θεοὶ μὲν ἦσαν, ἀνθρώπων δὲ γένη οὐκ ἦν.

Exercise B

Translate:

1. Who in the world said (use εἶπον) that the jurors would condemn Socrates to death?

2. And yet it is clear that you already know what must be done, since, of course, you care about our freedom and happiness. (Use an accusative absolute.)

3. At least Xenophon knew where he was going, didn't he?

4. If the thief is caught, how will he defend himself?

5. The majority feared that he might do something disgraceful to those who were with him.

17. τὸ Ἡφαιστεῖον. The Temple of Hephaestus, fifth century BC, located on the north-west side of the Agora, Athens.

Lesson 51

o-Contract Verbs. Conditional Adverbial Clauses
Temporal Clauses

o-Contract Verbs

Verbs with o as a stem vowel in the <u>present stem</u> contract in the present
and imperfect tenses as follows:

1. o + ω   or   η = ω
2. o + ει, οι or η = οι
3. o + ε, ο   or   ου = ου

<u>Note</u>: If the stem vowel (o) is accented, then the vowel(s) which result(s) from the
contraction receive(s) a circumflex.

<u>Present Active Indicative and Infinitive</u>

singular	person	plural
δηλῶ (δηλόω)	1	δηλοῦμεν (δηλόομεν)
δηλοῖς (δηλόεις)	2	δηλοῦτε (δηλόετε)
δηλοῖ (δηλόει)	3	δηλοῦσι(ν) (δηλόουσι)

<u>Infinitive</u>   δηλοῦν (δηλόειν = δηλόε-εν = δηλοῦν)

<u>Present Middle Passive Indicative and Infinitive</u>

singular	person	plural
δηλοῦμαι (δηλόομαι)	1	δηλούμεθα (δηλοόμεθα)
δηλοῖ (δηλόει, δηλόῃ)	2	δηλοῦσθε (δηλόεσθε)
δηλοῦται (δηλόεται)	3	δηλοῦνται (δηλόονται)

<u>Infinitive</u> δηλοῦσθαι (δηλόεσθαι)

<u>Imperfect Active Indicative</u>

singular	person	plural
ἐδήλουν (ἐδήλοον)	1	ἐδηλοῦμεν (ἐδηλόομεν)
ἐδήλους (ἐδήλοες)	2	ἐδηλοῦτε (ἐδηλόετε)
ἐδήλου (ἐδήλοε)	3	ἐδήλουν (ἐδήλοον)

Imperfect Middle-Passive Indicative

singular	person	plural
ἐδηλούμην (ἐδηλοόμην)	1	ἐδηλούμεθα (ἐδηλοόμεθα)
ἐδηλοῦ (ἐδηλόου)	2	ἐδηλοῦσθε (ἐδηλόεσθε)
ἐδηλοῦτο (ἐδηλόετο)	3	ἐδηλοῦντο (ἐδηλόοντο)

Present Active Subjunctive

singular	person	plural
δηλῶ (δηλόω)	1	δηλῶμεν (δηλόωμεν)
δηλοῖς (δηλόῃς)	2	δηλῶτε (δηλόητε)
δηλοῖ (δηλόῃ)	3	δηλῶσι (δηλόωσι)

Present Middle-Passive Subjunctive

singular	person	plural
δηλῶμαι (δηλόωμαι)	1	δηλώμεθα (δηλοώμεθα)
δηλοῖ (δηλόῃ)	2	δηλῶσθε (δηλόησθε)
δηλῶται (δηλόηται)	3	δηλῶνται (δηλόωνται)

Present Active Optative

singular	person	plural
δηλοίην (δηλοοίην)	1	δηλοῖμεν (δηλόοιμεν)
δηλοίης (δηλοοίης)	2	δηλοῖτε (δηλόοιτε)
δηλοίη (δηλοοίη)	3	δηλοῖεν (δηλόοιεν)

Present Middle-Passive Optative

singular	person	plural
δηλοίμην (δηλοοίμην)	1	δηλοίμεθα (δηλοοίμεθα)
δηλοῖο (δηλόοιο)	2	δηλοῖσθε (δηλόοισθε)
δηλοῖτο (δηλόοιτο)	3	δηλοῖντο (δηλόοιντο)

Present Active Imperative

singular	person	plural
δήλου (δήλοε)	2	δηλοῦτε (δηλόετε)
δηλούτω (δηλοέτω)	3	δηλούντων (δηλοόντων)

Present Middle-Passive Imperative

singular	person	plural
δηλοῦ (δηλόου)	2	δηλοῦσθε (δηλόεσθε)
δηλούσθω (δηλοέσθω)	3	δηλούσθων (δηλοέσθων)

Present Active Participle

Nominative singular
δηλῶν (δηλόων), δηλοῦσα (δηλόουσα), δηλοῦν (δηλόον)

Genitive singular
δηλοῦντος (δηλόοντος), δηλούσης (δηλοούσης),
δηλοῦντος (δηλόοντος)

Present Middle-Passive Participle

Nominative singular
δηλούμενος (δηλοόμενος), δηλουμένη (δηλοομένη),
δηλουμένου (δηλοομένου)

Genitive singular
δηλουμένου (δηλοομένου), δηλουμένης (δηλοομένης),
δηλουμένου (δηλοομένου)

Conditional Relative Clauses

Sentences that contain subordinate clauses introduced by relative pronouns (i.e. forms of ὅς or ὅστις) or relative adverbs (i.e. ὅπου, ὅποι, ὁπόθεν, etc.) follow the structural paradigms already established for conditions in Greek. In these conditional relative clauses, the εἰ or ἐάν of the protasis of the condition is simply replaced by a relative (ὅς, ὅστις, ὅπου, ὅποι, ὁπόθεν, etc.). Below, examples are only shown for sentences that contain conditional relative clauses following the paradigms for general and future conditions. The same structural correspondence exists, however, between all conditional and conditional relative clauses, including those that are contrary-to-fact (see Lesson 13), and particular (see Lessons 37, 39):

<u>Protasis</u> (negated by μή)   <u>Apodosis</u> (negated by οὐ)
<u>Present General</u>:   pres./aor. subj.   pres. indicative

Expressed as a Condition:

ἐὰν βλάπτῃ τοὺς φίλους ἀδικεῖ.
If ever he harms his friends, he does wrong.

Expressed with a Relative:

ὃς ἂν βλάπτῃ τοὺς φίλους ἀδικεῖ. (pronoun)
Whoever harms his friends does wrong.

ὅπου ἂν βλάπτῃ τοὺς φίλους, ἀδικεῖ. (adverb)
Wherever he harms his friends, he does wrong.

<u>Protasis</u> (negated by μή)   <u>Apodosis</u> (negated by οὐ)
<u>Past General</u>:   pres./aor. optative   imperfect indicative

Expressed with a Condition:

εἰ βλάπτοι τοὺς φίλους, ἠδίκει.
If anyone ever harmed his friends, he did wrong.

Expressed with a Relative:

ὅστις βλάπτοι τοὺς φίλους ἠδίκει. (pronoun)
Whoever harmed his friends did wrong.

ὅπου ἂν βλάπτοι τοὺς φίλους, ἀδικεῖ. (adverb)
Wherever he harmed his friends, he did wrong.

<u>Protasis</u> (negated by μή)   <u>Apodosis</u> (negated by οὐ)
<u>Future More Vivid</u>: pres./aor. subjunctive   future indicative

Expressed with a Condition:

πείσομαι τῷ ἀνδρί, ἐὰν (αὐτὸν) ἕλησθε.
I shall obey the man, if you choose (him).

Expressed with a Relative:

πείσομαι τῷ ἀνδρὶ ὃν ἂν ἕλησθε. (pronoun)
I shall obey whatever man you choose.

πείσομαι τῷ ἀνδρὶ ὅποι ἴῃ. (relative)
I shall obey the man, wherever he is going.

(negated by μή)   (negated by οὐ)
<u>Future Less Vivid</u>:   pres./aor. optative   pres./aor. optative + ἄν

Expressed with a Condition:

πειθοίμην ἄν τῷ ἀνδρὶ, <u>εἰ</u> (αὐτὸν) ἔλοισθε.
I would obey the man, <u>if</u> you should choose (him).

Expressed with a Relative:

πειθοίμην ἄν τῷ ἀνδρὶ <u>ὃν</u> ἔλοισθε. (pronoun)
I would obey <u>whatever</u> man you should choose.

πειθοίμην ἄν τῷ ἀνδρὶ <u>ὅποι</u> ἴοι. (adverb)
I would obey the man <u>wherever</u> he should go.

<u>Temporal Clauses</u>

Like conditional relative clauses, temporal clauses also tend to follow the same structural patterns as conditional sentences, replacing the εἰ (ἐάν) of the protasis of the condition with the temporal conjunctions ὅτε (ὅταν) (*when(ever)*), used typically to refer to events happening <u>at the same time</u> as the main verb, and ἐπεί (ἐπάν) or ἐπειδή (ἐπειδάν) (*after, when(ever); since*), used typically to refer to events happening <u>before</u> the main verb. Temporal clauses using πρίν (*before; until*) will be treated later in Lesson 55.

<u>Protasis</u> (negated by μή)   <u>Apodosis</u> (negated by οὐ)
<u>Present General</u>:   pres./aor. subj.   pres. indicative

Expressed as a Condition:

<u>ἐὰν</u> βλάπτῃ τοὺς φίλους, ἀδικεῖ.
<u>If ever</u> he harms his friends, he does wrong.

Expressed with a Temporal Conjunction:

<u>ἐπειδὰν</u> βλάπτῃ τοὺς φίλους, ἀδικεῖ.
<u>Whenever</u> he harms his friends, he does wrong.

<u>Protasis</u> (negated by μή)   <u>Apodosis</u> (negated by οὐ)
<u>Past General</u>:   pres./aor. optative   imperfect indicative

Expressed with a Condition:

<u>εἰ</u> βλάπτοι τοὺς φίλους, ἠδίκει.
<u>If</u> anyone <u>ever</u> harmed his friends, he did wrong.

Expressed with a Temporal Conjunction:

<u>ὅτε</u> βλάπτοι τοὺς φίλους, ἠδίκει.
<u>Whenever</u> he harmed his friends, he did wrong.

                   Protasis (negated by μή)   Apodosis (negated by οὐ)
Future More Vivid: pres./aor. subjunctive   future indicative

Expressed with a Condition:

πείσομαι τῷ ἀνδρί, ἐὰν (αὐτὸν) ἕλησθε.
I shall obey the man, if you choose (him).

Expressed with a Temporal Conjunction:

πείσομαι τῷ ἀνδρί, ὅταν (αὐτὸν) ἕλησθε.
I shall obey the man, whenever you choose (him).

                   Protasis (negated by μή)   Apodosis (negated by οὐ)
Future Less Vivid: pres./aor. optative   pres./aor. optative + ἄν

Expressed with a Condition:

πειθοίμην ἄν τῷ ἀνδρί, εἰ ἑλοίμην.
I would obey the man, if I should choose (sc. to do so).

Expressed with a Temporal Conjunction:

πειθοίμην ἄν τῷ ἀνδρὶ ὅτε ἑλοίμην.
I would obey the man, whenever I shall choose (sc. to do so).

Vocabulary

ἀξιόω, ἀξιώσω, ἠξίωσα, ἠξίωκα, ἠξίωμαι, ἠξιώθην *think worthy, think right; believe, expect, request* (+ acc. and infin.)

δηλόω, δηλώσω, ἐδήλωσα, δεδήλωκα, δεδήλωμαι, ἐδηλώθην *make clear, reveal, show* (governs participle in indirect statement)

δουλεύω, δουλεύσω, ἐδούλευσα *be a slave*

ἐπιθυμέω, ἐπιθυμήσω, ἐπεθύμησα *desire* (+ gen. or infin. or infin. and subj. acc.)

ἐπιτρέπω, ἐπιτρέψω, ἐπέτρεψα, ἐπιτέτροφα, ἐπιτέτραμμαι, ἐπετρέφθην *entrust, permit*

ἦν δ' ἐγώ *I said* (used for direct quotations)

ἦ δ' ὅς *he said* (used for direct quotations)

ἅρμα, ἅρματος, τό *chariot*

μισθός, -οῦ, ὁ *pay; reward*

ἄρα (postpositive particle) *therefore; as it seems*

σφόδρα (adverb) *very, very much*

ὧδε (adverb) *thus, as follows, in the following manner*

Drill

Give the following forms:

1. Imperfect active indicative, 3rd sg. of:
    ἀξιόω, ἐπιθυμέω, ἐάω, δουλεύω εἰμι

2. present middle-passive subjunctive, 2nd pl. of :
    δηλόω, ἐπιμελέομαι, εὔχομαι, ἀξιόω

3. present active optative, 3rd pl. of :
    δηλόω, σιγάω, εἶμι, ἀκολουθέω, εἰμί

Exercise A: Reading

Socrates and Lysis converse about bringing up children.

Ἐγὼ δὲ τὸν Λύσιν ἠρόμην, Ἦ που, ἦν δ᾽ ἐγώ, ὦ Λύσι,
σφόδρα φιλοῦσί σε ὁ πατὴρ καὶ ἡ μήτηρ;
    Πάνυ γε, ἦ δ᾽ ὅς.
    Οὐκοῦν ἀξιοῖεν ἄν σε ὡς εὐδαιμονέστατον εἶναι;
5   Πῶς γὰρ οὔ;
    Δοκεῖ δέ σοι εὐδαίμων εἶναι ἄνθρωπος δουλεύων τε καὶ
ᾧ μηδὲν ἂν ἐξείη ποιεῖν ὧν ἐπιθυμοίη;
    Μὰ Δί᾽ οὐκ ἔμοιγε, ἔφη.
    Οὐκοῦν εἴ σε φιλοῦσι ὁ πατὴρ καὶ ἡ μήτηρ καὶ
10 εὐδαίμονά σε ἐπιθυμοῦσι γενέσθαι, τοῦτο παντὶ πρόπῳ δηλοῦσι
ὅτι ἐπιμελοῦνται ὅπως εὐδαίμων ἔσει;
    Πῶς γὰρ οὔ; ἔφη.
    Ἐῶσιν ἄρα σε ἃ βούλει ποιεῖν οὐδὲ διακωλύουσι ποιεῖν
ὧν ἂν ἐπιθυμῇς;
15 Ναὶ μὰ Δία ἐμέ γε, ὦ Σώκρατες, καὶ μάλα γε πολλὰ
κωλύουσιν.
    Πῶς λέγεις; ἦν δ᾽ ἐγώ. βουλόμενοί σε εὐδαίμονα εἶναι
διακωλύουσι τοῦτο ποιεῖν ὃ ἂν βούλῃ; ὧδε δέ μοι λέγε· ἢν
ἐπιθυμήσῃς ἐπί τινος τῶν τοῦ πατρὸς ἁρμάτων ὀχεῖσθαι λαβὼν
20 τὰς ἡνίας, ὅταν ἁμιλλᾶται, οὐκ ἂν ἐῷέν σε ἀλλὰ διακωλύοιεν;
    Μὰ Δί᾽ οὐ μέντοι ἄν, ἔφη, ἐῷεν.
    Ἀλλὰ τίνα ἂν ἐῷεν;
    Ἔστιν τις ἡνίοχος παρὰ τοῦ πατρὸς μισθὸν φέρων.
    Πῶς λέγεις; ἢ ἐκεῖνον, ὡς δοκεῖ, ἡγοῦνται περὶ
25 πλείονος ἢ σὲ τὸν υἱόν, καὶ ἐπιτρέπουσι τὰ ἑαυτῶν μᾶλλον ἢ
σοί, καὶ ἐῶσι ποιεῖν ὅ τι βούλεται, σὲ δὲ διακωλύουσι;

Adapted from Plato, *Lysis* 207d-208c

1   Λύσιν from Λύσις, Λύσιδος, ὁ *Lysis*, an Athenian youth
5   Πῶς γὰρ οὔ; *Of course* (literally, *Indeed, why not?*)
8   Μά *by* (particle used with accusative in oaths)
15   Ναί *Yes* (particle used to express strong affirmation)
19   ὀχεῖσθαι from ὀχέομαι *ride*
20   ἡνίας from ἡνία, -ας, ἡ *rein*
     ἁμιλλᾶται from ἁμιλλάομαι *compete*
23   ἡνίοχος, -ου, ὁ *charioteer, driver*

Exercise B

Translate:

     1. "Whenever I go," he said, "the young men desire to hear me refuting others."

     2. He very much desired to entrust to the majority whatever seemed best.

     3. But in point of fact, whenever anyone is a slave, he can scarcely expect others to treat him justly.

     4. The messenger, as the evidence makes clear, was killed in the following manner: while seeking an escape-route he fell out of his chariot.

     5. Whoever wishes to accompany me instead of staying here will at some time get (use φέρω) a great reward from Cyrus.

18. Plato's Academy, mosaic from the House of
T. Siminius Stephanus, Pompeii, Italy, early first century BC.

Lesson 52

μι-Verbs: Present Active System. Dative of Manner

μι-Verbs: Present Active System

Unlike ω-verbs, μι-verbs lack a thematic vowel in the <u>present system</u>, <u>except</u> in the <u>subjunctive</u>. Instead, μι-verbs display a strong or a weak grade of their stem vowel in specific forms of the verb: η/α (for verbs like ἵστημι *stand*), η/ε (τίθημι *set*, ἵημι *send*), ω/ο (δίδωμι *give, donate*) or ῡ/υ (δείκνυμι *show*). The future, perfect, and aorist passive systems of μι-verbs are no different than those of ω-verbs. The remaining system – the aorist active system of μι-verbs – will be treated in Lesson 54.

Present Active Indicative

In the present active indicative, μι-verbs use the strong grade of their stem vowel in the singular forms and the weak grade in the plural forms and in the infinitive, as follows:

			<u>singular</u>		
1	ἵστημι	τίθημι	ἵημι	δίδωμι	δείκνυμι
2	ἵστης	τίθης	ἵης (ἱεῖς)	δίδως	δείκνυς
3	ἵστησι(ν)	τίθησι(ν)	ἵησι(ν)	δίδωσι(ν)	δείκνυσι(ν)
			<u>plural</u>		
1	ἵσταμεν	τίθεμεν	ἵεμεν	δίδομεν	δείκνυμεν
2	ἵστατε	τίθετε	ἵετε	δίδοτε	δείκνυτε
3	ἱστᾶσι(ν)	τιθέασι(ν)	ἱᾶσι(ν)	διδόασι(ν)	δεικνύασι(ν)

Infinitive

ἱστάναι	τιθέναι	ἱέναι	διδόναι	δεικνύναι

Imperfect Active Indicative

As in the present tense, the imperfect indicative uses the strong grade of the stem vowel in the singulars and the weak grade in the plurals.

			<u>singular</u>		
1	ἵστην	ἐτίθην	ἵην	ἐδίδουν	ἐδείκνυν
2	ἵστης	ἐτίθεις	ἵεις	ἐδίδους	ἐδείκνυς
3	ἵστη	ἐτίθει	ἵει	ἐδίδου	ἐδείκνυ

		plural		
1 ἵσταμεν	ἐτίθεμεν	ἵεμεν	ἐδίδομεν	ἐδείκνυμεν
2 ἵστατε	ἐτίθετε	ἵετε	ἐδίδοτε	ἐδείκνυτε
3 ἵστασαν	ἐτίθεσαν	ἵεσαν	ἐδίδοσαν	ἐδείκνυσαν

Present Active Subjunctive

μι-verbs are declined no differently than ω-verbs in the present subjunctive:

		singular		
1 ἱστῶ	τιθῶ	ἱῶ	διδῶ	δεικνύω
2 ἱστῇς	τιθῇς	ἱῇς	διδῷς	δεικνύῃς
3 ἱστῇ	τιθῇ	ἱῇ	διδῷ	δεικνύῃ

		plural		
1 ἱστῶμεν	τιθῶμεν	ἱῶμεν	διδῶμεν	δεικνύωμεν
2 ἱστῆτε	τιθῆτε	ἱῆτε	διδῶτε	δεικνύητε
3 ἱστῶσι(ν)	τιθῶσι(ν)	ἱῶσι(ν)	διδῶσι(ν)	δεικνύωσι(ν)

Present Active Optative

Here, the weak grade of the stem vowel combines with ι to create the sign of the optative mood, except in the case of δεικνύοιμι, which follows the ω-verb paradigm.

		singular		
1 ἱσταίην	τιθείην	ἱείην	διδοίην	δεικνύοιμι
2 ἱσταίης	τιθείης	ἱείης	διδοίης	δεικνύοις
3 ἱσταίη	τιθείη	ἱείη	διδοίη	δεικνύοι

		plural		
1 ἱσταῖμεν	τιθεῖμεν	ἱεῖμεν	διδοῖμεν	δεικνύοιμεν
2 ἱσταῖτε	τιθεῖτε	ἱεῖτε	διδοῖτε	δεικνύοιτε
3 ἱσταῖεν	τιθεῖεν	ἱεῖεν	διδοῖεν	δεικνύοιεν

Present Active Imperative

The weak grade of the verb is used. In the second person singular forms, however, an ε ending added to the stem vowel creates some predictable euphonic changes, as follows:

		singular		
2	ἵστη	τίθει	ἵει	δίδου	δείκνυ
3	ἱστάτω	τιθέτω	ἱέτω	διδότω	δεικύτω

		plural		
2	ἵστατε	τίθετε	ἵετε	δίδοτε	δείκνυτε
3	ἱστάντων	τιθέντων	ἱέντων	διδόντων	δεικνύντων

Present Active Participle

The weak grade is used. Compensatory lengthening (see Lesson 21) occurs – though it is not visible in the case of ἵστημι or δείκνυμι – when a ν or ντ drops from the ending of the participle on account of the presence of σ.

m.	ἱστάς,	τιθείς,	ἱείς,	διδούς,	δεικνύς,
f.	ἱστᾶσα,	τιθεῖσα,	ἱεῖσα,	διδοῦσα,	δεικνῦσα,
n.	ἱστάν	τιθέν	ἱέν	διδόν	δεικνύν

Dative of Manner (and Respect)

The manner in which something is done (Manner) or the point of view from which a statement is made (Respect) is expressed by the dative case. This construction answers the question "How?" (Manner) or "In respect to what?" (Respect). A preposition, however, is generally used in expressions of <u>manner</u> when no adjective occurs. Examples:

δίκῃ (or σὺν δίκῃ) τοὺς ἀδικήσαντας ἐδίωξεν.
With justice he prosecuted the wrongdoers.

πολλῇ ὕβρει ἡμῖν ἀποκέκρινται.
They have replied to us with much insolence.

λόγῳ μὲν φίλος ἐστίν, ἔργῳ δ᾽ οὔ.
He is a friend in word (allegedly), but not in deed (actually).

τῇ ἐμῇ γνώμῃ, αἴτιοί εἰσι τοῦ φόνου.
In my opinion, they are responsible for the murder.

Vocabulary

ἅπτομαι, ἅψομαι, ἡψάμην, ____, ἧμμαι, ____ (+ gen.) *touch*

γελάω, γελάσομαι, ἐγέλασα, ____, ____, ἐγελάσθην *laugh (at)*

δείκνυμι, δείξω, ἔδειξα, δέδειχα, δέδειγμαι, ἐδείχθην *show, point out* (with ὅτι or ὡς in indirect statement) (epideictic)

δίδωμι, δώσω, ἔδωκα, δέδωκα, δέδομαι, ἐδόθην *give* (antidote)

ἵημι, -ἥσω, -ἧκα, -εἷκα, -εἷμαι, -εἵθην *let go, throw, send*

ἵστημι, στήσω, ἔστησα, ἕστηκα, ἕσταμαι, ἐστάθην *cause to stand, set, set up, place* (active voice) (station)

ἐφίστημι (+ acc. and dat.) *place upon, set over*

τίθημι, θήσω, ἔθηκα, τέθηκα, ____, ἐτέθην *put, place; make* (with persons) (thesis)

τύπτω, τυπτήσω, ἔπαισα, πέπληγα, πέπληγμαι, ἐπλήγην *beat, strike*

ἐμός, -ή, -όν *my, mine*   σός, -ή, -όν *your, yours* (sg.)

ἡμέτερος, -α, -ον *our, ours*   οὐ μόνον . . . ἀλλὰ καί *not*

ὑμέτερος, -α, -ον *your, yours* (pl.)   *only . . . but also*

Note: The possessive adjectives listed above are used attributively (like the possessive genitive of demonstratives and reflexives). On the other hand, the possessive genitive of the corresponding personal pronouns and of αὐτός appears in the predicate position.

Drill A

Give the following forms:

1. present active optative, 1ˢᵗ pl. of:
    ἵημι, δείκνυμι, εἰμί, ἵστημι, δίδωμι

2. imperfect active indicative, 3ʳᵈ sg. of:
    τίθημι, ἵστημι, φιλέω, δίδωμι, εἶμι

3. present active indicative, 3ʳᵈ pl. of:
    ἵημι, δείκνυμι, φημί, δίδωμι, ἀξιόω

4. present active infinitive of:
    ἵστημι, ἐάω, δηλόω, εἶμι, ἵημι

Drill B

Make the verb in parentheses match the form of the verb to its left; translate the new verb form:

1. παιδεύεις (τίθημι)
2. ἱσταῖμεν (τίθημι)
3. ἐδήλους (δείκνυμι)
4. κρίνειν (ἵστημι)
5. πίπτοιεν (τίθημι)
6. ἵην (τύπτω)
7. εἴη (δείκνυμι)
8. δίδου (ἐφίστημι)
9. τίθησι (δίδωμι)
10. ἐδείκνυ (ἵημι)
11. ἀποκτενῶ (ἵστημι)
12. ἐπιτρέπετε (δίδωμι)

Exercise A: Reading

On bringing up children (continued)

Καί μοι, ὦ Λύσι, ἔτι τόδε εἰπέ· σὲ αὐτὸν ἐῶσιν ὁ
πατὴρ καὶ ἡ μήτηρ ἄρχειν σεαυτοῦ, ἢ οὐδὲ τοῦτο ἐπιτρέπουσί
σοι;
Πῶς γάρ, ἔφη, ἐπιτρέπουσιν;
5   Ἀλλ᾽ ἄρχει τίς σου;
Ὅδε, παιδαγωγός, ἔφη.
Μῶν δοῦλος ὤν;
Ἡμέτερός γε, ἔφη.
Ἦ δεινόν, ἦν δ᾽ ἐγώ, ἐλεύθερον ὄντα ὑπὸ δούλου
10   ἄρχεσθαι. τί δὲ ποιῶν οὗτος ὁ παιδαγωγός σου ἄρχει;
Ἄγων δήπου, ἔφη, εἰς διδασκάλου.
Μῶν μὴ καὶ οὗτοί σου ἄρχουσιν, οἱ διδάσκαλοι;
Πάντως γε.
Πολλοὺς ἄρα σοι δεσπότας καὶ ἄρχοντας ἑκὼν ὁ πατὴρ
15   ἐφίστησιν. ἀλλ᾽ ἄρα ἐπειδὰν εἰς οἰκίαν ἔλθῃς παρὰ τὴν μητέρα,
ἐκείνη σε ἐᾷ ποιεῖν ὃ ἂν βούλῃ, ἵνα εὐδαίμων ᾖς, ἢ περὶ τὰ ἔρια
ἢ περὶ τὸν ἱστὸν ὅταν ὑφαίνῃ; οὔ τι γάρ που διακωλύει σε ἢ
τῶν ἐρίων ἢ τοῦ ἱστοῦ ἢ ἄλλου τινὸς ἅπτεσθαι.
Καὶ ὅς γελάσας, Μὰ Δία, ἔφη, ὦ Σώκρατες, οὐ μόνον
20   γε διακωλύει, ἀλλὰ καὶ τυπτοίμην ἂν εἰ ἁπτοίμην.
Ἡράκλεις, ἦν δ᾽ ἐγώ, μῶν μή τι ἠδίκησας τὸν πατέρα ἢ
τὴν μητέρα;
Μὰ Δί᾽ οὐκ ἔγωγε, ἔφη.

Adapted from Plato, *Lysis* 208c-e

6   παιδαγωγός, -οῦ, ὁ *guardian* (who accompanied a boy to and from
     school)
11   δήπου (adverb) *obviously*
     διδασκάλου from διδάσκαλος, -ου, ὁ *teacher* (Supply οἰκίαν with
     εἰς.)
16   ἔρια from ἔριον, -ου, τό *wool*
17   ἱστόν from ἱστός, -οῦ, ὁ *loom*
     ὑφαίνῃ from ὑφαίνω *weave*
21   Ἡράκλεις vocative sg. of Ἡρακλῆς, -έους, ὁ *Heracles*

Exercise B

Translate:

     1. The victor (use perfect participle of νικάω) makes (use
τίθημι) our citizens seem to be happy, but I in fact make them happy.
     2. Your soldiers, I suppose, will set up as a general that man
who gives them the most pay.
     3. I want to show you how even base men will become better
by following (use χράομαι) the example of Socrates.
     4. May the gods somehow send us a clear proof of the oracle.
     5. In my opinion, anyone who accepts the orders of a tyrant
(lit., things ordered by a tyrant) is cowardly and not worthy of freedom.

19. ὁ Πλάτων.

Lesson 53

μι-Verbs: Present Middle-Passive System

μι-Verbs: Present Middle-Passive System

Present Middle-Passive Indicative

In the present middle-passive indicative, μι-verbs use the weak grade of their stem vowel throughout all forms.

			singular		
1	ἵσταμαι	τίθεμαι	ἵεμαι	δίδομαι	δείκνυμαι
2	ἵστασαι	τίθεσαι	ἵεσαι	δίδοσαι	δείκνυσαι
3	ἵσταται	τίθεται	ἵεται	δίδοται	δείκνυται
			plural		
1	ἱστάμεθα	τιθέμεθα	ἱέμεθα	διδόμεθα	δεικνύμεθα
2	ἵστασθε	τίθεσθε	ἵεσθε	δίδοσθε	δείκνυσθε
3	ἵστανται	τίθενται	ἵενται	δίδονται	δείκνυνται

Infinitive

ἵστασθαι	τίθεσθαι	ἵεσθαι	δίδοσθαι	δείνυσθαι

Imperfect Middle-Passive Indicative

In the imperfect middle-passive indicative, μι-verbs use the weak grade of their stem vowel throughout all forms.

			singular		
1	ἱστάμην	ἐτιθέμην	ἱέμην	ἐδιδόμην	ἐδεικνύμην
2	ἵστασο	ἐτίθεσο	ἵευο	ἐδίδοσο	ἐδείκνυσο
3	ἵστατο	ἐτίθετο	ἵετο	ἐδίδοτο	ἐδείκνυτο
			plural		
1	ἱστάμεθα	ἐτιθέμεθα	ἱέμεθα	ἐδιδόμεθα	ἐδεικνύμεθα
2	ἵστασθε	ἐτίθεσθε	ἵεσθε	ἐδίδοσθε	ἐδείκνυσθε
3	ἵσταντο	ἐθίθεντο	ἵεντο	ἐδίδοντο	ἐδείκνυντο

Present Middle-Passive Subjunctive

μι-verbs are declined no differently than ω-verbs in the present subjunctive. As a primary mood, the primary middle-passive endings are used.

singular

1	ἱστῶμαι	τιθῶμαι	ἱῶμαι	διδῶμαι	δεικνύωμαι
2	ἱστῇ	τιθῇ	ἱῇ	διδῷ	δεικνύῃ
3	ἱστῆται	τιθῆται	ἱῆται	διδῶται	δεικνύηται

plural

1	ἱστώμεθα	τιθώμεθα	ἱώμεθα	διδώμεθα	δεικνυώμεθα
2	ἱστῆσθε	τιθῆσθε	ἱῆσθε	διδῶσθε	δεικνύησθε
3	ἱστῶνται	τιθῶνται	ἱῶνται	διδῶνται	δεικνύωνται

Present Middle-Passive Optative

Here, the weak grade of the stem vowel combines with ι to create the sign of the optative mood, except in the case of δεικνύοιμι, which follows the ω-verb paradigm. As a secondary mood, the secondary middle-passive endings are used.

singular

1	ἱσταίμην	τιθείμην	ἱείμην	διδοίμην	δεικνυοίμην
2	ἱσταῖο	τιθεῖο	ἱεῖο	διδοῖο	δεικνύοιο
3	ἱσταῖτο	τιθεῖτο	ἱεῖτο	διδοῖτο	δεικνύοιτο

plural

1	ἱσταίμεθα	τιθείμεθα	ἱείμεθα	διδοίμεθα	δεικνυοίμεθα
2	ἱσταῖσθε	τιθεῖσθε	ἱεῖσθε	διδοῖσθε	δεικνύοισθε
3	ἱσταῖντο	τιθεῖντο	ἱεῖντο	διδοῖντο	δεικνύοιντο

Present Middle-Passive Imperative

The weak grade of the verb is used.

singular

2	ἵστασο	τίθεσο	ἵεσο	δίδοσο	δείκνυσο
3	ἱστάσθω	τιθέσθω	ἱέσθω	διδόσθω	δεικνύσθω

plural

2	ἵστασθε	τίθεσθε	ἵεσθε	δίδοσθε	δείκνυσθε
3	ἱστάσθων	τιθέσθων	ἱέσθων	διδόσθων	δεικνύσθων

Present Middle-Passive Participle

The weak grade of the verb is used.

m. ἱστάμενος,   τιθέμενος,   ἱέμενος,   διδόμενος,   δεικνύμενος,

f. ἱσταμένη,   τιθεμένη,   ἱεμένη,   διδομένη,   δεικνυμένη,

n. ἱστάμενον   τιθέμενος   ἱέμενον   διδόμενον   δεικνύμενον

Vocabulary

δύναμαι, δυνήσομαι, ____, ____, δεδύνημαι, ἐδυνήθην *be able, can*
(dynamic)

ἐπίσταμαι (imperf. ἠπιστάμην), ἐπιστήσομαι, ____, ____, ____,
ἠπιστήθην *know* (as a fact), *know how* (+ infin.) (governs participle or
ὅτι/ὡς in indirect statement)

ἵεμαι (mid. of ἵημι) *hasten, rush; be eager* (+ gen. or infin.)

ἵσταμαι (mid. of ἵστημι) *stand* (intransitive)

αἴτιον, -ου, τό *cause, reason*

γράμμα, γράμματος, τό *letter,* (pl.) *letters, writings* (monogram)

ἡλικία, -ας, ἡ *time of life, age, maturity*

δεύτερος, -α, -ον *second* (Deuteronomy)

τοιοῦτος, τοιαύτη, τοιοῦτο(ν) *such*

τοσοῦτος, τοσαύτη, τοσοῦτο(ν) *so great, so much*; (pl.) *so many*

ἀντί (+ gen.) *instead of, in return for* (antidote)
   ἀντὶ τίνος *why* (lit., *in return for what*)

ἄρτι (adverb) *just now, recently*

μήν (postpositive adverb) *in fact* (compare δή)

πω (enclitic) *yet, up to this time* (οὔτω or οὐ ... πω, *not yet*)

Drill A

Complete a full synopsis of the verbs listed below:

   1. τίθημι, 1st person plural
   2. δίδωμι, 2nd person singular

Drill B

Parse fully:

1. ἠπιστάμεθα	6. ἰῶνται
2. τίθεσο	7. διδοῖτο
3. ἐτίθεσο	8. δείκνυσθε
4. ἀξιοῦν	9. εἴργαστο
5. τιθεῖσι	10. γνῶθι

Drill C

Give the following forms:

1. present middle-passive imperative, 3rd plural of:
   δείκνυμι, ἀξιόω, ἐπίσταμαι, ἅπτομαι, φοβέομαι

2. imperfect middle-passive indicative, 2nd singular of:
   δύναμαι, ἵημι, ποιέω, βούλομαι, αἰτιάομαι

3. present middle-passive subjunctive, 1st plural of:
   δίδωμι, τίθημι, δηλόω, ἀπολογέομαι, πειράομαι

Exercise A: Reading

On bringing up children (continued)

  Ἀλλ' ἀντὶ τίνος μὴν οὕτω σε δεινῶς διακωλύουσιν
εὐδαίμονα εἶναι καὶ ποιεῖν ὃ ἂν βούλῃ, καὶ δι' ἡμέρας ὅλης
τρέφουσί σε ἀεί τῳ δουλεύοντα καὶ ἑνὶ λόγῳ ὀλίγου ὧν
ἐπιθυμεῖς οὐδὲν ποιοῦνται; ὥστε σοι, ὡς δοκεῖ, οὔτε τῶν
5 χρημάτων τοσούτων ὄντων οὐδὲν ὄφελός ἐστι, ἀλλὰ πάντες
αὐτῶν μᾶλλον ἄρχουσιν ἢ σύ, οὔτε τοῦ σώματος οὕτω καλοῦ
ὄντος, ἀλλὰ καὶ τούτου ἄλλος ἐπιμελεῖται· σὺ δὲ ἄρχεις
οὐδενός, ὦ Λύσι, οὐδὲ ποιεῖς οὐδὲν ὧν ἐπιθυμεῖς.
  Οὐ γὰρ πω, ἔφη, ἡλικίαν ἔχω, ὦ Σώκρατες.
10 Τοῦτό σε, ὦ παῖ, οὐ κωλύσει, ἐπεὶ τό γε τοσοῦτον,
ὡς ἐγῷμαι, καὶ ὁ πατὴρ καὶ ἡ μήτηρ σοι ἐπιτρέπουσι καὶ οὐκ
ἀναμένουσιν ἕως ἂν ἡλικίαν ἔχῃς· ὅταν γὰρ βούλωνται αὐτοῖς
τινα ἀναγνωσθῆναι ἢ γραφῆναι, σέ, ὡς ἐγῷμαι, πρῶτον τῶν ἐν
τῇ οἰκίᾳ ἐπὶ τοῦτο τάττουσιν· ἢ γάρ;
15 Πάνυ γε, ἔφη.

Οὐκοῦν δύνασαι ἐνταῦθ' ὃ ἂν βούλῃ πρῶτον τῶν
γραμμάτων γράφειν καὶ ὃ ἂν δεύτερον; καί σοι ἀναγιγνώσκειν
ὡσαύτως ἔξεστιν;

Πάντως δήπου, ἔφη.

20   Τί ποτ' ἂν οὖν εἴη τὸ αἴτιον, ὦ Λύσι, ὅτι ἐνταῦθα μὲν
οὐ διακωλύουσιν, ἐν οἷς δὲ ἄρτι ἐλέγομεν κωλύουσιν;

Ὅτι, οἶμαι, ἔφη, ταῦτα μὲν ἐπίσταμαι, ἐκεῖνα δ' οὔ.

Adapted from Plato, *Lysis* 208e-209c

3   τῳ alternate from of the interrogative τίνι
4   ὥστε means *therefore*, when used to begin an independent clause.
5   ὄφελος from ὄφελος, -ους, τό *advantage*
11   ἐγῷμαι crasis for ἐγὼ οἶμαι
12   ἀναμένουσιν from ἀναμένω *wait*
14   ἦ γάρ; *Is it not so?*
18   ὡσαύτως *in the same way*

<u>Exercise B</u>

Translate:

1. Why are you (sg.) so eager just now to read the ancient
writings of Xenophon?

2. When was it announced that the foreign rulers would set a
second tyrant over us?

3. Socrates' fame was such that many rushed to the market-
place where he was speaking about the causes of injustice.

4. Since your son has not yet reached (use ἔχω) maturity, how
will you be able to prevent him from doing something bad to someone? I
shall beat him.

5. If in fact Lysis knew how to refute Socrates, he would
become worthy of honor.

Lesson 54

μι-Verbs: Aorist System

Aorist System of μι-Verbs

μι-verbs in the aorist system show a wide variety of forms. δείκνυμι has a first aorist (ἔδειξα, *I showed*); ἵστημι has both a first and a second aorist, and a perfect, and pluperfect. The second aorist and perfects of ἵστημι are found only in the active voice and are intransitive (i.e. they do not take direct objects). Example:

First aorist	Second aorist
ἔστησα	ἔστην
I set/stood (up) (some object)	*I stood up* (i.e. myself)

The aorist of ἵημι is found only in compounds such as ἀφίημι.

Aorist Indicative

ἵστημι

	1st aorist		2nd aorist
	active	middle	active
1 sing.	ἔστησα	ἐστησάμην	ἔστην
2 sing.	ἔστησας	ἐστήσω	ἔστης
3 sing.	ἔστησε(ν)	ἐστήσατο	ἔστη
1 pl.	ἐστήσαμεν	ἐστησάμεθα	ἔστημεν
2 pl.	ἐστήσατε	ἐστήσασθε	ἔστητε
3 pl.	ἔστησαν	ἐστήσαντο	ἔστησαν

Aorist Infinitive

	στῆσαι	στήσασθαι	στῆναι

Aorist Indicative

	τίθημι		ἵημι	
	active	middle	active	middle
1 sing.	ἔθηκα	ἐθέμην	ἧκα	-εἵμην
2 sing.	ἔθηκας	ἔθου	ἧκας	-εἷσο
3 sing.	ἔθηκε(ν)	ἔθετο	ἧκε(ν)	-εἷτο

1 pl.	ἔθεμεν	ἐθέμεθα	-εῖμεν	εἵμεθα
2 pl.	ἔθετε	ἔθεσθε	-εῖτε	-εῖσθε
3 pl.	ἔθεσαν	ἔθεντο	-εῖσαν	-εἷντο

Aorist Infinitive

| | θεῖναι | θέσθαι | -εῖναι | -έσθαι |

Aorist Indicative

	δίδωμι		δείκνυμι	
	active	middle	active	middle
1 sing.	ἔδωκα	ἐδόμην	ἔδειξα	ἐδειξάμην
2 sing.	ἔδωκας	ἔδου	ἔδειξας	ἐδείξω
3 sing.	ἔδωκε(ν)	ἔδοτο	ἔδειξε(ν)	ἐδείξατο
1 pl.	ἔδομεν	ἐδόμεθα	ἐδείξαμεν	ἐδειξάμεθα
2 pl.	ἔδοτε	ἔδοσθε	ἐδείξατε	ἐδείξασθε
3 pl.	ἔδοσαν	ἔδοντο	ἔδειξαν	ἐδείξαντο

Aorist Infinitive

| | δοῦναι | δόσθαι | δεῖξαι | δείξασθαι |

Aorist Subjunctive

	ἵστημι		
	1st aorist		2nd aorist
	active	middle	active
1 sing.	στήσω	στήσωμαι	στῶ
2 sing.	στήσῃς	στήσῃ	στῇς
3 sing.	στήσῃ	στήσηται	στῇ
1 pl.	στήσωμεν	στησώμεθα	στῶμεν
2 pl.	στήσητε	στήσησθε	στῆτε
3 pl.	στήσωσι(ν)	στήσωνται	στῶσι(ν)

	τίθημι		ἵημι	
	<u>active</u>	<u>middle</u>	<u>active</u>	<u>middle</u>
1 sing.	θῶ	θῶμαι	-ῶ	-ῶμαι
2 sing.	θῆς	θῇ	-ῇς	-ῇ
3 sing.	θῇ	θῆται	-ῇ	-ῆται
1 pl.	θῶμων	θώμεθα	-ῶμεν	-ώμεθα
2 pl.	θῆτε	θῆσθε	-ῆτε	-ῆσθε
3 pl.	θῶσι(ν)	θῶνται	-ῶσι(ν)	-ῶνται

	δίδωμι		δείκνυμι	
	<u>active</u>	<u>middle</u>	<u>active</u>	<u>middle</u>
1 sing.	δῶ	δῶμαι	δείξω	δείξωμαι
2 sing.	δῷς	δῷ	δείξῃς	δείξῃ
3 sing.	δῷ	δῶται	δείξῃ	δείξηται
1 pl.	δῶμεν	δώμεθα	δείξωμεν	δειξώμεθα
2 pl.	δῶτε	δῶσθε	δείξητε	δείξησθε
3 pl.	δῶσι(ν)	δῶνται	δείξωσι(ν)	δείξωνται

<u>Aorist Optative</u>

ἵστημι

	1st aorist		2nd aorist
	<u>active</u>	<u>middle</u>	<u>active</u>
1 sing.	στήσαιμι	στησαίμην	σταίην
2 sing.	στήσειας/-σαις	στήσαιο	σταίης
3 sing.	στήσειε(ν)/-σαι	στήσαιτο	σταίη
1 pl.	στήσαιμεν	στησαίμεθα	σταῖμεν
2 pl.	στήσαιτε	στήσαισθε	σταῖτε
3 pl.	στήσειαν/-σαιεν	στήσαιντο	σταῖεν

	τίθημι		ἵημι	
	active	middle	active	middle
1 sing.	θείην	θείμην	-είην	-είμην
2 sing.	θείης	θεῖο	-είης	-εῖο
3 sing.	θείη	θεῖτο	-είη	-εῖτο
1 pl.	θεῖμεν	θείμεθα	-εῖμεν	-είμεθα
2 pl.	θεῖτε	θεῖσθε	-εῖτε	-εῖσθε
3 pl.	θεῖεν	θεῖντο	-εῖεν	-εῖντο

	δίδωμι		δείκνυμι	
	active	middle	active	middle
1 sing.	δοίην	δοίμην	δείξαιμι	δείξαίμην
2 sing.	δοίης	δοῖο	δείξειας/-ξαις	δείξαιο
3 sing.	δοίη	δοῖτο	δείξειε(ν)/-ξαι	δείξαιτο
1 pl.	δοῖμεν	δοίμεθα	δείξαιμεν	δειξαίμεθα
2 pl.	δοῖτε	δοῖσθε	δείξαιτε	δείξαισθε
3 pl.	δοῖεν	δοῖντο	δείξειαν/-ξαιεν	δείξαιντο

Aorist Imperative

ἵστημι

	1st aorist		2nd aorist
	active	middle	active
2 sing.	στῆσον	στῆσαι	στῆθι
3 sing.	στησάτω	στησάσθω	στήτω
2 pl.	στήσατε	στήσασθε	στῆτε
3 pl.	στησάντων	στησάσθων	στάντων

	τίθημι		ἵημι	
	<u>active</u>	<u>middle</u>	<u>active</u>	<u>middle</u>
2 sing.	θές	θοῦ	-ἕς	-οῦ
3 sing.	θέτω	θέσθω	-ἕτω	-ἕσθω
2 pl.	θέτε	θέσθε	-ἕτε	-ἕσθε
3 pl.	θέντων	θέσθων	-ἕντων	-ἕσθων

	δίδωμι		δείκνυμι	
	<u>active</u>	<u>middle</u>	<u>active</u>	<u>middle</u>
2 sing.	δός	δοῦ	δεῖξον	δεῖξαι
3 sing.	δότω	δόσθω	δειξάτω	δειξάσθω
2 sing.	δότε	δόσθε	δείξατε	δείξασθε
3 sing.	δόντων	δόσθων	δειξάντων	δειξάσθων

<u>Aorist Participle</u>

ἵστημι

	1st aorist		2nd aorist
<u>Nom.</u>	<u>active</u>	<u>middle</u>	<u>active</u>
m. sing.	στήσας,	στησάμενος,	στάς,
f. sing.	στήσασα,	στησαμένη,	στᾶσα,
n. sing.	στῆσαν	στησάμενον	στάν

	τίθημι		ἵημι	
	<u>active</u>	<u>middle</u>	<u>active</u>	<u>middle</u>
m. sing.	θείς	θέμενος,	-εἵς,	-ἕμενος,
f. sing.	θεῖσα,	θεμένη,	-εῖσα,	-ἑμένη,
n. sing.	θέν	θέμενον	-ἕν	-ἕμενον

	δίδωμι		δείκνυμι	
	active	middle	active	middle
m. sing.	δούς,	δόμενος,	δείξας,	δειξάμενος,
f. sing.	δοῦσα,	δομένη,	δείξασα,	δειξαμένη,
n. sing.	δόν	δόμενον	δεῖξαν	δειξάμενον

The Perfect System of ἵστημι

	First Perfect Indicative		First Pluperfect Indicative	
	active	mid.-pass.	active	mid.-pass.
1 sing.	ἕστηκα	ἕστημαι	εἱστήκη	εἱστήμην
2 sing.	ἕστηκας	ἕστησαι	εἱστήκης	εἵστησο
3 sing.	ἕστηκε(ν)	ἕστηται	εἱστήκει(ν)	εἵστητο
1 pl.	ἑστήκαμεν	ἑστήμεθα	εἱστήκεμεν	εἱστήμεθα
2 pl.	ἑστήκατε	ἕστησθε	εἱστήκετε	εἵστησθε
3 pl.	ἑστήκασι(ν)	ἕστηνται	εἱστήκεσαν	εἵστηντο

First Perfect Infinitive
ἑστηκέναι

First Perfect Participle

	active	mid.-pass.
N. sing.	ἑστηκώς, -κυῖα, -κός	ἑστημένος, -μένη, -μένον
G. sing.	ἑστηκότος, -κυίας, -κότος	ἑστημένου, -μένης, -μένου

	Second Perfect Indicative	Second Pluperfect Indicative
	active	active
1 sing.	[ἕστηκα]	[εἱστήκη]
2 sing.	[ἕστηκας]	[εἱστήκης]
3 sing.	[ἕστηκε(ν)]	[εἱστήκει(ν)]

1 pl.	ἕσταμεν	ἕσταμεν
2 pl.	ἕστατε	ἕστατε
3 pl.	ἑστᾶσι(ν)	ἕστασαν

Second Perfect Infinitive

active

ἑστάναι

Second Perfect Active Participle

N. sing. ἑστώς, ἑστῶσα, ἑστός

G. sing. ἑστῶτος, ἑστώσης, ἑστῶτος

Vocabulary

ἐπιτίθημι (+ acc. and dat.) *place upon, apply, impose* (epithet)

συγχωρέω, συγχωρήσω, συνεχώρησα, συγκεχώρηκα, συγκεχώρημαι, συνεχωρήθην (+ dat.) *agree, concede*

ὑπολαμβάνω *take up; suppose, interrupt, reply* (governs infinitive or ὅτι/ὡς in indirect statement)

φρονέω, φρονήσω, ἐφρόνησα, πεφρόνηκα *have understanding, think, mean* (governs ὅτι or ὡς in indirect statement)

Ἑλλάς, Ἑλλάδος, ἡ *Greece*

νοῦς, νοῦ, νῷ, νοῦν, ὁ *mind, intelligence, sense*

ὅρος, ὅρου, ὁ *boundary, standard* (horizon)

ὀφθαλμός, -οῦ, ὁ *eye* (opthalmologist)

φάρμακον, -ου, τό *remedy, medicine, drug* (pharmacist)

ὀρθός, -ή, -όν *straight, upright; right, correct* (orthography)

ὅσος, -η, -ον *how great, as great as, how far, as far as;* (pl.) *how many, as many as*

εἶεν (adverb) *well then; very well*

Drill A

Give synopses of the following verbs in the indicative, subjunctive, optative, and imperative moods:

1. ἵστηνι in the 1ˢᵗ aorist active and middle, 3ʳᵈ sg.
2. ἵημι in the present active and middle-passive, 2ⁿᵈ pl.
3. τίθημι in the present active and middle-passive, 2ⁿᵈ sg.
4. ἵστημι in the 2ⁿᵈ aorist active, 3ʳᵈ pl.

Drill B

Make the verb in parentheses match the form of the verb to its left; translate the new verb:

1. ἐπαίδευσας (δίδωμι)
2. ἱσταίμεθα (τίθημι)
3. μανθάνειν (ἵστημι)
4. ἐπιτρέποιεν (τίθημι)
5. ἐτίθεμεν (ἵημι)
6. ἵης (δείκνυμι)

Drill C

Parse the following verbs completely:

1. θῶμαι
2. δοῦναι
3. ἔθηκε(ν)
4. δεικνύοιτο
5. σταίην
6. διδοίη
7. ἱᾶσι
8. τιθῶμεν

Exercise A: Reading

On bringing up children (conclusion)

Εἶεν, ἦν δ᾽ ἐγώ, ὦ ἄριστε, οὐκ ἄρα τὴν ἡλικίαν σου περιμένει ὁ πατὴρ ἐπιτρέπειν πάντα, ἀλλ᾽ ᾗ ἂν ἡμέρᾳ ἡγήσηταί σε βέλτιον αὐτοῦ φρονεῖν, ταύτῃ ἐπιτρέψει σοι καὶ αὐτὸν καὶ τὰ αὐτοῦ.

5   Οἶμαι ἔγωγε, ἔφη.

Εἶεν, ἦν δ᾽ ἐγώ, τί δέ; τῷ γείτονι ἆρ᾽ οὐχ ὁ αὐτὸς ὅρος ὅσ τῷ πατρὶ περὶ σοῦ; πότερον οἴει αὐτὸν ἐπιτρέψειν σοι τὴν αὐτοῦ οἰκίαν οἰκονομεῖν ὅταν σε ἡγήσηται βέλτιον περὶ οἰκονομίας ἑαυτοῦ φρονεῖν, ἢ αὐτὸν οἰκονομήσειν;

10   Ἐμοὶ ἐπιτρέψειν οἶμαι.
            Τί δ’; Ἀθηναίους οἴει σοι οὐκ ἐπιτρέψειν τὰ αὑτῶν,
        ὅταν αἰσθάνωνται ὅτι ἱκανῶς φρονεῖς;
            Ἔγωγε.
            Πρὸς Διός, ἦν δ’ ἐγώ, τί ἄρα ὁ μέγας βασιλεύς; εἰ
15   τοὺς ὀφθαλμοὺς ὁ υἱὸς αὐτοῦ ἀσθενὴς εἴη, ἆρα ἐῴη ἂν αὐτὸν
        ἅπτεσθαι τῶν ἑαυτοῦ ὀφθαλμῶν, μὴ αὐτὸν εἶναι ἰατρὸν
        ἡγούμενος, ἢ κωλύοι ἄν;
            Κωλύοι ἄν.
            Ἡμᾶς δέ γε εἰ ὑπολαμβάνοι ἰατροὺς εἶναι, κἂν εἰ
20   βουλοίμεθα φάρμακα ἐπιτιθέναι, οἶμαι οὐκ ἂν κωλύσειεν,
        ἡγούμενος ἡμᾶς ὀρθῶς φρονεῖν.
            Ἀληθῆ λέγεις.
            Ἆρ’ οὖν καὶ τἆλλα πάντα ἡμῖν ἐπιτρέποι ἂν μᾶλλον ἢ
        ἑαυτῷ καὶ τῷ υἱῷ περὶ ὅσων ἂν δόξωμεν αὐτῷ σοφώτεροι
25   ἐκείνων εἶναι;
            Πάνυ γε, ἔφη, ὦ Σώκρατες.
            Οὕτως ἄρα ἔχει, ἦν δ’ ἐγώ, ὦ φίλε Λύσι: εἰς μὲν ταῦτα,
        ἃ ἂν ἱκανοὶ γενώμεθα, ἅπαντες ἡμῖν ἐπιτρέψουσιν, Ἕλληνές τε
        καὶ βάρβαροι καὶ ἄνδρες καὶ γυναῖκες, ποιήσομέν τε ἐν
30   τούτοις ὃ ἂν βουλώμεθα, καὶ οὐδεὶς ἡμᾶς ἑκὼν κωλύσει, ἀλλ’
        αὐτοί τε ἐλεύθεροι ἐσόμεθα ἐν αὐτοῖς καὶ ἄλλων ἄρχοντες,
        ἡμέτερά τε ταῦτα ἔσται. πρὸς ἃ δ’ ἂν νοῦν μὴ κτησώμεθα,
        οὐδεὶς ἡμῖν ἐπιτρέψει περὶ αὐτὰ ποιεῖν τὰ ἡμῖν δοκοῦντα,
        ἀλλ’ κωλύσουσι πάντες καθ’ ὅ τι ἂν δύνωνται, οὐ μόνον οἱ
35   βάρβαροι ἀλλὰ καὶ ὁ πατὴρ καὶ ἡ μήτηρ. συγχωρεῖς
        οὕτως ἔχειν;
            Συγχωρῶ.

                        Adapted from Plato, *Lysis* 209c-210c

    2   περιμένει from περιμένω *wait for*
    6   τί δέ; *What about this?*
         γείτονι from γείτων, γείτονος, ὁ *neighbor*
    7   αὐτόν refers to γείτονι (6).
    8   οἰκονομεῖν from οἰκονομέω *manage*
    9   οἰκονομίας from οἰκονομία, -ας, ἡ What must this noun mean in
         view of its relationship to οἰκονομεῖν?
         αὐτόν <u>intensive</u>! Refers to γείτονι (6).

Exercise B

Translate:

     1. Whenever a youth is able to think correctly and has maturity and intelligence, his father and mother allow him to do what seems best to him.

     2. "Well, then, Socrates," I said, "do you suppose that all men use the same common standards for judging (lit., "of judging") each other?"

     3. After giving me medicine, the doctor ordered me to apply it to my eyes each day.

     4. As many of the jurors as condemned Socrates to death in order not to be refuted did not know that such a remedy would be worse than the disease.

     5. When the barbarians arrived in Greece (use genitive absolute), the Greeks deliberated not only how they would wage (use middle of ἵστημι) the war but also from where they would summon allies.

20. The Charioteer of Delphi, cast in bronze, c. 470 BC.

Lesson 55

Numbers. Temporal Clauses with πρίν. Genitive of Measure

Cardinal Numbers

one	εἷς, μία, ἕν
two	δύο
three	τρεῖς, τρία
four	τέτταρες, τέτταρα
five	πέντε
six	ἕξ
seven	ἑπτά
eight	ὀκτώ
nine	ἐννέα
ten	δέκα
eleven	ἕνδεκα
twelve	δώδεκα
thirteen	τρεῖς (τρία) καὶ δέκα or τρεισκαίδεκα
fourteen	τέτταρες (τέτταρα) καὶ δέκα
fifteen	πεντεκαίδεκα
sixteen	ἐκκαίδεκα
seventeen	ἑπτακαίδεκα
eighteen	ὀκτωκαίδεκα
nineteen	ἐννεακαίδεκα
twenty	εἴκοσι(ν)
twenty-one	εἷς καὶ εἴκοσι(ν) or εἴκοσι (καὶ) εἷς
thirty	τριάκοντα
forty	τετταράκοντα
fifty	πεντήκοντα
sixty	ἑξήκοντα
seventy	ἑβδομήκοντα
eighty	ὀγδοήκοντα
ninety	ἐνενήκοντα
one hundred	ἑκατόν
two hundred	διακόσιοι, -αι, -α
three hundred	τριακόσιοι, -αι, -α
four hundred	τετρακόσιοι, -αι, -α
five hundred	πεντακόσιοι, -αι, -α
six hundred	ἑξακόσιοι, -αι, -α
seven hundred	ἑπτακόσιοι, -αι, -α

eight hundred	ὀκτακόσιοι, -αι, -α
nine hundred	ἐνακόσιοι, -αι, -α
one thousand	χίλιοι, -αι, -α
ten thousand	μύριοι, -αι, -α

Declension of δύο, τρεῖς, and τέττερες

The declension of εἷς has already been presented (see Lesson 31). The numbers δύο (*two*), τρεῖς (*three*), and τέττερες (*four*) are declined as follows:

	sing.	m./f./ pl.	n. pl.	m./f. pl.	n. pl.
Nom.	δύο	τρεῖς	τρία	τέτταρες	τέτταρα
Gen.	δυοῖν	τριῶν	τριῶν	τεττάρων	τεττάρων
Dat.	δυοῖν	τρισί(ν)	τρισί(ν)	τέτταροι(ν)	τέτταροι(ν)
Acc.	δύο	τρεῖς	τρία	τέτταρας	τέτταρα

Ordinal Numbers

first	πρῶτος, -η, -ον
second	δεύτερος, -α, -ον
third	τρίτος, -η, -ον
fourth	τέταρτος, -η, -ον
fifth	πέμπτος, -η, -ον
sixth	ἕκτος, -η, -ον
seventh	ἕβδομος, -η, -ον
eighth	ὄγδοος, -η, -ον
ninth	ἔνατος, -η, -ον
tenth	δέκατος, -η, -ον

Temporal Clauses with πρίν

a. After an __affirmative__ main clause πρίν, meaning *before*, introduces a temporal clause. The verb of the temporal clause is in the __infinitive__ mood, and the subject, when it differs from the subject of the independent clause, is expressed in the __accusative__ case.
Example:

ἧκε __πρὶν__ αὐτοὺς ἐξιέναι.
He came __before__ they left.

b. After a negative independent clause, πρίν means *until*. To express a past action, it takes the indicative (usually aorist). To express a future action, πρίν takes a construction similar to the protases of future more vivid and less vivid conditions (see Lessons 37, 39). The subjunctive with ἄν is used in primary sequence, and the optative alone in secondary sequence (not common). Examples:

ὁ κλὼψ οὐχ ἑάλω πρὶν τὸ τεκμήριον εὑρέθη.
The thief was not caught until the evidence was found.

ὁ κλὼψ οὐχ ἁλώσεται πρὶν τὸ τεκμήριον ἂν εὑρεθῇ.
The thief will not be caught until the evidence is found.

Genitive of Measure

The genitive is used in Greek to denote amount or quantity. Examples:

τὸ μειράκιόν ἐστιν ἐτῶν ὀκτωκαίδεκα.
The youth is eighteen years old.

ἡ κατὰ γῆν πορεία ἦν ἑκατὸν ἡμερῶν.
The journey by land took one hundred days.

Vocabulary

διαλέγομαι, διαλέξομαι, διελεξάμην, ____, διείλεγμαι, διελέχθην
(+ dat.) *converse (with)* (dialogue)

κρατέω, κρατήσομαι, ἐκράτησα, κεκράτηκα, κεκράτημαι, ἐκρατήθην
be strong; (+ gen.) *rule, be master of*

φράζω, φράσω, ἔφρασα, πέφρακα, πέφρασμαι, ἐφράσθην *tell, declare, explain*; (mid.) *ponder, contrive, perceive* (governs ὅτι or ὡς in indirect statement) (phrase)

Ἀλκιβιάδης, -ου, ὁ (voc. Ἀλκιβιάδη) *Alcibiades*

ἔπαινος, -ου, ὁ *praise, approval*

κράτος, κράτους, τό *power, might* (democrat)

μειράκιον, -ου, τό *youth, boy, young man* (14-20 years old)

Περικλῆς, Περικλέους, Περικλεῖ, Περικλέα (voc. Περίκλεις), ὁ *Pericles*

τοιόσδε, τοιάδε, τοιόνδε *such as this, such as follows*

πρίν *before, until*

ὥσπερ *just as, just as if* (+ εἰ or participle); *as it were*

Drill

Translate:

1. I was once small and four years old, just as you are now.
2. Tell me now, who is really worthy of praise and prosperity?
3. Ponder well the following: does anyone do wrong unwillingly?
4. Is Alcibiades cleverer than Pericles or not?
5. In my opinion, just government has great power (Express in two ways).

Exercise A: Reading

What is a law?

Λέγεται δὴ Ἀλκιβιάδην, πρὶν εἴκοσιν ἐτῶν εἶναι,
Περικλεῖ ἐπιτρόπῳ μὲν ὄντι αὐτοῦ, προστάτῃ δὲ τῆς πόλεως,
τοιάδε διαλεχθῆναι περὶ νόμων·
Εἰπέ μοι, ἦ δ᾽ ὅς, ὦ Περίκλεις, ἔχοις ἄν με διδάξαι
5 τί ἐστι νόμος;
Πάντως δήπου, ἔφη ὁ Περικλῆς.
Δίδαξον δὴ πρὸς τῶν θεῶν, ἔφη ὁ Ἀλκιβιάδης· ὡς ἐγὼ
ἀκούων τινῶν ἐπαινουμένων, ὅτι δίκαιοι ἄνδρες εἰσίν, οἶμαι
οὐκ ἂν δικαίως τούτου τυχεῖν τοῦ ἐπαίνου τὸν μὴ εἰδότα ὅ
10 τί ἐστι νόμος.
Ἀλλ᾽ οὐδέν τι χαλεποῦ πράγματος ἐπιθυμεῖς, ὦ
Ἀλκιβιάδη, ἔφη ὁ Περικλῆς, βουλόμενος γνῶναι τί ἐστι νόμος·
πάντες γὰρ οὗτοι νόμοι εἰσίν, οὓς τὸ πλῆθος συνελθὸν καὶ
βουλευσάμενον ἔγραψε, φράζον ἅ τε δεῖ ποιεῖν καὶ ἃ μή.
15 Πότερον δὲ τἀγαθὰ νομίσαν δεῖν ποιεῖν ἢ τὰ κακά;
Τἀγαθὰ μὰ Δία, ἦ δ᾽ ὅς, ὦ μειράκιον, τὰ δὲ κακὰ οὔ.
Ἐὰν δὲ μὴ τὸ πλῆθος, ἀλλ᾽, ὥσπερ ὅπου ὀλιγαρχία
ἐστίν, ὀλίγοι συνελθόντες γράψωσιν ὅ τι χρὴ ποιεῖν, ταῦτα τί
ἐστί;
20 Πάντα, ἦ δ᾽ ὅς, ὅσα ἂν τὸ κρατοῦν τῆς πόλεως
βουλευσάμενον, ἃ χρὴ ποιεῖν, γράψῃ, νόμος καλεῖται.
Κἂν τύραννος οὖν κρατῶν τῆς πόλεως γράψῃ τοῖς
πολίταις ἃ χρὴ ποιεῖν, καὶ ταῦτα νόμος ἐστί;
Καὶ ὅσα τύραννος ἄρχων, ἔφη, γράφει, καὶ ταῦτα
25 νόμος καλεῖται.

Adapted from Xenophon, *Memorabilia* 1.2.40-43

2   ἐπιτρόπῳ from ἐπίτροπος, -ου, ὁ *guardian*
     προστάτῃ from προστάτης, -ου, ὁ *leader*
6   δήπου (adverb) *obviously*
16   μὰ Δία *by Zeus* (See the reading selection from Lesson 51, line 8.)
17   ὀλιγαρχία, -ας, ἡ For meaning, compare the English derivative.
22   Κἄν = καὶ ἄν

Exercise B

Translate:

1. Make (use middle of ποιέω) no one your friend, Alcibiades, until you inquire how he has treated his other friends.

2. Before Socrates persuaded the Athenians to care for their souls, they considered even small portions of money more important than virtue.

3. But in point of fact Athens was a free city until the thirty tyrants ruled it.

4. Whenever a young man is twenty years old, let him take care that he not become weak in mind or body.

5. Before Pericles conversed with Alcibiades, he thought that he could explain what a law is.

21. ὁ Ἀλκιβιάδης.

Lesson 56

Review of Conditional Sentences and Wishes

Conditional Sentences

	protasis (neg. μή)	apodosis (neg. οὐ)
a. Present Particular (see Lesson 37)	εἰ + pres. indic. εἰ ταῦτα ποιεῖ, *If he does this,*	pres. indic. ἁμαρτάνει *he errs.*
b. Present General (see Lesson 37)	ἐάν (ἤν, ἄν) + pres./aor. subj. ἐάν τις ταῦτα ποιῇ, *If anyone (ever) does this,* ὅς ἄν ταῦτα ποιῇ, *Whoever does this,*	pres. indic. ἁμαρτάνει. *he errs.* ἁμαρτάνει. *errs.*
c. Past Particular (See Lesson 37)	εἰ + past tense indic. εἰ ταῦτα ἐποίησεν, *If he did this,*	past tense indic. ἥμαρτεν. *he erred.*
d. Past General (See Lesson 39)	εἰ + pres./aor. opt. εἴ τις ταῦτα ποιοίη, *If anyone (ever) did this,* ὅτε τις ταῦτα λέξειεν, *Whenever anyone said this,*	imperf. indic. ἡμάρτανεν. *he erred.* ἐψεύδετο. *he lied.*
e. Fut. More Vivid (see Lesson 37)	ἐάν (ἤν, ἄν) + pres./aor. subj. ἐάν ταῦτα ποιήσῃ, *If he does this,*	future indic. οὐχ ἁμαρτήσεται. *he will not err.*
f. Future Less Vivid (see Lesson 38)	εἰ + pres./aor. opt. εἰ ταῦτα ποιήσειεν, If he should do this,	pres./aor. opt. + ἄν ἁμάρτοι ἄν. he would err.

g. Present   εἰ + imperf. indic.   imperf. indic. + ἄν
   Contrary-to-Fact   εἰ ταῦτα ἐποίει,   ἡμάρτανεν ἄν.
   (see Lesson 13)   *If he were doing this,*   *he would be wrong.*

h. Past   εἰ + aor. indic.   aor. indic. + ἄν
   Contrary-to-Fact   εἰ μὴ ταῦτα ἐποίησαν,   ἥμαρτεν ἄν.
   (see Lesson 13)   *If he had not done this,*   *he would have erred.*

Wishes (neg. μή)

a. Possible   εἴθε (εἰ γάρ) + pres./aor. opt.
   (see Lesson 44)   εἰ γὰρ μὴ ταῦτα ποιήσειεν.
                      May he not do this!
                      or
                      If only he would not do this!

b. Present   εἴθε (εἰ γάρ) + imperf. indic.
   Impossible   εἴθε ταῦτα ἐποίει.
   (see Lesson 44)   *If only he were doing this!*

c. Past Impossible   εἴθε (εἰ γάρ) + aor. indic.
   (see Lesson 44)   εἴθε μὴ ταῦτα ἐποίησεν.
                      I wish that he had not done this!
                      or
                      If only he had not done this!

Vocabulary

ἀναγκάζω, ἀναγκάσω, ἠνάγκασα, ἠνάγκακα, ἠνάγκασμαι,
   ἠναγκάσθην *force, compel*

ἀνατίθημι *refer; dedicate;* (mid.) *retract* (an opinion)

βιάζομαι, βιασθήσομαι, ἐβιασάμην, ____, βεβίασμαι, ἐβιάσθην *force,
   constrain, act violently*

μελετάω, μελετήσω, ἐμελέτησα, μεμελέτηκα, μεμελέτημαι,
   ἐμελετήθην *attend to, study, practice*

ἀνομία, -ας, ἡ *lawlessness, illegal conduct*

βία, -ας, ἡ *force, strength*

ἥττων, -ον *inferior, weaker;* ἧττον (adv.) *less;* ἥκιστα (adv.) *least; not at all*

οἷος, -α, -ον *of what sort, such as*

τηλικόσδε, τηλικήδε, τηλικόνδε *of such an age, so old, so young*

τηλικοῦτος, τηλικαύτη, τηλικοῦτον *of such an age, so old, so young*

εἴτε … εἴτε *either … or, whether … or*

τοι (enclitic particle) *you know, you see, I tell you*

<u>Drill</u>

Give the following forms:

1. present middle-passive subjunctive, 3ʳᵈ pl. of:
    βιάζομαι, ἀνατίθημι, μελετάω, ἵημι, κρατέω

2. present active optative, 3ʳᵈ sg. of:
    ἀναγκάζω, δίδωμι, φρονέω, εἰμί, γελάω

3. aorist passive subjunctive, 2ⁿᵈ sg. of:
    φράζω, ἵστημι, σφάττω, δύναμαι, ὑπολαμβάνω

4. aorist active optative, 3ʳᵈ pl. of:
    βαίνω, γιγνώσκω, συγχωρέω, τρέχω, ἐπιτίθημι

<u>Exercise A: Reading</u>

What is a law? (conclusion)

Βία δέ, ἔφη ὁ Ἀλκιβιάδης, καὶ ἀνομία τί ἐστιν, ὦ
Περίκλεις; ἆρ᾽ οὐχ ὅταν ὁ κρείττων τὸν ἥττω μὴ πείσας, ἀλλὰ
βιασάμενος, ἀναγκάσῃ ποιεῖν ὅ τι ἂν αὐτῷ δοκῇ;
    Ἔμοιγε δοκεῖ, ἔφη ὁ Περικλῆς.
5   Καὶ ὅσα ἄρα τύραννος μὴ πείσας τοὺς πολίτας
ἀναγκάζει ποιεῖν γράφων, ἀνομία ἐστί;
    Δοκεῖ μοι, ἔφη ὁ Περικλῆς· ἀνατίθεμαι γὰρ τὸ ὅσα
τύραννος μὴ πείσας γράφει νόμον εἶναι.
    Ὅσα δὲ οἱ ὀλίγοι τοὺς πολλοὺς μὴ πείσαντες, ἀλλὰ
10   κρατοῦντες γράφουσι πότερον βίαν φῶμεν ἢ μὴ φῶμεν εἶναι;
    Πάντα μοι δοκεῖ, ἔφη ὁ Περικλῆς, ὅσα τις
μὴ πείσας ἀναγκάζει τινὰ ποιεῖν, εἴτε γράφων εἴτε μή, βία
μᾶλλον ἢ νόμος εἶναι.
    Καὶ ὅσα ἄρα τὸ πᾶν πλῆθος κρατοῦν τῶν τὰ χρήματα

15   ἐχόντων γράφει μὴ πείσαν, βία μᾶλλον ἢ νόμος ἂν εἴη;
           Μάλα τοι, ἔφη ὁ Περικλῆς, ὦ Ἀλκιβιάδη, καὶ ἡμεῖς
        τηλικοῦτοι ὄντες δεινοὶ τὰ τοιαῦτα ἦμεν· τοιαῦτα γὰρ καὶ
        ἐμελετῶμεν καὶ ἐσοφιζόμεθα οἷά περ καὶ σὺ νῦν ἐμοὶ δοκεῖς
        μελετᾶν.
20   Ὁ δὲ Ἀλκιβιάδης ἔφη· Εἴθε σοι, ὦ Περίκλεις, τότε
        συνεγενόμην, ὅτε δεινότατος ταῦτα ἦσθα.

                        Adapted from Xenophon, *Memorabilia* 1.2.44-46

7   τό accusative with εἶναι, which is used as an articular infinitive.
16   ἡμεῖς editorial "we." Pericles is referring to himself.
18   ἐσοφιζόμεθα from σοφίζομαι, *devise cleverly*

                        <u>Exercise B</u>

Translate:

      1. If Pericles were not so old, he would be practicing these
same things day by day.
      2. If only you (sg.) would retract what you have said in the
assembly, father, before someone accuses you!
      3. It would be lawlessness, I tell you, if anyone were to force
the weaker to obey him.
      4. Whether the majority agrees or not (μή), I shall not willingly
stop doing such things as I have often done in the market-place.
      5. Who in the world uses force if it is possible to use reason?
      6. In addition to this, you will suffer least if you agree eagerly
with the tyrant.
      7. Finally, if I had not chosen the weaker argument (use
λόγος), I would not have been convicted by the jurors.
      8. Whoever remained where he was stationed was praised by
Pericles himself after the battle.
      9. If only we had perceived that the three defendants (literally,
fleeing ones) were being saved contrary to the law!
      10. Where did you happen to be standing when the storm
destroyed your house? I cannot remember.

Lesson 57

Cognate Accusative
Review of Subjunctive and Optative: Purpose and Fear Clauses,
Hortatory and Deliberative Subjunctive, Prohibitions,
Potential Optative, Optative in Indirect Statement

Cognate Accusative

A verb may govern an object of <u>kindred meaning or origin</u> known as a
<u>cognate accusative</u>. A neuter adjective or a pronoun may be substituted for a noun
when the meaning of the verb permits it. Examples:

    a. <u>Kindred origin</u>:

        ὁ Μέλητος τὸν Σωκράτη γραφὴν ἐγράψατο.
        Meletus brought an indictment against Socrates.

    b. <u>Kindred meaning</u>:

        ὁ Μέλητος ἐνίκησε δίκην κατὰ τοῦ Σωκράτους.
        Meletus won his case against Socrates.

    c. <u>Pronoun</u>:

      ποῖος ἂν εἴη θάνατος καλλίων ἢ ὃν κάλλιστά τις ἀποθάνοι;
What kind of death would be more honorable than that which a person met most honorably?

    d. <u>Neuter adjective</u>:

        πόσα ἡμάρτηκεν ὁ νεανίας;
        How many faults has the young man committed?

Review of Subjunctive and Optative

<u>Purpose Clauses</u> (see Lessons 37 and 39).

    a. <u>primary</u>:

παρασκευάζονται ἵνα (ὅπως, ὡς) τοὺς τεθνηκότας θάψωσιν.
They are making preparations (in order) to bury the dead.

    b. <u>secondary</u>:

παρεσκευάζοντο ἵνα (ὅπως, ὡς) τοὺς τεθνηκότας θάψειαν.
They were making preparations (in order) to bury the dead.

Fear Clauses (see Lessons 37 and 39).

    a. primary:

        δέδιμεν μὴ οὐ τοὺς τεθνηκότας θάψωσιν.
        We are afraid that they will not bury the dead.

    b. secondary:

        ἐδέδιμεν μὴ οὐ τοὺς τεθνηκότας θάψειαν.
        We were afraid that they would not bury the dead.

Deliberative Subjunctive (see Lesson 42).

        μὴ θάψωμεν τοὺς τεθνηκότας;
        Are we not to bury the dead?

Hortatory Subjunctive (see Lesson 42).

        θάψωμεν τοὺς τεθνηκότας.
        Let us bury the dead.

Prohibitions (see Lesson 42).

        μὴ θάψητε τοὺς τεθνηκότας.
        Don't bury the dead.

Potential Optative (see Lesson 44).

        πάντα γὰρ ἂν πύθοιό μου.
        For you can learn everything from me.

Optative in Indirect Statement (see Lesson 49).

        εἶπον ὅτι τοὺς τεθνηκότας οὐ θάψοιεν.
        They said that they would not bury the dead.

Vocabulary

βιόω, βιώσομαι, ἐβίων (2nd aor.), βεβίωκα, βεβίωται, ____ *live, be alive*

γραφὴν γράφεσθαι (+ acc. of person) *bring an indictment (against), indict*

ζάω (imperf. ἔζων), ζήσω, ____, ____, ____, ____, *live, be alive*

ὁμολογέω, ὁμολογήσω, ὡμολόγησα, ὡμολόγηκα, ὡμολόγημαι
    ὡμολογήθην (+ dat.) *agree with, agree* (governs infinitive in indirect
    statement)

σκοπέω, σκέψομαι, ἐσκεψάμην, ____, ἔσκεμμαι, ____ *consider, examine*
    (sceptical)

ἀνάγκη, -ης, ἡ *necessity*

ἀνάγκη ἐστί(ν) (+ dat.) *it is*

   necessary

μήν, μηνός, ὁ *month*

ἀλλοῖος, -α, -ον *different, of another*
   kind

ποῖος, -α, -ον *what kind of*

πόσος, -η, -ον *how much, how great,*

   (pl.) how many

φανερός, -ά, -όν *evident, conspicuous,*

   manifest

ἔμπροσθεν (adverb or prep. + gen.)
   before

οἱ ἔμπροσθεν *ancestors*

Notes: ζάω, like χράομαι (see Lesson 19), contracts to η, not α; hence ζῇς ("you live"), ζῇ ("he lives"), and the present infinitive ζῆν.

   The fifth principal part of βιόω is impersonal and so appears only in the third person singular; it is used with a dative of agent. Example:

$$\text{πολὺν χρόνον αὐτῷ βεβίωται.}$$
He has lived for a long time.

Exercise A: Reading

Socrates' last days: Part I

      Ὁμολογεῖται γὰρ οὐδένα πω τῶν μνημονευομένων
ἀνθρώπων κάλλιον θάνατον ἐνεγκεῖν. ἀνάγκη μὲν γὰρ ἐγένετο
αὐτῷ μετὰ τὴν κρίσιν τριάκοντα ἡμέρας βιῶναι διὰ τὸ Δήλια
μὲν ἐκείνου τοῦ μηνὸς εἶναι, τὸν δὲ νόμον μηδένα ἐᾶν δημοσίᾳ
5 ἀποθνήσκειν ἕως ἂν ἡ θεωρία ἐκ Δήλου ἐπανέλθη, καὶ τὸν
χρόνον τοῦτον ἅπασι τοῖς φίλοις φανερὸς ἐγένετο οὐδὲν
ἀλλοιότερον διαβιοὺς ἢ τὸν ἔμπροσθεν χρόνον· καίτοι τὸν
ἔμπροσθέν γε χρόνον, πάντων ἀνθρώπων μάλιστα ἐθαυμάζετο
ἐπὶ τῷ ὀρθῶς τε καὶ δικαίως ζῆν. καὶ πῶς ἄν τις κάλλιον ἢ
10 οὕτως ἀποθάνοι; ἢ ποῖος ἂν εἴη θάνατος καλλίων ἢ ὃν
κάλλιστά τις ἀποθάνοι; ποῖος δ' ἂν γένοιτο θάνατος·
εὐδαιμονέστερος τοῦ καλλίστου; ἢ ποῖος θάνατος θεοῖς
φιλώτερος τοῦ εὐδαιμονεστάτου; λέξω δὲ καὶ ἃ Ἑρμογένους
ἤκουσα περὶ αὐτοῦ. ἔφη γάρ, ἤδη Μελήτου γεγραμμένου αὐτὸν
15 τὴν γραφήν, αὐτὸς ἀκούων Σωκράτους πάντα μᾶλλον ἢ περὶ
τῆς δίκης διαλεγομένου λέγειν αὐτῷ ὡς χρὴ σκοπεῖν ὅ τι
ἀπολογήσεται.

Adapted from Xenophon, *Memorabilia* 4.8.2-4

1   μνημονευομένων passive participle of μνημονεύομαι, *be remembered*
3   κρίσιν from κρίσις, κρίσεως, ἡ *judgment, verdict*
     Δήλια, -ων, τά, *festival of Apollo* (celebrated on the island of Delos)
4   δημοσίᾳ from δημοσία, -ας, ἡ Translate: *by state execution.*
5   θεωρία, -ας, ἡ *religious embassy*
6   φανερός ἐγένετο Translate impersonally: *it was clear that...*
13   Ἑρμογένους from Ἑρμογένης, -ους, ὁ *Hermogenes*, an acquaintance
     of Socrates and Xenophon
16   δίκης does not mean *justice* here, but rather *case.*

Exercise B

Translate:

    1. The king's daughter was slain in order that the storm might cease and the ships might sail back to Greece.

    2. I am afraid that a man so old may not live (use ζάω) for more than three months.

    3. Let us examine what kind of indictment those base accusers have brought against Alcibiades.

    4. Perhaps someone of you might suppose that Socrates is different from (ἤ) the rest.

    5. How many victories must we win before Cyrus gives us even a small reward?

    6. Don't practice evil willingly, boy, if you don't want anyone to blame (use αἰτιάομαι) you.

    7. Long ago our ancestors taught (use imperfect) that the immortal gods are weaker than necessity.

    8. Where am I to run? Where am I to turn? Am I to rush to Delphi, from where I shall learn what I am to suffer?

    9. How could you agree with a disgraceful old man whose insolence is so evident to all?

    10. Are we in fact to believe that no one except Socrates corrupts the mind of Alcibiades?

Lesson 58

Genitive of Separation
Review of Indirect Statement and Indirect Question

Genitive of Separation

The genitive case without a preposition is used to express separation after verbs meaning: to cease, release, prevent, refrain, be away from, etc. This genitive may also occur after adjectives of similar meaning. Examples:

τούτους οὐ παύσω τῆς ἀρχῆς.
I shall not stop (depose) them from their rule.

πράττει τὰ δίκαια καὶ τῶν ἀδίκων ἀπέχεται.
He does just things and refrains from unjust things.

οἱ Ἀθηναῖοι ἦσαν τοῦ φόβου ἐλεύθεροι.
The Athenians were free from fear.

Review of Indirect Statement

a. Infinitive (see Lesson 32).

τύραννόν φασι τῆς πόλεως ἄρχειν.
They say that a tyrant is ruling the city.

ἐλπίζουσι τῆς πόλεως ἄρξειν.
They hope that they will rule the city.

ᾤμην τύραννον τῆς πόλεως οὐκ ἄρχειν.
I thought that a tyrant was not ruling the city.

οὐκ ἔφαμεν τὴν πόλιν ὑπὸ τυράννου ἀρχθῆναι.
We said that the city had not been ruled by a tyrant.

b. ὅτι or ὡς (see Lessons 34 and 49).

ἀπεκρίνατο ὅτι τύραννός τις τῆς πόλεως ἄρχει (or ἄρχοι).
He answered that a tyrant was ruling the city.

εἴπετε ὡς τύραννός τις τῆς πόλεως ἄρξοι (or ἄρξει).
You said that a tyrant would rule the city.

θαυμάζομεν ὅτι αἱ πόλεις ὑπὸ τυράννων ἠργμέναι εἰσίν.
We are amazed that the cities have been ruled by tyrants.

c. Participle (see Lesson 34).

ἠκούσαμεν τύραννόν τινα τῆς πόλεως ἄρχοντα.
We heard that a tyrant was ruling the city.

ᾔδειν ἡμᾶς τοῦ αὐτοῦ ὀνόματος ἐπιλησομένους.
He knew that we would forget his name.

ᾔσθετο ἁμαρτών.
He learned that he had erred.

Review of Indirect Question (see Lesson 49)

σκοπῶμεν εἴτε τις ἑκὼν ἀδικεῖ εἴτε μή.
Let us consider whether anyone does wrong willingly or not.

ἤρετό με ὅστις Σωκράτη τοιαύτην γραφὴν γράψαιτο (or ἐγράψατο).
He asked me who brought such an indictment against Socrates.

Vocabulary

διαγίγνομαι *go through, pass* (of time); *go through life, live, survive*

διατελέω, διατελέσω, διετέλεσα, διατετέλεκα, ____, ____ (+ participle)
continue

ἐναντιόομαι, ἐναντιώσομαι, ____, ____, ἠναντίωμαι, ἠναντιώθην (+
dat.) *oppose, forbid*

ἐντυγχάνω (+ dat.) *meet*

ἐπιχειρέω *put one's hand to, attempt*

συμβαίνω *agree; happen*

τελευτάω, τελευτήσω, ἐτελεύτησα, τετελεύτηκα, ____, ἐτελευτήθην
finish; die

φροντίζω, φροντιῶ, ἐφρόντισα, πεφρόντικα, ____, ____ *consider, ponder*
(+ acc. or governs participle in indirect statement); *think about, take
thought for* (+ gen.)

ἀπολογία, -ας, ἡ *speech in defense, defense*

δαιμόνιον, -ου, τό *divine sign*

μέχρι (+ gen.) *as far as, until, up to*

Exercise A: Reading

Socrates' last days: Part II

Ὁ δὲ Σωκράτης τὸ μὲν πρῶτον εἶπεν· Οὐ γὰρ δοκῶ σοι
τοῦτο μελετῶν διαβεβιωκέναι; ἐπεὶ δὲ αὐτὸν ἤρετο ὅπως,
εἶπεν αὐτὸς ὅτι οὐδὲν ἄλλο ποιῶν διαγεγένηται ἢ διασκοπῶν
μὲν τά τε δίκαια καὶ τὰ ἄδικα, πράττων δὲ τὰ δίκαια καὶ τῶν
5   ἀδίκων ἀπεχόμενος, ἥν νομίζοι καλλίστην μελέτην ἀπολογίας
εἶναι.

Αὐτὸς δὲ πάλιν εἶπεν· Οὐχ ὁρᾷς, ὦ Σώκρατες, ὅτι οἱ ἐν
Ἀθήναις δικασταὶ πολλοὺς μὲν ἤδη μηδὲν ἀδικοῦντας λόγῳ
παραχθέντες ἀπέκτειναν, πολλοὺς δὲ ἀδικοῦντας ἀπέλυσαν;
10   Ἀλλὰ νὴ τὸν Δία, ἔφη, ὦ Ἑρμόγενες, ἤδη μου
ἐπιχειροῦντος φροντίσαι τῆς πρὸς τοὺς δικαστὰς ἀπολογίας
ἠναντιώθη τὸ δαιμόνιον.

Καὶ αὐτὸς εἰπεῖν· Θαυμαστὰ λέγεις.

Ὁ δὲ Σωκράτες, θαυμάζεις, ἔφη, εἰ τῷ θεῷ δοκεῖ
15   βέλτιον εἶναι ἐμὲ τελευτᾶν τὸν βίον ἤδη; οὐκ οἶσθ᾽ ὅτι μέχρι
μὲν τοῦδε τοῦ χρόνου ἐγὼ οὐδενὶ ἀνθρώπων ὑφείμην ἂν οὔτε
βέλτιον οὔθ᾽ ἥδιον ἐμαυτοῦ βεβιωκέναι; ἄριστα μὲν γὰρ οἶμαι
ζῆν τοὺς ἄριστα ἐπιμελομένους τοῦ ὡς βελτίστους γίγνεσθαι,
ἥδιστα δὲ τοὺς μάλιστα αἰσθανομένους ὅτι βελτίους γίγνονται.
20   ἃ ἐγὼ μέχρι τοῦδε τοῦ χρόνου ᾐσθανόμην ἐμαυτῷ συμβαίνοντα,
καὶ τοῖς ἄλλοις ἀνθρώποις ἐντυγχάνων καὶ πρὸς τοὺς ἄλλους
παραβάλλων ἐμαυτὸν οὕτω διατετέλεκα περὶ ἐμαυτοῦ
γιγνώσκων· καὶ οὐ μόνον ἐγώ, ἀλλὰ καὶ οἱ ἐμοὶ φίλοι οὕτως
ἔχοντες περὶ ἐμοῦ διατελοῦσιν, οὐ διὰ τὸ φιλεῖν ἐμέ (καὶ γὰρ οἱ
τοὺς ἄλλους φιλοῦντες οὕτως ἂν εἶχον πρὸς τοὺς ἑαυτῶν
25   φίλους), ἀλλὰ καὶ ὅτι αὐτοὶ ἂν οἴονται ἐμοὶ συνόντες βέλτιστοι
γίγνεσθαι.

Adapted from Xenophon, *Memorabilia* 4.8.4-7

5   μελέτην from μελέτη, -ης, ἡ; for the meaning of this noun cf. the verb
μελετάω.
9   παραχθέντες from παράγω, *mislead*
10   νή *by* (particle of strong affirmation governing the accusative).
13   Θαυμαστά from θαυμαστός, -ή, -όν; for the meaning cf. the verb
θαυμάζω.
16   ὑφείμην from ὑφίημι, *yield, concede*
19   ἃ a connecting relative equal to καὶ ταῦτα.
21   παραβάλλων from παραβάλλω, *compare*
24   ἄν modifies γίγνεσθαι (line 26).

Exercise B

Translate:

     1. Socrates thought that he could make (use τίθημι) the young men associating with him as good as possible.

     2. Our ancestors taught us that by fighting for our fatherland we shall continue to be free.

     3. It is agreed that up to this time no one bore misfortune more nobly than Socrates.

     4. Pericles perceived that his opinion was the opposite of Alcibiades'.

     5. As we were going up to Delphi to pray to Apollo, we met Xenophon, an Athenian by birth, who asked us who we were and where we came from.

     6. Consider that no one has lived a happy life until he dies.

     7. In his defense Socrates answered that his divine sign always forbade him to take part in public affairs (= τὰ πολιτικὰ πράττειν).

     8. If at that time he had attempted to oppose the government, he would not have survived even for a little time.

     9. If some terrible experience happens to you, know that the cause is the envy and retribution of the gods.

     10. Now be silent and consider (use σκοπέω) whether you are ready to retract such an accusation or not.

22. The Death of Socrates, Jacques Louis David, 1787.

Lesson 59

Genitive of Value. Review of Participles

Genitive of Value

The genitive case without a preposition is used to express price or value. Example:

πόσου διδάσκει; πέντε μνῶν.
For how much does he teach? For five minas.

Review of Participles

a. Attributive (see Lesson 27).

τῷ τὴν γνώμην ταύτην εἰπόντι ὡμολογήσαμεν.
We agreed with the man who expressed this opinion.

b. Circumstantial (see Lessons 27 29 and 48).

Causal:

ἅτε οὖν νίκης ἱέμενοι, μένοντες μάχεσθε.
Therefore, since you desire victory, stay and fight.

Genitive Absolute:

μηδενὸς κωλύοντος, διὰ τῆς πολεμίας χώρας πορευώμεθα.
If no one prevents (us), let us proceed through the hostile country.

Accusative Absolute:

δόξαν ὑμῖν τοῦτο, εἵλεσθε ἄνδρας εἴκοσιν.
Since this seemed best to you, you chose twenty men.

Purpose:

ἐπὶ τὰς ναῦς ἦλθε ὁ γέρων τὴν θυγατέρα λυσόμενος.
The old man came to the ships to ransom his daughter.

c. Supplementary (see Lessons 29 and 34).

πότε παύσεται λέγων ὁ ῥήτωρ;
When will the orator stop speaking?

διατελεῖ πάντας μισῶν.
He continues to hate everyone.

ἐδήλωσεν ὁ Περικλῆς τοὺς νόμους ἐπαινῶν
Pericles showed that he approved of the laws.

Vocabulary

διανοέομαι, διανοήσομαι, διενοησάμην, ____, διανενόημαι,
διενοήθην *think, have in mind, intend*

μαρτυρέω, μαρτυρήσω, ____, ____, μεμαρτύρημαι, ἐμαρτυρήθην
bear witness, testify (governs ὅτι or ὡς in indirect statement)

γῆρας, γήρως, γήρᾳ, γῆρας, τό *old age* (geriatrics)

δόξα, -ης, ἡ *reputation, opinion, expectation* (paradox)

δραχμή, -ῆς, ἡ *drachma* (a silver coin worth six obols)

μάρτυς, μάρτυρος, ὁ *witness* (martyr)

μνᾶ, -ᾶς, ἡ *mina* (a sum of money worth 100 drachmas)

ὀβολός, -οῦ, ὁ *obol* (a small Athenian coin)

τάλαντον, -ου, τό *talent* (a sum of money worth 60 minas or 6,000
drachmas)

βιωτός, -ή, -όν *worth living*

ἕτερος, -α, -ον (with article) *the other* (of two); (without article) *another, other*

ὁστισοῦν (ὁτιοῦν) *anyone (anything) whatever, anyone (anything) at all*

πώποτε *ever*

Exercise A: Reading

Socrates' last days: Part III

Εἰ δὲ βιώσομαι πλείω χρόνον, ἴσως ἀνάγκη ἔσται τὰ
τοῦ γήρως ἐπιτελεῖσθαι καὶ ὁρᾶν τε καὶ ἀκούειν ἧττον καὶ
διανοεῖσθαι χεῖρον, καὶ καὶ ὧν πρότερον βελτίων ἦν, τούτων
χείρω γίγνεσθαι· ἀλλὰ μὴν ταῦτά γε μὴ αἰσθανομένῳ μὲν
5   ἀβίωτος ἂν εἴη ὁ βίος, αἰσθανομένῳ δὲ πῶς οὐκ ἀνάγκη χεῖρόν
τε καὶ ἀηδέστερον ζῆν; ἀλλὰ μὴν εἴ γε ἀδίκως ἀποθανοῦμαι,
τοῖς μὲν ἀδίκως ἐμὲ ἀποκτείνασιν αἰσχρὸν ἂν εἴη τοῦτο·

εἰ γὰρ τὸ ἀδικεῖν αἰσχρόν ἐστι, πῶς οὐκ αἰσχρὸν καὶ τὸ ἀδίκως
ὁτιοῦν ποιεῖν; ἐμοὶ δὲ τί αἰσχρὸν τὸ ἑτέρους μὴ δύνασθαι περὶ
10   ἐμοῦ τὰ δίκαια μήτε γνῶμαι μήτε ποιῆσαι; ὁρῶ δ' ἔγωγε καὶ τὴν
δόξαν τῶν προγεγονότων ἀνθρώπων ἐν τοῖς ἐπιγιγνομένοις
οὐχ ὁμοίαν καταλειπομένην τῶν τε ἀδικησάντων καὶ τῶν
ἀδικηθέντων. οἶδα δ' ὅτι καὶ ἐγὼ δόξης τεύξομαι ὑπ'
ἀνθρώπων, καὶ ἐὰν νῦν ἀποθάνω, οὐχ ὁμοίως τοῖς ἐμὲ
15   ἀποκτείνασιν· οἶδα γὰρ τοὺς ἐπιγιγνομένους ἀεὶ ὑπὲρ ἐμαυτοῦ
μαρτυρήσοντας ὅτι ἐγὼ ἠδίκησα μὲν οὐδένα πώποτε ἀνθρώπων
οὐδὲ χείρω ἐποίησα, βελτίους δὲ ποιεῖν ἐπειρώμην ἀεὶ τοὺς
ἐμοὶ συνόντας.
     Τοιαῦτα μὲν πρὸς Ἑρμογένην τε διελέχθη καὶ πρὸς
20   τοὺς ἄλλους.

Adapted from Xenophon, *Memorabilia* 4.8.8-10

1   βιώσομαι Note the future tenses in <u>both</u> protasis <u>and</u> apodosis. This
     construction is known as a <u>future most vivid</u> condition.
2   ἐπιτελεῖσθαι from ἐπιτελέομαι (+ acc.), *be subject to, pay the price of*
6   ἀηδέστερον With the root ἡδύς plus the α privative, what must this
     adverb mean?
9   τί supply ἐστί.
     ἑτέρους A subject accusative with the articular infinitive τὸ ...
     δύνασθαι.
11   προγεγονότων from προγίγνομαι, the antonym of ἐπιγίγνομαι, *be
     born after*
12   ὁμοίαν Construe as a predicate adjective.
12-13 τῶν τε ἀδικήσαντων ... ἀδικηθέντων: These words are in apposition
     to ἀνθρώπων (line 11).

<u>Exercise B</u>

Translate (using participles wherever possible):

     1. Although the guard was present, the thieves stole fifteen
drachmas from the bank.
     2. After reading the letter, the boy was at a loss. "What am I to
do about this difficult journey?" he said.
     3. For those who have suffered in war, a life worth living is not
only contrary to expectation but also beyond hope.
     4. While the other witnesses were testifying, the jurors perceived
that the defendant (literally, "the fleeing one") had lied.

5. Old age prevented the father from accompanying his three daughters to the gates of our city.

6. Whose son do you boast that you are?

7. Will old age ever be able to run faster than death?

8. I say that no one of men, either good or bad, has ever escaped fate.

9. Summoned from Greece, the Lacedaemonians crossed the sea in order to ransom their captured allies for twelve talents.

10. For neither in court nor in war should anyone try to survive by doing anything whatsoever (that is) base.

23. Phidias Showing the Frieze of the Parthenon to his Friends,
Lawrence Alma-Tadema, 1868.

Lesson 60

Synopsis of ὡς

Review of ὡς

a. With participles and prepositional phrases:

1. Future participles expressing purpose (see Lesson 27).

παρασκευάζοντο ὡς μαχούμενοι.
They made preparations to fight.

2. Participles other than future (see Lesson 28).

αὐτῷ ὡς φίλῳ ὄντι ἐπίστευον.
I trusted him on the grounds that he was a friend.

3. Prepositional phrases.

παρασκευάζονται ὡς ἐπὶ τοὺς Ἕλληνας.
They are making preparations as if against the Greeks.

b. Indirect Statement (see Lesson 34).

εἶπεν ὡς ὁ Κῦρος ἀπώλετο.
He said that Cyrus had perished.

c. With Indicative (see Lesson 37):

ὁ Σωκράτης εὐσεβὴς ἦν, ὡς ὑμεῖς ἐπίστασθε.
Socrates was pious, as you know.

ἡμᾶς πέμψαι δεῖ φύλακας, ὡς διανοεῖται τὴν γέφυραν λῦσαι ὁ βασιλεύς.
We must send the guards, since the king intends to destroy the bridge.

ὡς ἀπῆλθεν, ᾠήθημεν οὔποτε πάλιν ἐκεῖνον ὄψεσθαι.
When he left, we thought that we would never see him again.

d. With Purpose Clauses (see Lessons 37 and 39):

ᾔτησαν ναῦς ὡς ἀποπλέοιεν.
They asked for ships in order that they might sail away.

e. <u>With Superlatives</u> (see Lesson 41):

ὡς τάχιστα ἔδραμον.
They ran <u>as</u> quickly <u>as possible</u>.

Other Uses of ὡς

a. "how" before adjectives or adverbs in direct and indirect exclamations:

ὡς αὐτάρκης ὁ ἄνθρωπος.
<u>How</u> self-reliant the man is!

ἐθαυμάζομεν τοῦτο, ὡς ἡδέως θάνατον ἔπαθεν.
We were amazed at <u>how</u> gladly he suffered death.

b. "about" or "approximately" before numbers:

ὁ παῖς ὡς ἑπτὰ ἐτῶν ἦν.
The child was <u>about</u> seven years old.

c. "to" as a preposition with the <u>accusative</u> where the object is a person:

ὡς τὸν τύραννον ἥκουσιν.
They have come <u>to</u> the tyrant.

d. "as" before nouns:

ἔλαβε Ξενοφῶντα ὡς φίλον.
He took Xenophon <u>as</u> a friend.

e. ὡς = ὥστε in result clauses (usually with the infinitive):

ἐμοὶ οὕτω χρῆσθε ὡς ὑμῖν μὴ πιστεύειν.
You treat me in such a way <u>that</u> I cannot trust you.

Vocabulary

ἀπόλλυμι, ἀπολῶ, ἀπώλεσα, (2nd aor. mid. ἀπωλόμην), ἀπολώλεκα,
    ____, ____ (act.) *destroy, lose;* (mid. & 2nd perf. act. [ἀπόλωλα]) *die, perish*
διηγέομαι, διηγήσομαι, διηγησάμην, ____, διήγημαι, ____ *describe*

δοκιμάζω, δοκιμάσω, ἐδοκίμασα, ____, δεδοκίμασμαι, ἐδοκιμάσθην
test, put to the test, approve

ἦθος, -ους, τό *character* (ethics)

αὐτάρκης, -ες *independent, self-reliant*

ἐγκρατής, -ές *self-controlled, self-restrained*

εὐσεβής, -ές *pious, righteous*

φρόνιμος, -ον *reasonable, prudent, sensible*

ὠφέλιμος, -ον *helpful, beneficial*

ἀνά (+ acc.) *up; throughout* (analysis, analogy)

ἄνευ (+ gen.) *without*

Exercise A: Reading

Socrates' last days: Part IV

Τῶν δὲ Σωκράτην γιγνωσκότων οἷος ἦν οἱ ἀρετῆς
ἐφιέμενοι πάντες ἔτι καὶ νῦν διατελοῦσι πάντων μάλιστα
μεμνημένοι ἐκείνου, ὡς ὠφελιμωτάτου ὄντος πρὸς τὸ ἀρετῆς
ἐπιμελεῖσθαι. ἐμοὶ μὲν δή, τοιοῦτος ὢν οἷον ἐγὼ διήγημαι,
5   εὐσεβὴς μὲν οὕτως ὥστε μηδὲν ἄνευ τῆς τῶν θεῶν γνώμης
ποιεῖν, δίκαιος δὲ ὥστε βλάπτειν μὲν μηδὲ μικρὸν μηδένα,
ὠφελεῖν δὲ τὰ μέγιστα τοὺς χρωμένους αὐτῷ, ἐγκρατὴς δὲ ὥστε
μήποτε προαιρεῖσθαι τὸ ἥδιον ἀντὶ τοῦ βελτίονος, φρόνιμος δὲ
ὥστε μὴ διαμαρτάνειν κρίνων τὰ βελτίω καὶ τὰ χείρω μηδὲ
10   ἄλλου προσδεῖσθαι, ἀλλ'αὐτάρκης εἶναι πρὸς τὸ ταῦτα
γιγνώσκειν, ἱκανὸς δὲ καὶ λόγῳ εἰπεῖν τε καὶ δηλῶσαι τὰ
τοιαῦτα, ἱκανὸς δὲ καὶ ἄλλους δοκιμάσαι τε καὶ ἁμαρτάνοντας
ἐλέγξαι καὶ ἄριστός τε ἀνὴρ καὶ εὐδαιμονέστατος. εἰ δέ τῳ μὴ
ἱκανὰ δοκεῖ εἶναι ταῦτα, παραβάλλων τὸ ἄλλων ἦθος πρὸς
15   ταῦτα οὕτω κρινέτω.

Adapted from Xenophon, *Memorabilia* 4.8.11

2   ἐφιέμενοι from ἐφίημι, (mid.) *desire, long for*
4   ἐμοί here = τῇ ἐμῇ γνώμῃ
14   παραβάλλων from παραβάλλω, *compare*

<u>Exercise B</u>

Translate:

      1. His ships cannot sail up the river because of the terrible storm.

      2. How pious in character and independent in thought Socrates was!

      3. They forgot us as if we were dead (use ἀπόλλυμι in 2nd perfect).

      4. Throughout the war, as I have described (it), dreadful experiences were common to those who did not actually perish; for often they had to bury their sons.

      5. He was so self-restrained as to be silent even if someone accused him of insolence.

      6. Without the gods even a prudent, self-reliant man will not survive if he takes part in politics (= τὰ πολιτικὰ πράττειν).

      7. The thirty brought an indictment against Socrates on the grounds that he put them to the test and opposed their rule.

      8. Throughout Greece our ancestors placed one obol on each eye of a dead person with the intention of providing pay in return for the journey of his soul beyond the river of death.

      9. Is it ever beneficial to destroy (use ἀπόλλυμι) men contrary to the opinion of the majority?

      10. Since I have given him about four minas, he is eager to accompany me as an ally.

24. Theseus Slaying a Centaur, Antonio Canova,
Kunsthistorisches Museum, Vienna, Austria, 1804-1819.

Declensions

Declensions

The Definite Article

	Masculine	Feminine	Neuter
		Singular	
Nominative	ὁ	ἡ	τό
Genitive	τοῦ	τῆς	τοῦ
Dative	τῷ	τῇ	τῷ
Accusative	τόν	τήν	τό

	Plural		
Nominative	οἱ	αἱ	τά
Genitive	τῶν	τῶν	τῶν
Dative	τοῖς	ταῖς	τοῖς
Accusative	τούς	τάς	τά

Nouns

The First Declension

Category	1a(Fem.)	b(Fem.)	2a(Fem.)	b(Fem.)	3a(Masc.)	b(Masc.)
			Singular			
Nom.	ἀρετή	οἰκία	θάλαττα	μοῖρα	πολίτης	νεανίας
Gen.	ἀρετῆς	οἰκίας	θαλάττης	μοίρας	πολίτου	νεανίου
Dat.	ἀρετῇ	οἰκίᾳ	θαλάττῃ	μοίρᾳ	πολίτῃ	νεανίᾳ
Acc.	ἀρετήν	οἰκίαν	θάλατταν	μοῖραν	πολίτην	νεανίαν

			Plural			
Nom.	ἀρεταί	οἰκίαι	θάλατται	μοῖρα	πολῖται	νεανίαι
Gen.	ἀρετῶν	οἰκιῶν	θαλαττῶν	μοιρῶν	πολιτῶν	νεανιῶν
Dat.	ἀρεταῖς	οἰκίαις	θαλάτταις	μοίραις	πολίταις	νεανίαις
Acc.	ἀρετάς	οἰκίας	θαλάττας	μοίρας	πολίτας	νεανίας

The Second Declension

	Masculine	Feminine	Neuter
		Singular	
Nom.	ἄνθρωπος	ὁδός	παιδίον
Gen.	ἀνθρώπου	ὁδοῦ	παιδίου
Dat.	ἀνθρώπῳ	ὁδῷ	παιδίῳ
Acc.	ἄνθρωπον	ὁδόν	παιδίον

Declensions

	Plural		
Nom.	ἄνθρωποι	ὁδοί	παιδία
Gen.	ἀνθρώπων	ὁδῶν	παιδίων
Dat.	ἀνθρώποις	ὁδοῖς	παιδίοις
Acc.	ἀνθρώπους	ὁδούς	παιδία

The Third Declension

Masculine & Feminine Consonant Stems

Singular

	Labial (π,β,φ)	Palatal (κ,γ,ξ)	Dental (τ,δ,θ)	Nasal (-ων)
Nom.	κλώψ	κῆρυξ	ἀσπίς	χειμών
Gen.	κλωπός	κήρυκος	ἀσπίδος	χειμῶνος
Dat.	κλωπί	κήρυκι	ἀσπίδι	χειμῶνι
Acc.	κλῶπα	κήρυκα	ἀσπίδα	χειμῶνα

Plural

	Labial (π,β,φ)	Palatal (κ,γ,ξ)	Dental (τ,δ,θ)	Nasal (-ων)
Nom.	κλῶπες	κήρυκες	ἀσπίδες	χειμῶνες
Gen.	κλωπῶν	κηρύκων	ἀσπίδων	χειμώνων
Dat.	κλωψί(ν)	κήρυξι(ν)	ἀσπίσι(ν)	χειμῶσι(ν)
Acc.	κλῶπας	κήρυκας	ἀσπίδας	χειμῶνας

Singular

	Nasal/Dental (-οντ)	Sibilant (-εσ)	Liquid (-ρ)	(-ηρ/-ερ/-ρ(α))	
Nom.	γέρων	τριήρης	ῥήτωρ	μήτηρ	ἀνήρ
Gen.	γέροντος	τριήρους	ῥήτορος	μητρός	ἀνδρός
Dat.	γέροντι	τριήρει	ῥήτορι	μητρί	ἀνδρί
Acc.	γέροντα	τριήρη	ῥήτορα	μητέρα	ἄνδρα

Plural

	Nasal/Dental (-οντ)	Sibilant (-εσ)	Liquid (-ρ)	(-ηρ/-ερ/-ρ(α))	
Nom.	γέροντες	τριήρεις	ῥήτορες	μητέρες	ἄνδρες
Gen.	γερόντων	τριήρων	ῥητόρων	μητέρων	ἀνδρῶν
Dat.	γέρουσι(ν)	τριήρεσι(ν)	ῥήτορσι(ν)	μητράσι(ν)	ἀνδράσι(ν)
Acc.	γέροντας	τριήρεις	ῥήτορας	μητέρας	ἄνδρας

Neuter Consonant Stems

	Sibilant (-εσ)		Dental (-ατ)	
	Singular	Plural	Singular	Plural
Nom.	κέρδος	κέρδη	χρῆμα	χρήματα
Gen.	κέρδους	κερδῶν	χρήματος	χρημάτων
Dat.	κέρδει	κέρδεσι(ν)	χρήματι	χρήμασι(ν)
Acc.	κέρδος	κέρδη	χρῆμα	χρήματα

Declensions

Masculine and Feminine Variable Vowel Stems

Singular

	-ευ(ϝ)/-ηυ(ϝ)	-αυ(ϝ)/-ευ(ϝ)/-ηυ(ϝ)	-ι/-ει(ϝ)/-ηι(ϝ)
Nom.	βασιλεύς	ναῦς	πόλις
Gen.	βασιλέως	νεώς	πόλεως
Dat.	βασιλεῖ	νηί	πόλει
Acc.	βασιλέα	ναῦν	πόλιν

Plural

Nom.	βασιλῆς (-εῖς)	νῆες	πόλεις
Gen.	βασιλέων	νεῶν	πόλεων
Dat.	βασιλεῦσι(ν)	ναυσί(ν)	πόλεσι(ν)
Acc.	βασιλέας	ναῦς	πόλεις

Adjectives

First and Second Declension

	Three Terminations			Two Terminations	
			Singular		
	Masculine	Feminine	Neuter	Masc./Fem.	Neuter
Nom.	πρῶτος	πρώτη	πρῶτον	ἄδικος	ἄδικον
Gen.	πρώτου	πρώτης	πρώτου	ἀδίκου	ἀδίκου
Dat.	πρώτῳ	πρώτῃ	πρώτῳ	ἀδίκῳ	ἀδίκῳ
Acc.	πρῶτον	πρώτην	πρῶτον	ἄδικον	ἄδικον

Plural

	Masculine	Feminine	Neuter	Masc./Fem.	Neuter
Nom.	πρῶτοι	πρῶται	πρῶτα	ἄδικοι	ἄδικα
Gen.	πρώτων	πρώτων	πρώτων	ἀδίκων	ἀδίκων
Dat.	πρώτοις	πρώταις	πρώτοις	ἀδίκοις	ἀδίκοις
Acc.	πρώτους	πρώτας	πρῶτα	ἀδίκους	ἄδικα

Irregular First and Second Declension

Singular

	Masculine	Feminine	Neuter	Masculine	Feminine	Neuter
Nom.	μέγας	μεγάλη	μέγα	πολύς	πολλή	πολύ
Gen.	μεγάλου	μεγάλης	μεγάλου	πολλοῦ	πολλῆς	πολλοῦ
Dat.	μεγάλῳ	μεγάλη	μεγάλῳ	πολλῷ	πολλῇ	πολλῷ
Acc.	μέγαν	μεγάλην	μέγα	πολύν	πολλήν	πολύ

Declensions

	Plural					
Nom.	μεγάλοι	μεγάλαι	μεγάλα	πολλοί	πολλαί	πολλά
Gen.	μεγάλων	μεγάλων	μεγάλων	πολλῶν	πολλῶν	πολλῶν
Dat.	μεγάλοις	μεγάλαις	μεγάλοις	πολλοῖς	πολλαῖς	πολλοῖς
Acc.	μεγάλους	μεγάλας	μεγάλα	πολλούς	πολλάς	πολλά

Third Declension

Two Terminations
Singular

	Nasal (-ων)		Sibilant (-εσ)	
	Masc./Fem.	Neuter	Masc./Fem.	Neuter
Nom.	εὐδαίμων	εὔδαιμον	ἀληθής	ἀληθές
Gen.	εὐδαίμονος	εὐδαίμονος	ἀληθοῦς	ἀληθοῦς
Dat.	εὐδαίμονι	εὐδαίμονι	ἀληθεῖ	ἀληθεῖ
Acc.	εὐδαίμονα	εὔδαιμον	ἀληθῆ	ἀληθές

	Plural			
Nom.	εὐδαίμονες	εὐδαίμονα	ἀληθεῖς	ἀληθῆ
Gen.	εὐδαιμόνων	εὐδαιμόνων	ἀληθῶν	ἀληθῶν
Dat.	εὐδαίμοσι(ν)	εὐδαίμοσι(ν)	ἀληθέσι(ν)	ἀληθέσι(ν)
Acc.	εὐδαίμονας	εὐδαίμονα	ἀληθεῖς	ἀληθῆ

Three Terminations

	Singular			Plural		
	Masculine	Feminine	Neuter	Masculine	Feminine	Neuter
Nom.	ἡδύς	ἡδεῖα	ἡδύ	ἡδεῖς (ἡδέες)	ἡδεῖαι	ἡδέα
Gen.	ἡδέος	ἡδείας	ἡδέος	ἡδέων	ἡδειῶν	ἡδέων
Dat.	ἡδεῖ (ἡδέϊ)	ἡδείᾳ	ἡδεῖ (ἡδέϊ)	ἡδέσι(ν)	ἡδείαις	ἡδέσι(ν)
Acc.	ἡδύν	ἡδεῖαν	ἡδύ	ἡδεῖς	ἡδείας	ἡδέα

The Irregular Adjective πᾶς

	Singular			Plural		
	Masculine	Feminine	Neuter	Masculine	Feminine	Neuter
Nom.	πᾶς	πᾶσα	πᾶν	πάντες	πᾶσαι	πάντα
Gen.	παντός	πάσης	παντός	πάντων	πασῶν	πάντων
Dat.	παντί	πάσῃ	παντί	πᾶσι(ν)	πάσαις	πᾶσι(ν)
Acc.	πάντα	πᾶσαν	πᾶν	πάντας	πάσας	πάντα

Declensions

Participles

Present Active (Regular ω-Verbs)
Singular

	Masculine	Feminine	Neuter
Nom.	παιδεύων	παιδεύουσα	παιδεῦον
Gen.	παιδεύοντος	παιδευούσης	παιδεύοντος
Dat.	παιδεύοντι	παιδευούσῃ	παιδεύοντι
Acc.	παιδεύοντα	παιδεύουσαν	παιδεῦον

Plural

	Masculine	Feminine	Neuter
Nom.	παιδεύοντες	παιδεύουσαι	παιδεύοντα
Gen.	παιδευόντων	παυδευουσῶν	παιδευόντων
Dat.	παιδεύουσι(ν)	παιδευούσαις	παιδεύουσι(ν)
Acc.	παιδεύοντας	παιδευούσας	παιδεύοντα

Present Active (ε-contract Verbs / o-contract Verbs)
Singular

	Masculine	Feminine	Neuter
Nom.	ποιῶν	ποιοῦσα	ποιοῦν
Gen.	ποιοῦντος	ποιούσης	ποιοῦντος
Dat.	ποιοῦντι	ποιούσῃ	ποιοῦντι
Acc.	ποιοῦντα	ποιοῦσαν	ποιοῦν

Plural

	Masculine	Feminine	Neuter
Nom.	ποιοῦντες	ποιοῦσαι	ποιοῦντα
Gen.	ποιούντων	ποιουσῶν	ποιούντων
Dat.	ποιοῦουσι(ν)	ποιούσαις	ποιοῦουσι(ν)
Acc.	ποιοῦντας	ποιούσας	ποιοῦντα

Present Active (α-contract Verbs)
Singular

	Masculine	Feminine	Neuter
Nom.	τιμῶν	τιμῶσα	τιμῶν
Gen.	τιμῶντος	τιμώσης	τιμῶντος
Dat.	τιμῶντι	τιμώσῃ	τιμῶντι
Acc.	τιμῶντα	τιμῶσαν	τιμῶν

Plural

	Masculine	Feminine	Neuter
Nom.	τιμῶντες	τιμῶσαι	τιμῶντα
Gen.	τιμώντων	τιμωσῶν	τιμώντων
Dat.	τιμῶσι(ν)	τιμώσαις	τιμῶσι(ν)
Acc.	τιμῶντας	τιμώσας	τιμῶντα

Declensions

Present Active (ἵστημι)
Singular

	Masculine	Feminine	Neuter
Nom.	ἱστάς	ἱστᾶσα	ἱστάν
Gen.	ἱστάντος	ἱστάσης	ἱστάντος
Dat.	ἱστάντι	ἱστάσῃ	ἱστάντι
Acc.	ἱστάντα	ἱστᾶσαν	ἱστάν

Plural

	Masculine	Feminine	Neuter
Nom.	ἱστάντες	ἱστᾶσαι	ἱστάντα
Gen.	ἱστάντων	ἱστασῶν	ἱστάντων
Dat.	ἱστᾶσι(ν)	ἱστάσαις	ἱστᾶσι(ν)
Acc.	ἱστάντας	ἱστάσας	ἱστάντα

Present Active (τίθημι / ἵημι)
Singular

	Masculine	Feminine	Neuter
Nom.	τιθείς	τιθεῖσα	τιθέν
Gen.	τιθέντος	τιθείσης	τιθέντος
Dat.	τιθέντι	τιθείσῃ	τιθέντι
Acc.	τιθέντα	τιθεῖσαν	τιθέν

Plural

	Masculine	Feminine	Neuter
Nom.	τιθέντες	τιθεῖσαι	τιθέντα
Gen.	τιθέντων	τιθεισῶν	τιθέντων
Dat.	τιθεῖσι(ν)	τιθείσαις	τιθεῖσι(ν)
Acc.	τιθέντας	τιθείσας	τιθέντα

Present Active (δίδωμι)
Singular

	Masculine	Feminine	Neuter
Nom.	διδούς	διδοῦσα	διδόν
Gen.	διδόντος	διδούσης	διδόντος
Dat.	διδόντι	διδούσῃ	διδόντι
Acc.	διδόντα	διδοῦσαν	διδόν

Plural

	Masculine	Feminine	Neuter
Nom.	διδόντες	διδοῦσαι	διδόντα
Gen.	διδόντων	διδουσῶν	διδόντων
Dat.	διδοῦσι(ν)	διδούσαις	διδοῦσι(ν)
Acc.	διδόντας	διδούσας	διδόντα

Declensions

Present Active (δείκνυμι)
Singular

	Masculine	Feminine	Neuter
Nom.	δεικνύς	δεικνῦσα	δεικνύν
Gen.	δεικνύντος	δεικνύσης	δεικνύντος
Dat.	δεικνύντι	δεικνύσῃ	δεικνύντι
Acc.	δεικνύντα	δεικνῦσαν	δεικνύντα

Plural

	Masculine	Feminine	Neuter
Nom.	δεικνύντες	δεικνῦσαι	δεικνύντα
Gen.	δεικνύντων	δεικνυσῶν	δεικνύντων
Dat.	δεικνῦσι(ν)	δεικνύσαις	δεικνῦσι(ν)
Acc.	δεικνύντας	δεικνύσας	δεικνύντα

Future Active (Regular ω-Verbs / μι-Verbs)
Singular

	Masculine	Feminine	Neuter
Nom.	παιδεύσων	παιδεύσουσα	παιδεῦσον
Gen.	παιδεύσοντος	παιδευσούσης	παιδεύσοντος
Dat.	παιδεύσοντι	παιδευσούσῃ	παιδεύσοντι
Acc.	παιδεύσοντα	παιδεύσουσαν	παιδεῦσον

Plural

	Masculine	Feminine	Neuter
Nom.	παιδεύσοντες	παιδεύσουσαι	παιδεύσοντα
Gen.	παιδευσόντων	παιδευσουσῶν	παιδευσόντων
Dat.	παιδεύσουσι(ν)	παιδευσούσαις	παιδεύσουσι(ν)
Acc.	παιδεύσοντας	παιδευσούσας	παιδεύσοντα

Future Active (Liquid Verbs)
Singular

	Masculine	Feminine	Neuter
Nom.	φανῶν	φανοῦσα	φανοῦν
Gen.	φανοῦντος	φανούσης	φανοῦντος
Dat.	φανοῦντι	φανούσῃ	φανοῦντι
Acc.	φανοῦντα	φανοῦσαν	φανοῦν

Plural

	Masculine	Feminine	Neuter
Nom.	φανοῦντες	φανοῦσαι	φανοῦντα
Gen.	φανούντων	φανουσῶν	φανούντων
Dat.	φανοῦουσι(ν)	φανούσαις	φανοῦουσι(ν)
Acc.	φανοῦντας	φανούσας	φανοῦντα

Declensions

First Aorist Active
Singular

	Masculine	Feminine	Neuter
Nom.	παιδεύσας	παιδεύσασα	παιδεῦσαν
Gen.	παιδεύσαντος	παιδευσάσης	παιδεύσαντος
Dat.	παιδεύσαντι	παιδευσάσῃ	παιδεύσαντι
Acc.	παιδεύσαντα	παιδεύσασαν	παιδεῦσαν

Plural

	Masculine	Feminine	Neuter
Nom.	παιδεύσαντες	παιδεύσασαι	παιδεύσαντα
Gen.	παιδευσάντων	παιδευσασῶν	παιδευσάντων
Dat.	παιδεύσασι(ν)	παιδευσάσαις	παιδεύσασι(ν)
Acc.	παιδεύσαντας	παιδευσάσας	παιδεύσαντα

Second Aorist Active (ω-Verbs)
Singular

	Masculine	Feminine	Neuter
Nom.	λιπών	λιποῦσα	λιπόν
Gen.	λιπόντος	λιπούσης	λιπόντος
Dat.	λιπόντι	λιπούσῃ	λιπόντι
Acc.	λιπόντα	λιποῦσαν	λιπόν

Plural

	Masculine	Feminine	Neuter
Nom.	λιπόντες	λιποῦσαι	λιπόντα
Gen.	λιπόντων	λιπουσῶν	λιπόντων
Dat.	λιποῦσι(ν)	λιπούσαις	λιποῦσι(ν)
Acc.	λιπόντας	λιπούσας	λιπόντα

Second Aorist Active (ἵστημι)
Singular

	Masculine	Feminine	Neuter
Nom.	στάς	στᾶσα	στάν
Gen.	στάντος	στάσης	στάντος
Dat.	στάντι	στάσῃ	στάντι
Acc.	στάντα	στᾶσαν	στάν

Plural

	Masculine	Feminine	Neuter
Nom.	στάντες	στᾶσαι	στάντα
Gen.	στάντων	στασῶν	στάντων
Dat.	στᾶσι(ν)	στάσαις	στᾶσι(ν)
Acc.	στάντας	στάσας	στάντα

Declensions

Second Aorist Active (τίθημι / ἵημι)
Singularθ

	Masculine	Feminine	Neuter
Nom.	θείς	θεῖσα	θέν
Gen.	θέντος	θείσης	θέντος
Dat.	θέντι	θείσῃ	θέντι
Acc.	θέντα	θεῖσαν	θέν

Plural

	Masculine	Feminine	Neuter
Nom.	θέντες	θεῖσαι	θέντα
Gen.	θέντων	θεισῶν	θέντων
Dat.	θεῖσι(ν)	θείσαις	θεῖσι(ν)
Acc.	θέντας	θείσας	θέντα

Second Aorist Active (δίδωμι)
Singular

	Masculine	Feminine	Neuter
Nom.	δούς	δοῦσα	δόν
Gen.	δόντος	δούσης	δόντος
Dat.	δόντι	δούσῃ	δόντι
Acc.	δόντα	δοῦσα	δόν

Plural

	Masculine	Feminine	Neuter
Nom.	δόντες	δοῦσαι	δόντα
Gen.	δόντων	δουσῶν	δόντων
Dat.	δοῦσι(ν)	δούσαις	δοῦσι(ν)
Acc.	δόντας	δούσας	δόντα

Perfect Active
Singular

	Masculine	Feminine	Neuter
Nom.	πεπαιδευκώς	πεπαιδευκυῖα	πεπαιδευκός
Gen.	πεπαιδευκότος	πεπαιδευκυίας	πεπαιδευκότος
Dat.	πεπαιδευκότι	πεπαιδευκυίᾳ	πεπαιδευκότι
Acc.	πεπαιδευκότα	πεπαιδευκυῖαν	πεπαιδευκός

Plural

	Masculine	Feminine	Neuter
Nom.	πεπαιδευκότες	πεπαιδευκυῖαι	πεπαιδευκότα
Gen.	πεπαιδευκότων	πεπαιδευκυιῶν	πεπαιδευκότων
Dat.	πεπαιδευκόσι(ν)	πεπαιδευκυίαις	πεπαιδευκόσι(ν)
Acc.	πεπαιδευκότας	πεπαιδευκυίας	πεπαιδευκότα

Present Middle-Passive (Regular ω-Verbs)
Singular

	Masculine	Feminine	Neuter
Nom.	παιδευόμενος	παιδευομένη	παιδευόμενον
Gen.	παιδευομένου	παιδευομένης	παιδευομένου
Dat.	παιδευομένῳ	παιδευομένῃ	παιδευομένῳ
Acc.	παιδευόμενον	παιδευομένην	παιδευόμενον

Plural

	Masculine	Feminine	Neuter
Nom.	παιδευόμενοι	παιδευόμεναι	παιδευόμενα
Gen.	παιδευομένων	παιδευομένων	παιδευομένων
Dat.	παιδευομένοις	παιδευομέναις	παιδευομένοις
Acc.	παιδευομένους	παιδευομένας	παιδευόμενα

Present Middle-Passive (ε-contract Verbs / o-contract Verbs)
Singular

	Masculine	Feminine	Neuter
Nom.	ποιούμενος	ποιουμένη	ποιούμενον
Gen.	ποιουμένου	ποιουμένης	ποιουμένου
Dat.	ποιουμένῳ	ποιουμένῃ	ποιουμένῳ
Acc.	ποιούμενον	ποιουμένην	ποιούμενον

Plural

	Masculine	Feminine	Neuter
Nom.	ποιούμενοι	ποιούμεναι	ποιούμενα
Gen.	ποιουμένων	ποιουμένων	ποιουμένων
Dat.	ποιουμένοις	ποιουμέναις	ποιουμένοις
Acc.	ποιουμένους	ποιουμένας	ποιούμενα

Present Middle-Passive (α-contract Verbs)
Singular

	Masculine	Feminine	Neuter
Nom.	τιμώμενος	τιμωμένη	τιμώμενον
Gen.	τιμωμένου	τιμωμένης	τιμωμένου
Dat.	τιμωμένῳ	τιμωμένῃ	τιμωμένῳ
Acc.	τιμώμενον	τιμωμένην	τιμώμενον

Plural

	Masculine	Feminine	Neuter
Nom.	τιμώμενοι	τιμώμεναι	τιμώμενα
Gen.	τιμωμένων	τιμωμένων	τιμωμένων
Dat.	τιμωμένοις	τιμωμέναις	τιμωμένοις
Acc.	τιμωμένους	τιμωμένας	τιμώμενα

Present Middle-Passive (ἵστημι)
Singular

	Masculine	Feminine	Neuter
Nom.	ἱστάμενος	ἱσταμένη	ἱστάμενον
Gen.	ἱσταμένου	ἱσταμένης	ἱσταμένου
Dat.	ἱσταμένῳ	ἱσταμένῃ	ἱσταμένῳ
Acc.	ἱστάμενον	ἱσταμένην	ἱστάμενον

Plural

	Masculine	Feminine	Neuter
Nom.	ἱστάμενοι	ἱστάμεναι	ἱστάμενα
Gen.	ἱσταμένων	ἱσταμένων	ἱσταμένων
Dat.	ἱσταμένοις	ἱσταμέναις	ἱσταμένοις
Acc.	ἱσταμένους	ἱσταμένας	ἱστάμενα

Present Middle-Passive (τίθημι / ἵημι)
Singular

	Masculine	Feminine	Neuter
Nom.	τιθέμενος	τιθεμένη	τιθέμενον
Gen.	τιθεμένου	τιθεμένης	τιθεμένου
Dat.	τιθεμένῳ	τιθεμένῃ	τιθεμένῳ
Acc.	τιθέμενον	τιθεμένην	τιθέμενον

Plural

	Masculine	Feminine	Neuter
Nom.	τιθέμενοι	τιθέμεναι	τιθέμενα
Gen.	τιθεμένων	τιθεμένων	τιθεμένων
Dat.	τιθεμένοις	τιθεμέναις	τιθεμένοις
Acc.	τιθεμένους	τιθεμένας	τιθέμενα

Present Middle-Passive (δίδωμι)
Singular

	Masculine	Feminine	Neuter
Nom.	διδόμενος	διδομένη	διδόμενον
Gen.	διδομένου	διδομένης	διδομένου
Dat.	διδομένῳ	διδομένῃ	διδομένῳ
Acc.	διδόμενον	διδομένην	διδόμενον

Plural

	Masculine	Feminine	Neuter
Nom.	διδόμενοι	διδόμεναι	διδόμενα
Gen.	διδομένων	διδομένων	διδομένων
Dat.	διδομένοις	διδομέναις	διδομένοις
Acc.	διδομένους	διδομένας	διδόμενα

Declensions

Present Middle-Passive (δείκνυμι)
Singular

	Masculine	Feminine	Neuter
Nom.	δεικνύμενος	δεικνυμένη	δεικνύμενον
Gen.	δεικνυμένου	δεικνυμένης	διδομένου
Dat.	δεικνυμένῳ	δεικνυμένῃ	διδομένῳ
Acc.	δεικνύμενον	δεικνυμένην	δεικνύμενον

Plural

Nom.	δεικνύμενοι	δεικνύμεναι	δεικνύμενα
Gen.	δεικνυμένων	δεικνυμένων	δεικνυμένων
Dat.	δεικνυμένοις	δεικνυμέναις	δεικνυμένοις
Acc.	δεικνυμένους	δεικνυμένας	δεικνύμενα

Future Middle (Regular ω-Verbs / μι-Verbs)
Singular

	Masculine	Feminine	Neuter
Nom.	παιδευσόμενος	παιδευσομένη	παιδευσόμενον
Gen.	παιδευσομένου	παιδευσομένης	παιδευσομένου
Dat.	παιδευσομένῳ	παιδευσομένη	παιδευσομένῳ
Acc.	παιδευσόμενον	παιδευσομένην	παιδευσόμενον

Plural

Nom.	παιδευσόμενοι	παιδευσόμεναι	παιδευσόμενα
Gen.	παιδευσομένων	παιδευσομένων	παιδευσομένων
Dat.	παιδευσομένοις	παιδευσομέναις	παιδευσομένοις
Acc.	παιδευσομένους	παιδευσομένας	παιδευσόμενα

Future Middle (Liquid Verbs)
Singular

	Masculine	Feminine	Neuter
Nom.	φανούμενος	φανουμένη	φανούμενον
Gen.	φανουμένου	φανουμένης	φανουμένου
Dat.	φανουμένῳ	φανουμένῃ	φανουμένῳ
Acc.	φανούμενον	φανουμένην	φανούμενον

Plural

Nom.	φανούμενοι	φανούμεναι	φανούμενα
Gen.	φανουμένων	φανουμένων	φανουμένων
Dat.	φανουμένοις	φανουμέναις	φανουμένοις
Acc.	φανουμένους	φανουμένας	φανούμενα

Declensions

First Aorist Middle
Singular

	Masculine	Feminine	Neuter
Nom.	παιδευσάμενος	παιδευσαμένη	παιδευσάμενον
Gen.	παιδευσαμένου	παιδευσαμένης	παιδευσαμένου
Dat.	παιδευσαμένῳ	παιδευσαμένῃ	παιδευσαμένῳ
Acc.	παιδευσάμενον	παιδευσαμένην	παιδευσάμενον

Plural

Nom.	παιδευσάμενοι	παιδευσάμεναι	παιδευσάμενα
Gen.	παιδευσαμένων	παιδευσαμένων	παιδευσαμένων
Dat.	παιδευσαμένοις	παιδευσαμέναις	παιδευσαμένοις
Acc.	παιδευσαμένους	παιδευσαμένας	παιδευσάμενα

Second Aorist Middle (ω-Verbs)
Singular

	Masculine	Feminine	Neuter
Nom.	λιπόμενος	λιπομένη	λιπόμενον
Gen.	λιπομένου	λιπομένης	λιπομένου
Dat.	λιπομένῳ	λιπομένῃ	λιπομένῳ
Acc.	λιπόμενον	λιπομένην	λιπόμενον

Plural

Nom.	λιπόμενοι	λιπόμεναι	λιπόμενα
Gen.	λιπομένων	λιπομένων	λιπομένων
Dat.	λιπομένοις	λιπομέναις	λιπομένοις
Acc.	λιπομένους	λιπομένας	λιπόμενα

Second Aorist Middle (τίθημι / ἵημι)
Singular

	Masculine	Feminine	Neuter
Nom.	θέμενος	θεμένη	θέμενον
Gen.	θεμένου	θεμένης	θεμένου
Dat.	θεμένῳ	θεμένῃ	θεμένῳ
Acc.	θέμενον	θεμένην	θέμενον

Plural

Nom.	θέμενοι	θέμεναι	θέμενα
Gen.	θεμένων	θεμένων	θεμένων
Dat.	θεμένοις	θεμέναις	θεμένοις
Acc.	θεμένους	θεμένας	θέμενα

Declensions

Second Aorist Middle (δίδωμι)
Singular

	Masculine	Feminine	Neuter
Nom.	δόμενος	δομένη	δόμενον
Gen.	δομένου	δομένης	δομένου
Dat.	δομένῳ	δομένῃ	δομένῳ
Acc.	δόμενον	δομένην	δόμενον

Plural

	Masculine	Feminine	Neuter
Nom.	δόμενοι	δόμεναι	δόμενα
Gen.	δομένων	δομένων	δομένων
Dat.	δομένοις	δομέναις	δομένοις
Acc.	δομένους	δομένας	δόμενα

Perfect Middle-Passive
Singular

	Masculine	Feminine	Neuter
Nom.	πεπαιδευμένος	πεπαιδευμένη	πεπαιδευμένον
Gen.	πεπαιδευμένου	πεπαιδευμένης	πεπαιδευμένου
Dat.	πεπαιδευμένῳ	πεπαιδευμένη	πεπαιδευμένῳ
Acc.	πεπαιδεύμενον	πεπαιδευμένην	πεπαιδεύμενον

Plural

	Masculine	Feminine	Neuter
Nom.	πεπαιδεύμενοι	πεπαιδεύμεναι	πεπαιδεύμενα
Gen.	πεπαιδευμένων	πεπαιδευμένων	πεπαιδευμένων
Dat.	πεπαιδευμένοις	πεπαιδευμέναις	πεπαιδευμένοις
Acc.	πεπαιδευμένους	πεπαιδευμένας	πεπαιδεύμενα

Aorist Passive
Singular

	Masculine	Feminine	Neuter
Nom.	παιδευθείς	παιδευθεῖσα	παιδευθέν
Gen.	παιδευθέντος	παιδευθείσης	παιδευθέντος
Dat.	παιδευθέντι	παιδευθείσῃ	παιδευθέντι
Acc.	παιδευθέντα	παιδευθεῖσαν	παιδευθέν

Plural

	Masculine	Feminine	Neuter
Nom.	παιδευθέντες	παιδευθεῖσαι	παιδευθέντα
Gen.	παιδευθέντων	παιδευθεισῶν	παιδευθέντων
Dat.	παιδευθεῖσι(ν)	παιδευθείσαις	παιδευθεῖσι(ν)
Acc.	παιδευθέντας	παιδευθείσας	παιδευθέντα

Declensions

Pronouns

Demonstrative

	Singular			Plural		
	Masculine	Feminine	Neuter	Masculine	Feminine	Neuter
Nom.	ἐκεῖνος	ἐκείνη	ἐκεῖνο	ἐκεῖνοι	ἐκεῖναι	ἐκεῖνα
Gen.	ἐκείνου	ἐκείνης	ἐκείνου	ἐκείνων	ἐκείνων	ἐκείνων
Dat.	ἐκείνῳ	ἐκείνῃ	ἐκείνῳ	ἐκείνοις	ἐκείναις	ἐκείνοις
Acc.	ἐκεῖνον	ἐκείνην	ἐκεῖνο	ἐκείνους	ἐκείνας	ἐκεῖνα

	Singular			Plural		
	Masculine	Feminine	Neuter	Masculine	Feminine	Neuter
Nom.	οὗτος	αὕτη	τοῦτο	οὗτοι	αὗται	ταῦτα
Gen.	τούτου	ταύτης	τούτου	τούτων	τούτων	τούτων
Dat.	τούτῳ	ταύτῃ	τούτῳ	τούτοις	ταύταις	τούτοις
Acc.	τοῦτον	ταύτην	τοῦτο	τούτους	ταύτας	ταῦτα

	Singular			Plural		
	Masculine	Feminine	Neuter	Masculine	Feminine	Neuter
Nom.	ὅδε	ἥδε	τόδε	οἵδε	αἵδε	τάδε
Gen.	τοῦδε	τῆσδε	τοῦδε	τῶνδε	τῶνδε	τῶνδε
Dat.	τῷδε	τῇδε	τῷδε	τοῖσδε	ταῖσδε	τοῖσδε
Acc.	τόνδε	τήνδε	τόδε	τούσδε	τάσδε	τάδε

Indefinite Relative

	Singular		
	Masculine	Feminine	Neuter
Nom.	ὅστις	ἥτις	ὅ τι
Gen.	οὗτινος (ὅτου)	ἧστινος	οὗτινος (ὅτου)
Dat.	ᾧτινι (ὅτῳ)	ᾗτινι	ᾧτινι (ὅτῳ)
Acc.	ὅντινα	ἥντινα	ὅ τι

	Plural		
	Masculine	Feminine	Neuter
Nom.	οἵτινες	αἵτινες	ἅτινα (ἅττα)
Gen.	ὧντινα (ὅτων)	ὧντινα	ὧντινα (ὅτων)
Dat.	οἷστισι(ν) (ὅτοις)	αἷστισι(ν)	οἷστισι(ν) (ὅτοις)
Acc.	οὕστινας	ἅστινας	ἅτινα (ἅττα)

Declensions

Interrogative / Indefinite (enclitic forms)

	Singular		Plural	
	Masculine-Feminine	Neuter	Masculine-Feminine	Neuter
Nom.	τίς	τί	τίνες	τίνα
Gen.	τίνος (τοῦ)	τίνος (τοῦ)	τίνων	τίνων
Dat.	τίνι (τῷ)	τίνι (τῷ)	τίσι(ν)	τίσι(ν)
Acc.	τίνα	τί	τίνας	τίνα

1st & 2nd Person Personal

	First Person		Second Person	
	Singular	Plural	Singular	Plural
Nom.	ἐγώ	ἡμεῖς	σύ	ὑμεῖς
Gen.	ἐμοῦ (μου)	ἡμῶν	σοῦ (σου)	ὑμῶν
Dat.	ἐμοί (μοι)	ἡμῖν	σοί (σοι)	ὑμῖν
Acc.	ἐμέ (με)	ἡμᾶς	σέ (σε)	ὑμᾶς

3rd Person Personal/Intensive/Identifying

	Singular			Plural		
	Masculine	Feminine	Neuter	Masculine	Feminine	Neuter
Nom.	αὐτός	αὐτή	αὐτό	αὐτοί	αὐταί	αὐτά
Gen.	αὐτοῦ	αὐτῆς	αὐτοῦ	αὐτῶν	αὐτῶν	αὐτῶν
Dat.	αὐτῷ	αὐτῇ	αὐτῷ	αὐτοῖς	αὐταῖς	αὐτοῖς
Acc.	αὐτόν	αὐτήν	αὐτό	αὐτούς	αὐτάς	αὐτά

Reflexive

First Person

	Singular	Plural
Nom.		
Gen.	ἐμαυτοῦ, -ῆς	ἡμῶν αὐτῶν
Dat.	ἐμαυτῷ, -ῇ	ἡμῖν αὐτοῖς, -αῖς
Acc.	ἐμαυτόν, -ήν	ἡμᾶς αὐτούς, -άς

Second Person

	Singular	Plural
Nom.		
Gen.	σεαυτοῦ, -ῆς (σαυτοῦ, -ῆς)	ὑμῶν αὐτῶν
Dat.	σεαυτῷ, -ῇ (σαυτῷ, -ῇ)	ὑμῖν αὐτοῖς, -αῖς
Acc.	σεαυτόν, -ήν (σαυτόν, -ήν)	ὑμᾶς αὐτούς, -άς

Declensions

Third Person

	Singular	Plural
Nom.		
Gen.	ἑαυτοῦ, -ῆς, -οῦ	ἑαυτῶν
	(αὐτοῦ, -ῆς, -οῦ)	(αὐτῶν)
Dat.	ἑαυτῷ, -ῇ, -ῷ	ἑαυτοῖς, -αῖς, -οῖς
	(αὐτῷ, -ῇ, -ῷ)	(αὐτοῖς, -αῖς, -οῖς)
Acc.	ἑαυτόν, -ήν, -ό	ἑαυτούς, -άς, -ά
	(αὐτόν, -ήν, -ό)	(αὐτούς, -άς, -ά)

Relative

	Singular			Plural		
	Masculine	Feminine	Neuter	Masculine	Feminine	Neuter
Nom.	ὅς	ἥ	ὅ	οἵ	αἵ	ἅ
Gen.	οὗ	ἧς	οὗ	ὧν	ὧν	ὧν
Dat.	ᾧ	ᾗ	ᾧ	οἷς	αἷς	οἷς
Acc.	ὅν	ἥν	ὅ	οὕς	ἅς	ἅ

ω-Verbs

Present Stem = first principal part - ω

Indicative

Present Active			Present Middle-Passive		
Singular	Person	Plural	Singular	Person	Plural
παιδεύω	1	παιδεύομεν	παιδεύομαι	1	παιδευόμεθα
παιδεύεις	2	παιδεύετε	παιδεύει (-η)	2	παιδεύεσθε
παιδεύει	3	παιδεύουσι(ν)	παιδεύεται	3	παιδεύονται

Present Active (ε-contract)			Present Middle-Passive (ε-contract)		
Singular	Person	Plural	Singular	Person	Plural
ποιῶ	1	ποιοῦμεν	ποιοῦμαι	1	ποιούμεθα
ποιεῖς	2	ποιεῖτε	ποιεῖ	2	ποιεῖσθε
ποιεῖ	3	ποιοῦσι(ν)	ποιεῖται	3	ποιοῦνται

Present Active (α-contract)			Present Middle-Passive (α-contract)		
Singular	Person	Plural	Singular	Person	Plural
τιμῶ	1	τιμῶμεν	τιμῶμαι	1	τιμώμεθα
τιμᾷς	2	τιμᾶτε	τιμᾷ	2	τιμᾶσθε
τιμᾷ	3	τιμῶσι(ν)	τιμᾶται	3	τιμῶνται

Present Active (o-contract)			Present Middle-Passive (o-contract)		
Singular	Person	Plural	Singular	Person	Plural
δηλῶ	1	δηλοῦμεν	δηλοῦμαι	1	δηλούμεθα
δηλοῖς	2	δηλοῦτε	δῆλοι	2	δηλοῦσθε
δηλοῖ	3	δηλοῦσι(ν)	δηλοῦται	3	δηλοῦνται

Infinitive

Present Active	Present Middle-Passive
παιδεύειν	παιδεύεσθαι
Present Active (ε-contract)	Present Middle-Passive (ε-contract)
ποιεῖν	ποιεῖσθαι
Present Active (α-contract)	Present Middle-Passive (α-contract)
τιμᾶν	τιμᾶσθαι
Present Active (o-contract)	Present Middle-Passive (o-contract)
δηλοῦν	δηλοῦσθαι

Participle

Present Active	Present Middle-Passive
παιδευόμενος, -η, -ον	παιδευόμενος, -η, -ον

Present Active (ε-contract)   Present Middle-Passive (ε-contract)
ποιῶν, -οῦσα, -οῦν   ποιούμενος, -η, -ον

Present Active (α-contract)   Present Middle-Passive (α-contract)
τιμῶν, -ῶσα, -ῶν   τιμώμενος, -η, -ον

Present Active (ο-contract)   Present Middle-Passive (ο-contract)
δηλῶν, -οῦσα, -οῦν   δηλούμενος, -η,-ον

Imperative
 Present Active   Present Middle-Passive

Singular	Person	Plural	Singular	Person	Plural
παίδευε	2	παιδεύετε	παιδεύου	2	παιδεύεσθε
παιδευέτω	3	παιδευόντων	παιδευέσθω	3	παιδευέσθων

 Present Active (ε-contract)   Present Middle-Passive (ε-contract)

Singular	Person	Plural	Singular	Person	Plural
ποίει	2	ποιεῖτε	ποιοῦ	2	ποιεῖσθε
ποιείτω	3	ποιούντων	ποιείσθω	3	ποιείσθων

 Present Active (α-contract)   Present Middle-Passive (α-contract)

Singular	Person	Plural	Singular	Person	Plural
τίμα	2	τιμᾶτε	τιμῶ	2	τιμᾶσθε
τιμάτω	3	τιμώντων	τιμάσθω	3	τιμάσθων

 Present Active (ο-contract)   Present Middle-Passive (ο-contract)

Singular	Person	Plural	Singular	Person	Plural
δήλου	2	δηλοῦτε	δηλοῦ	2	δηλοῦσθε
δηλούτω	3	δηλούντων	δηλούσθω	3	δηλούσθων

Subjunctive
 Present Active   Present Middle-Passive

Singular	Person	Plural	Singular	Person	Plural
παιδεύω	1	παιδεύωμεν	παιδεύωμαι	1	παιδευώμεθα
παιδεύῃς	2	παιδεύητε	παιδεύῃ	2	παιδεύησθε
παιδεύῃ	3	παιδεύωσι(ν)	παιδεύηται	3	παιδεύωνται

 Present Active (ε-contract)   Present Middle-Passive (ε-contract)

Singular	Person	Plural	Singular	Person	Plural
ποιῶ	1	ποιῶμεν	ποιῶμαι	1	ποιώμεθα
ποιῇς	2	ποιῆτε	ποιῇ	2	ποιῆσθε
ποιῇ	3	ποιῶσι(ν)	ποιῆται	3	ποιῶμαι

ω-Verbs

Present Active (α-contract)			Present Middle-Passive (α-contract)		
Singular	Person	Plural	Singular	Person	Plural
τιμῶ	1	τιμῶμεν	τιμῶμαι	1	τιμώμεθα
τιμᾷς	2	τιμᾶτε	τιμᾷ	2	τιμᾶσθε
τιμᾷ	3	τιμῶσι(ν)	τιμᾶται	3	τιμῶνται

Present Active (o-contract)			Present Middle-Passive (o-contract)		
Singular	Person	Plural	Singular	Person	Plural
δηλῶ	1	δηλῶμεν	δηλῶμαι	1	δηλώμεθα
δηλοῖς	2	δηλῶτε	δηλοῖ	2	δηλῶσθε
δηλοῖ	3	δηλῶσι	δηλῶται	3	δηλῶνται

Optative

Present Active			Present Middle-Passive		
Singular	Person	Plural	Singular	Person	Plural
παιδεύοιμι	1	παιδεύοιμεν	παιδευοίμην	1	παιδευοίμεθα
παιδεύοις	2	παιδεύοιτε	παιδεύοιο	2	παιδεύοισθε
παιδεύοι	3	παιδεύοιεν	παιδεύοιτο	3	παιδεύοιντο

Present Active (ε-contract)			Present Middle-Passive (ε-contract)		
Singular	Person	Plural	Singular	Person	Plural
ποιοίην	1	ποιοῖμεν	ποιοίμην	1	ποιοίμεθα
ποιοίης	2	ποιοῖτε	ποιοῖο	2	ποιοῖσθε
ποιοίη	3	ποιοῖεν	ποιοῖτο	3	ποιοῖντο

Present Active (α-contract)			Present Middle-Passive (α-contract)		
Singular	Person	Plural	Singular	Person	Plural
τιμῴην	1	τιμῶμεν	τιμῴμην	1	τιμώμεθα
τιμῴης	2	τιμῷτε	τιμῷο	2	τιμῷσθε
τιμῴη	3	τιμῷεν	τιμῷτο	3	τιμῷντο

Present Active (o-contract)			Present Middle-Passive (o-contract)		
Singular	Person	Plural	Singular	Person	Plural
δηλοίην	1	δηλοῖμεν	δηλοίμην	1	δηλοίμεθα
δηλοίης	2	δηλοῖτε	δηλοῖο	2	δηλοῖσθε
δηλοίη	3	δηλοῖεν	δηλοῖτο	3	δηλοῖντο

Imperfect Stem = augment + first principal part - ω

Indicative

Imperfect Active			Imperfect Middle-Passive		
Singular	Person	Plural	Singular	Person	Plural
ἐπαίδευον	1	ἐπαιδεύομεν	ἐπαιδευόμην	1	ἐπαιδευόμεθα
ἐπαίδευες	2	ἐπαιδεύετε	ἐπαιδεύου	2	ἐπαιδεύεσθε
ἐπαίδευε	3	ἐπαίδευον	ἐπαιδεύετο	3	ἐπαιδεύοντο

ω-Verbs

Imperfect Active (ε-contract)				Imperfect Middle-Passive (ε-contract)		
Singular	Person	Plural		Singular	Person	Plural
ἐποίουν	1	ἐποιοῦμεν		ἐποιούμην	1	ἐποιούμεθα
ἐποίεις	2	ἐποιεῖτε		ἐποιοῦ	2	ἐποιεῖσθε
ἐποίει	3	ἐποίουν		ἐποιεῖτο	3	ἐποιοῦντο

Imperfect Active (α-contract)				Imperfect Middle-Passive (α-contract)		
Singular	Person	Plural		Singular	Person	Plural
ἐτίμων	1	ἐτιμῶμεν		ἐτιμώμην	1	ἐτιμώμεθα
ἐτίμας	2	ἐτιμᾶτε		ἐτιμῶ	2	ἐτιμᾶσθε
ἐτίμα	3	ἐτίμων		ἐτιμᾶτο	3	ἐτιμῶντο

Imperfect Active (ο-contract)				Imperfect Active (ο-contract)		
Singular	Person	Plural		Singular	Person	Plural
ἐδήλουν	1	ἐδηλοῦμεν		ἐδηλούμην	1	ἐδηλούμεθα
ἐδήλους	2	ἐδηλοῦτε		ἐδηλοῦ	2	ἐδηλοῦσθε
ἐδήλου	3	ἐδήλουν		ἐδηλοῦτο	3	ἐδηλοῦντο

Future Active/Middle Stem = second principal part - ω

Indicative

Future Active				Future Middle		
Singular	Person	Plural		Singular	Person	Plural
παιδεύσω	1	παιδεύσομεν		παιδεύσομαι	1	παιδευσόμεθα
παιδεύσεις	2	παιδεύσετε		παιδεύσει (-ῃ)	2	παιδεύσεσθε
παιδεύσει	3	παιδεύσουσι(ν)		παιδεύσεται	3	παιδεύσονται

Liquid Future Active				Liquid Future Middle		
Singular	Person	Plural		Singular	Person	Plural
φανῶ	1	φανοῦμεν		φανοῦμαι	1	φανούμεθα
φανεῖς	2	φανεῖτε		φανεῖ	2	φανεῖσθε
φανεῖ	3	φανοῦσι(ν)		φανεῖται	3	φανοῦνται

Infinitive

Future Active	Future Middle
παιδεύσειν	παιδεύσεσθαι

Liquid Future Active	Liquid Future Middle
φανεῖν	φανεῖσθαι

Participle

Future Active	Future Middle
παιδεύσων, -ουσα, -ον	παιδευσόμενος, -η, -ον

ω-Verbs

Liquid Future Active
φανῶν, -οῦσα, -οῦν

Liquid Future Middle
φανούμενος,-η, -ον

First Aorist Active/Middle Stem = 3ʳᵈ principal part - (σ)α
Note: the temporal augment is lost in all moods except for the indicative.

Indicative
First Aorist Active

Singular	Person	Plural
ἐπαίδευσα	1	ἐπαιδεύσαμεν
ἐπαίδευσας	2	ἐπαιδεύσατε
ἐπαίδευσε(ν)	3	ἐπαίδευσαν

First Aorist Middle

Singular	Person	Plural
ἐπαιδευσαμην	1	ἐπαιδευσάμεθα
ἐπαιδεύσω	2	ἐπαιδεύσασθε
ἐπαιδεύσατο	3	ἐπαιδεύσαντο

Liquid Aorist Active

Singular	Person	Plural
ἔφηνα	1	ἐφήναμεν
ἔφηνας	2	ἐφήνατε
ἔφηνε(ν)	3	ἔφηναν

Liquid Aorist Middle

Singular	Person	Plural
ἐφηνάμην	1	ἐφηνάμεθα
ἐφήνω	2	ἐφήνασθε
ἐφήνατο	3	ἐφήναντο

Infinitive
First Aorist Active
παιδεῦσαι

First Aorist Middle
παιδεύσασθαι

Liquid Aorist Active
φῆναι

Liquid Aorist Middle
φήνασθαι

Participle
First Aorist Active
παιδεύσας, -σασα, -σαν

First Aorist Middle
παιδευσάμενος, -η, -ον

Liquid Aorist Active
φήνας,-νασα, -ναν

Liquid Aorist Middle
φηνάμενος, -η, -ον

Imperative
First Aorist Active

Singular	Person	Plural
παίδευσον	2	παιδεύσατε
παιδεύσατε	3	παιδευσάντων

First Aorist Middle

Singular	Person	Plural
παιδεύου	2	παιδεύσασθε
παιδευσάσθω	3	παιδευσάσθων

Liquid Aorist Active

Singular	Person	Plural
φῆνον	2	φήνατε
φηνάτω	3	φηνάντων

Liquid Aorist Middle

Singular	Person	Plural
φῆναι	2	φήνασθε
φηνάσθω	3	φήνασθων

ω-Verbs

Subjunctive

First Aorist Active

Singular	Person	Plural
παιδεύσω	1	παιδεύσωμεν
παιδεύσῃς	2	παιδεύσητε
παιδεύσῃ	3	παιδεύσωσι(ν)

First Aorist Middle

Singular	Person	Plural
παιδεύσωμαι	1	παιδευσώμεθα
παιδεύσῃ	2	παιδεύσησθε
παιδεύσηται	3	παιδεύσωνται

Liquid Aorist Active

Singular	Person	Plural
φήνω	1	φήνωμεν
φήνῃς	2	φήνητε
φήνῃ	3	φήνωσι(ν)

Liquid Aorist Middle

Singular	Person	Plural
φήνωμαι	1	φηνώμεθα
φήνῃ	2	φήνησθε
φήνηται	3	φήνωνται

Optative

First Aorist Active

Singular	Person	Plural
παιδεύσαιμι	1	
παιδεύσειας (παιδευσαις)	2	παιδεύσαιτε
παιδεύσειε(ν) (παιδεύσαι)	3	παιδεύσειαν (παιδεύσαιεν)

First Aorist Middle

Singular	Person	Plural
παιδευσαίμην	1	παιδευσαίμεθα
παιδεύσαιο	2	παιδεύσαισθε
παιδεύσαιτο	3	παιδεύσαιντο

Liquid Aorist Active

Singular	Person	Plural
φήναιμι	1	
φήνειας (φήναις)	2	φήναιτε
φήνειε(ν) (φήναι)	3	φήνειαν (φήναιεν)

Liquid Aorist Middle

Singular	Person	Plural
φηναίμην	1	φηναίμεθα
φήναιο	2	φήναισθε
φήναιτο	3	φήναιντο

Second Aorist Active/Middle Stem = 3rd principal part - ον
Note: the temporal augment is lost in all moods except for the indicative.

Indicative

Second Aorist Active

Singular	Person	Plural
ἔλιπον	1	ἐλίπομεν
ἔλιπες	2	ἐλίπετε
ἔλιπε	3	ἔλιπον

Second Aorist Middle

Singular	Person	Plural
ἐλιπόμην	1	ἐλιπόμεθα
ἐλίπου	2	ἐλίπεσθε
ἐλίπετο	3	ἐλίποντο

Infinitive

Second Aorist Active
λιπεῖν

Second Aorist Middle
λιπέσθαι

ω-Verbs

Participle

Second Aorist Active
λιπών, -οῦσα, -όν

Second Aorist Middle
λιπόμενος, -η, -ον

Imperative

Second Aorist Active

Singular	Person	Plural
λίπε	2	λίπετε
λιπέτω	3	λιπόντων

Second Aorist Middle

Singular	Person	Plural
λιποῦ	2	λίπεσθε
λιπέσθω	3	λιπέσθων

Subjunctive

Second Aorist Active

Singular	Person	Plural
λίπω	1	λίπωμεν
λίπῃς	2	λίπητε
λίπῃ	3	λίπωσι(ν)

Second Aorist Middle

Singular	Person	Plural
λίπωμαι	1	λιπώμεθα
λίπῃ	2	λίπησθε
λίπηται	3	λίπωνται

Optative

Second Aorist Active

Singular	Person	Plural
λίποιμι	1	λίποιμεν
λίποις	2	λίποιτε
λίποι	3	λίποιεν

Second Aorist Middle

Singular	Person	Plural
λιποίμην	1	λιποίμεθα
λίποιο	2	λίποισθε
λίποιτο	3	λίποιντο

Perfect Active Stem =
    4th principal part - (κ)α

Perfect Middle-Passive Stem =
    5th principal part - μαι

Indicative

Perfect Active

Singular	Person	Plural
πεπαίδευκα	1	πεπαιδεύκαμεν
πεπαίδευκας	2	πεπαιδεύκατε
πεπαίδευκε(ν)	3	πεπαιδεύκασι(ν)

Perfect Middle-Passive

Singular	Person	Plural
πεπαίδευμαι	1	πεπαιδεύμεθα
πεπαίδευσαι	2	πεπαίδευσθε
πεπαίδευται	3	πεπαίδευνται

Infinitive

Perfect Active
πεπαιδευκέναι

Perfect Middle-Passive
πεπαιδεῦσθαι

Participle

Perfect Active
πεπαιδευκώς, -κυῖα, -κός

Perfect Middle-Passive
πεπαιδευμένος, -η, -ον

ω-Verbs

Pluperfect Active Stem =
  augment + 4ᵗʰ principal part - (κ)α

Pluperfect Middle-Passive Stem =
  augment + 5ᵗʰ principal part - μαι

Indicative

Pluperfect Active			Pluperfect Middle-Passive		
Singular	Person	Plural	Singular	Person	Plural
ἐπεπαιδεύκη	1	ἐπεπαιδεύκεμεν	ἐπεπαιδεύμην	1	ἐπεπαιδεύμεθα
ἐπεπαιδεύκης	2	ἐπεπαιδεύκετε	ἐπεπαίδευσο	2	ἐπεπαίδευσθε
ἐπεπαιδεύκει(ν)	3	ἐπεπαιδεύκεσαν	ἐπεπαίδευτο	3	ἐπεπαίδευντο

Aorist Passive Stem =
  6ᵗʰ principal part - ν
Note: the temporal augment is lost in the
infinitive and participle.

Future Passive Stem =
  6ᵗʰ principal part - augment -ν

Indicative

Aorist Passive			Future Passive		
Singular	Person	Plural	Singular	Person	Plural
ἐπαιδεύθην	1	ἐπαιδεύθημεν	παιδευθήσομαι	1	παιδευθησόμεθα
ἐπαιδεύθης	2	ἐπαιδεύθητε	παιδευθήσει (-ῃ)	2	παιδευθήσεσθε
ἐπαιδεύθη	3	ἐπαιδεύθησαν	παιδευθήσεται	3	παιδευθήσονται

Infinitive

Aorist Passive	Future Passive
παιδευθῆναι	παιδευθήσεσθαι

Participle

Aorist Passive
παιδευθείς, -εῖσα, -έν

Imperative

First Aorist Passive			Second Aorist Passive		
Singular	Person	Plural	Singular	Person	Plural
παιδεύθητι	2	παιδεύθητε	φάνηθι	2	φάνητε
παιδευθήτω	3	παιδευθέντων	φανήτω	3	φανέντων

Subjunctive

First Aorist Passive			Second Aorist Passive		
Singular	Person	Plural	Singular	Person	Plural
παιδευθῶ	1	παιδευθῶμεν	φανῶ	1	φανῶμεν
παιδευθῇς	2	παιδευθῆτε	φανῇς	2	φανῆτε
παιδευθῇ	3	παιδευθῶσι(ν)	φανῇ	3	φανῶσι(ν)

μι-Verbs

Present Stem = first principal part – stem vowel – μι

ἵστημι

Indicative

Present Active			Present Middle-Passive		
Singular	Person	Plural	Singular	Person	Plural
ἵστημι	1	ἵσταμεν	ἵσταμαι	1	ἱστάμεθα
ἵστης	2	ἵστατε	ἵστασαι	2	ἵστασθε
ἵστησι(ν)	3	ἱστᾶσι(ν)	ἵσταται	3	ἵστανται

Infinitive

Present Active	Present Middle-Passive
ἱστάναι	ἵστασθαι

Participle

Present Active	Present Middle-Passive
ἱστάς, -ᾶσα, -άν	ἱστάμενος, -η, -ον

Imperative

Present Active			Present Middle-Passive		
Singular	Person	Plural	Singular	Person	Plural
ἵστη	2	ἵστατε	ἵστασο	2	ἵστασθε
ἱστάτω	3	ἱστάντων	ἱστάσθω	3	ἱστάσθων

Subjunctive (*See paradigms listed under ω-verbs*)

Optative

Present Active			Present Middle-Passive		
Singular	Person	Plural	Singular	Person	Plural
ἱσταίην	1	ἱσταῖμεν	ἱσταίμην	1	ἱσταίμεθα
ἱσταίης	2	ἱσταῖτε	ἱσταῖο	2	ἱσταῖσθε
ἱσταίη	3	ἱσταῖεν	ἱσταῖτο	3	ἱσταῖντο

τίθημι

Indicative

Present Active			Present Middle-Passive		
Singular	Person	Plural	Singular	Person	Plural
τίθημι	1	τίθεμεν	τίθεμαι	1	τιθέμεθα
τίθης	2	τίθετε	τίθεσαι	2	τίθεσθε
τίθησι(ν)	3	τιθέασι(ν)	τίθεται	3	τίθενται

Infinitive

Present Active	Present Middle-Passive
τιθέναι	τίθεσθαι

μι-Verbs

Participle
Present Active	Present Middle-Passive
τιθείς, -εῖσα, -έν	τιθέμενος, -η, -ον

Imperative
Present Active
Singular	Person	Plural
τίθει	2	τίθετε
τιθέτω	3	τιθέντων

Present Middle-Passive
Singular	Person	Plural
τίθεσο	2	τίθεσθε
τιθέσθω	3	τιθέσθων

Subjunctive (*See paradigms listed under ω-verbs*)

Optative
Present Active
Singular	Person	Plural
τιθείην	1	τιθεῖμεν
τιθείης	2	τιθεῖτε
τιθείη	3	τιθεῖεν

Present Middle-Passive
Singular	Person	Plural
τιθείμην	1	τιθείμεθα
τιθεῖο	2	τιθεῖσθε
τιθεῖτο	3	τιθεῖντο

ἵημι

Indicative
Present Active
Singular	Person	Plural
ἵημι	1	ἵεμεν
ἵης (ἱεῖς)	2	ἵετε
ἵησι(ν)	3	ἱᾶσι(ν)

Present Middle-Passive
Singular	Person	Plural
ἵεμαι	1	ἱέμεθα
ἵεσαι	2	ἵεσθε
ἵεται	3	ἵεντο

Infinitive
Present Active	Present Middle-Passive
ἱέναι	ἵεσθαι

Participle
Present Active	Present Middle-Passive
ἱείς, -εῖσα, -έν	ἱέμενος, -η, -ον

Imperative
Present Active
Singular	Person	Plural
ἵει	2	ἵετε
ἱέτω	3	ἱέντων

Present Middle-Passive
Singular	Person	Plural
ἵεσο	2	ἵεσθε
ἱέσθω	3	ἱέσθων

Subjunctive (*See paradigms listed under ω-verbs*)

μι-Verbs

Optative

Present Active			Present Middle-Passive		
Singular	Person	Plural	Singular	Person	Plural
ἱείην	1	ἱεῖμεν	ἱείμην	1	ἱείμεθα
ἱείης	2	ἱεῖτε	ἱεῖο	2	ἱεῖσθε
ἱείη	3	ἱεῖεν	ἱεῖτο	3	ἱεῖντο

δίδωμι

Indicative

Present Active			Present Middle-Passive		
Singular	Person	Plural	Singular	Person	Plural
δίδωμι	1	δίδομεν	δίδομαι	1	διδόμεθα
δίδως	2	δίδοτε	δίδοσαι	2	δίδοσθε
δίδωσι(ν)	3	διδόασι(ν)	δίδοται	3	δίδονται

Infinitive

Present Active	Present Middle-Passive
διδόναι	δίδοσθαι

Participle

Present Active	Present Middle-Passive
διδούς, -οῦσα, -όν	διδόμενος, -η, -ον

Imperative

Present Active			Present Middle-Passive		
Singular	Person	Plural	Singular	Person	Plural
δίδου	2	δίδοτε	δίδοσο	2	δίδοσθε
διδότω	3	διδόντων	διδόσθω	3	διδόσθων

Subjunctive (*See paradigms listed under ω-verbs*)

Optative

Present Active			Present Middle-Passive		
Singular	Person	Plural	Singular	Person	Plural
διδοίην	1	διδοῖμεν	διδοίμην	1	διδοίμεθα
διδοίης	2	διδοῖτε	διδοῖο	2	διδοῖσθε
διδοίη	3	διδοῖεν	διδοῖτο	3	διδοῖντο

δείκνυμι

Indicative

Present Active			Present Middle-Passive		
Singular	Person	Plural	Singular	Person	Plural
δείκνυμι	1	δείκνυμεν	δείκνυμαι	1	δεικνύμεθα
δείκνυς	2	δείκνυτε	δείκνυσαι	2	δείκνυσθε
δείκνυσι(ν)	3	δεικνύασι(ν)	δείκνυται	3	δείκνυνται

Infinitive

    Present Active   Present Middle-Passive

        δεικνύναι   δείκνυσθαι

Participle

    Present Active   Present Middle-Passive

    δεικνύς, -ῦσα, -ύν   δεικνύμενος, -η, -ον

Imperative

Present Active			Present Middle-Passive		
Singular	Person	Plural	Singular	Person	Plural
δείκνυ	2	δείκνυτε	δείκνυσο	2	δείκνυσθε
δεικνύτω	3	δεικνύντων	δεικνύσθω	3	δεικνύσθων

Subjunctive (*See paradigms listed under ω-verbs*)

Optative

Present Active			Present Middle-Passive		
Singular	Person	Plural	Singular	Person	Plural
δεικνύοιμι	1	δεικνύοιμεν	δεικνυοίμην	1	δεικνυοίμεθα
δεικνύοις	2	δεικνύοιτε	δεικνύοιο	2	δεικνύοισθε
δεικνύοι	3	δεικνύοιεν	δεικνύοιτο	3	δεικνύοιντο

Imperfect Stem = augment + first principal part – stem vowel – μι

ἵστημι

Indicative

Imperfect Active			Imperfect Middle-Passive		
Singular	Person	Plural	Singular	Person	Plural
ἵστην	1	ἵσταμεν	ἵσταμαι	1	ἱστάμεθα
ἵστης	2	ἵστατε	ἵστασαι	2	ἵστασθε
ἵστη	3	ἵστασαν	ἵστατο	3	ἵστανται

τίθημι

Indicative

Imperfect Active			Imperfect Middle-Passive		
Singular	Person	Plural	Singular	Person	Plural
ἐτίθην	1	ἐτίθεμεν	ἐτιθέμην	1	ἐτιθέμεθα
ἐτίθεις	2	ἐτίθετε	ἐτίθεσο	2	ἐτίθεσθε
ἐτίθει	3	ἐτίθεσαν	ἐτίθετο	3	ἐθίθεντο

μι-Verbs

ἵημι

Indicative

Imperfect Active			Imperfect Middle-Passive		
Singular	Person	Plural	Singular	Person	Plural
ἵην	1	ἵεμεν	ἱέμην	1	ἱέμεθα
ἵεις	2	ἵετε	ἵεσο	2	ἵεσθε
ἵει	3	ἵεσαν	ἵετο	3	ἵεντο

δίδωμι

Indicative

Imperfect Active			Imperfect Middle-Passive		
Singular	Person	Plural	Singular	Person	Plural
ἐδίδουν	1	ἐδίδομεν	ἐδιδόμην	1	ἐδιδόμεθα
ἐδίδους	2	ἐδίδοτε	ἐδίδοσο	2	ἐδίδοσθε
ἐδίδου	3	ἐδίδοσαν	ἐδίδοτο	3	ἐδίδοντο

δείκνυμι

Indicative

Imperfect Active			Imperfect Middle-Passive		
Singular	Person	Plural	Singular	Person	Plural
ἐδείκνυν	1	ἐδείκνυμεν	ἐδεικνύμην	1	ἐδεικνύμεθα
ἐδείκνυς	2	ἐδείκνυτε	ἐδείκνυσο	2	ἐδείκνυσθε
ἐδείκνυ	3	ἐδείκνυσαν	ἐδείκνυτο	3	ἐδείκνυντο

Future Active/Middle Stem = second principal part - ω
See paradigms listed under ω-verbs

First Aorist Active/Middle Stem = 3rd principal part - (σ)α
See paradigms listed under ω-verbs for the first aorists of ἵστημι and δείκνυμι

Second Aorist Active/Middle Stem = 3rd principal part – stem vowel - ν
Note: the temporal augment is lost in all moods <u>except for</u> the indicative.

ἵστημι

Note: The first aorist of ἵστημι (transitive) has middle and passive forms, the second aorist (intransitive) below does not.

Indicative

Second Aorist Active		
Singular	Person	Plural
ἔστην	1	ἔστημεν
ἔστης	2	ἔστητε
ἔστη	3	ἔστησαν

Infinitive

Second Aorist Active
στῆναι

Participle

Second Aorist Active
στάς, -ᾶσα, -άν

μι-Verbs

Imperative
    Second Aorist Active

Singular	Person	Plural
στῆθι	2	στῆτε
στήσω	3	στάντων

Subjunctive
    (*See paradigms listed under ω-verbs*)

Optative
    Second Aorist Active

Singular	Person	Plural
σταίην	1	σταῖμεν
σταίης	2	σταῖτε
σταίη	3	σταῖεν

τίθημι

Indicative

Singular	Person	Plural
	Second Aorist Active	
ἔθηκα	1	ἔθεμεν
ἔθηκας	2	ἔθετε
ἔθηκε(ν)	3	ἔθεσαν

Second Aorist Middle

Singular	Person	Plural
ἐθέμην	1	ἐθέμεθα
ἔθου	2	ἔθεσθε
ἔθετο	3	ἔθεντο

Infinitive
    Second Aorist Active   Second Aorist Middle
         θεῖναι   θέσθαι

Participle
    Second Aorist Active   Second Aorist Middle
    θείς, -εῖσα, -έν   θέμενος, -η, -ον

Imperative
    Second Aorist Active

Singular	Person	Plural
θές	2	θέτε
θέτω	3	θέντων

Second Aorist Middle

Singular	Person	Plural
θοῦ	2	θέσθε
θέσθω	3	θέσθων

Subjunctive (*See paradigms listed under ω-verbs*)

Optative
    Second Aorist Active

Singular	Person	Plural
θείην	1	θεῖμεν
θείης	2	θεῖτε
θείη	3	θεῖεν

Second Aorist Middle

Singular	Person	Plural
θείμην	1	θείμεθα
θεῖο	2	θεῖσθε
θεῖτο	3	θεῖντο

 μι-Verbs

ἵημι

Indicative

	Second Aorist Active			Second Aorist Middle	
Singular	Person	Plural	Singular	Person	Plural
ἧκα	1	-εἷμεν	-εἵμην	1	-εἵμεθα
ἧκας	2	-εἷτε	-εἷσο	2	-εἷσθε
ἧκε(ν)	3	-εἷσαν	-εἷτο	3	-εἷντο

Infinitive

Second Aorist Active	Second Aorist Middle
-εἷναι	-έσθαι

Participle

Second Aorist Active	Second Aorist Middle
-εἵς, -εἷσα, -έν	-έμενος, -η, -ον

Imperative

	Second Aorist Active			Second Aorist Middle	
Singular	Person	Plural	Singular	Person	Plural
-ἕς	2	-ἕτε	-οὗ	2	-ἕσθε
-ἕτω	3	-ἕντων	-ἕσθω	3	-ἕσθων

Subjunctive (*See paradigms listed under ω-verbs*)

Optative

	Second Aorist Active			Second Aorist Middle	
Singular	Person	Plural	Singular	Person	Plural
-εἵην	1	-εἷμεν	-εἵμην	1	-εἵμεθα
-εἵης	2	-εἷτε	-εἷο	2	-εἷσθε
-εἵη	3	-εἷεν	-εἷτο	3	-εἷντο

δίδωμι

Indicative

	Second Aorist Active			Second Aorist Middle	
Singular	Person	Plural	Singular	Person	Plural
ἔδωκα	1	ἔδομεν	ἐδόμην	1	ἐδόμεθα
ἔδωκας	2	ἔδοτε	ἔδου	2	ἔδοσθε
ἔδωκε(ν)	3	ἔδοσαν	ἔδοτο	3	ἔδοντο

Infinitive

Second Aorist Active	Second Aorist Middle
δοῦναι	δόσθαι

μι-Verbs

Participle
Second Aorist Active
δούς, -οῦσα, -όν

Second Aorist Middle
δόμενος, -η, -ον

Imperative

	Second Aorist Active				Second Aorist Middle	
Singular	Person	Plural		Singular	Person	Plural
δός	2	δότε		δοῦ	2	δόσθε
δότω	3	δόντων		δόσθω	3	δόσθων

Subjunctive (*See paradigms listed under ω-verbs*)

Optative

	Second Aorist Active				Second Aorist Middle	
Singular	Person	Plural		Singular	Person	Plural
δοίην	1	δοῖμεν		δοίμην	1	δοίμεθα
δοίης	2	δοῖτε		δοῖο	2	δοῖσθε
δοίη	3	δοῖεν		δοῖτο	3	δοῖντο

First Perfect Active Stem = fourth principal part - κα
First Pluperfect Active Stem = augment + fourth principal part - κα
First Perfect Middle-Passive Stem = fifth principal part - μαι
First Pluperfect Middle-Passive Stem = augment + fifth principal part - μαι
See paradigms listed under ω-verbs

Second Perfect Active Stem =   Second Pluperfect Active Stem =
    4th principal part - κα   augment + 4th principal part - κα
Note: ἵστημι, which also has first perfect/pluperfect forms (transitive), is the only
μι-verb with second perfect forms (intransitive).

Indicative

	Second Perfect Active				Second Pluperfect Active	
Singular	Person	Plural		Singular	Person	Plural
[ἕστηκα]	1	ἕσταμεν		[εἱστήκη]	1	ἕσταμεν
[ἕστηκας]	2	ἕστατε		[εἱστήκης]	2	ἕστατε
[ἕστηκε(ν)]	3	ἑστᾶσι(ν)		[εἱστήκει(ν)]	3	ἕστασαν

Infinitive
Second Perfect Active
ἑστάναι

Participle
Second Perfect Active
ἑστώς, ἑστῶσα, ἑστός

Aorist Passive Stem =   Future Passive Stem =
    6th principal part - ν   6th principal part - augment -ν
See paradigms listed under ω-verbs

ἀγαθός, -ή, -όν good, brave 31
ἀγγέλλω announce, report 27
ἄγγελος, -ου, ὁ messenger 32
ἀγορά, -ᾶς, ἡ market-place 7
ἄγω lead, bring 2
ἀδελφός, -οῦ, ὁ brother 3
ἀδικέω injure, wrong, do wrong (to) 17
ἀδικία, -ας, ἡ injustice, injury, wrong 17
ἄδικος, -ον unjust 9
ἀεί (adverb) always 35
ἀθάνατος, -ον immortal 9
Ἀθῆναι, -ῶν, αἱ Athens 14
Ἀθηναῖος, -ου, ὁ Athenian 13
ἀθροίζω collect 23
αἱρέω take, seize, capture; (mid.) choose 17
αἰσθάνομαι perceive, learn (by perception), hear (+ gen. &,acc.) 34
αἰσχρός, -ά, -όν shameful, base, disgraceful 48
αἰτέω ask (for), demand 27
αἰτιάομαι blame 47
αἴτιον, -ου, τό cause, reason 53
αἴτιος, -α, -ον (+gen.) responsible (for) 41
ἀκολουθέω (+dat.) follow, accompany 46
ἀκούω (+ gen.) hear, listen to 11
ἄκων, -ουσα, -ον unwilling 32
ἀλήθεια, -ας, ἡ truth 18
ἀληθής, -ές true 38
ἁλίσκομαι be taken, be caught, be captured, be convicted 46
Ἀλκιβιάδης, -ου, ὁ Alcibiades 55
ἀλλά but 6
ἀλλὰ γάρ but in point of fact 49
ἀλλήλων each other, one another 43
ἀλλοῖος, -α, -ον different, of another kind 57

ἄλλο τι ἤ (sign of a question, expecting an affirmative answer) 48
ἁμαρτάνω (+gen.) miss; err 41
ἀμείνων, -ον better 41
ἄν postpositive adverb (untranslatable) 13
ἄν = ἐάν if 37
ἀνά (+ acc.) up; throughout 60
ἀναβαίνω go up 46
ἀναγιγνώσκω read 46
ἀναγκάζω force, compel 56
ἀνάγκη, -ης, ἡ necessity 57
ἀνατίθημι refer; dedicate; (mid.) retract (an opinion) 56
ἄνευ (+ gen.) without 60
ἀνήρ, -δρός, ὁ man, husband 22
ἄνθρωπος, -ου, ὁ man; human being 3
ἀνομία, -ας, ἡ lawlessness 56
ἀντί (+ gen.) instead of, in return for 53
ἀντὶ τίνος why 53
ἄξιος, -α, -ον (+ gen.) worthy (of) 9
ἀξιόω, think worthy, think right; believe, expect, request 51
ἅπας, ἅπασα, ἅπαν every, all 48
ἀπέχω keep away; (+ gen.) be away (from); (mid.) abstain from (+ gen.) 25
ἀπό (+ gen.) from, away from 4
ἀποθνῄσκω die, be killed 17
ἀποκρίνομαι answer, reply 34
ἀποκτείνω kill 17
ἀπόλλυμι (act.) destroy, lose; (mid. & 2nd perf. act.) die, perish 60
Ἀπόλλων, -ωνος, ὁ Apollo 33
ἀπολογέομαι defend oneself, make a defense 35
ἀπολογία, -ας, ἡ speech in defense, defense 58
ἀπορέω be at a loss 42
ἅπτομαι (+ gen.) touch 52

ἄρα therefore; as it seems 51
ἆρα (sign of a question) 48
ἀρετή, -ῆς, ἡ excellence, virtue 7
ἄριστος, -η, -ον best, very good,
    bravest 41
ἅρμα, -ατος, τό chariot 51
ἁρπάζω seize 23
ἄρτι just now, recently 53
ἀρχαῖος, -α, -ον old, ancient 46
ἀρχή, -ῆς, ἡ beginning; rule,
    government 44
ἄρχω (+ gen.) rule; (mid.) begin 11
ἄρχων, -οντος, ὁ ruler 27
ἀσθενής, -ές weak 42
ἀσπίς, -ίδος, ἡ shield 21
ἀσφαλής, -ές safe, secure 38
ἅτε (+ part.) since 28
αὐτάρκης, -ες independent, self-
    reliant 60
αὐτός, -ή, -ό (3rd person pronoun);
    -self; same 16
ἀφικνέομαι (with εἰς or ἐπί +
    acc.) arrive (in/at), reach 24

βάλλω throw, hit 23
βάρβαροι, -ων, οἱ the
    foreigners, barbarians 33
βάρβαρος, -ον foreign 33
βασιλεύς, -έως, ὁ king 22
βέλτιστος, -η, -ον (morally) best,
    very good 41
βελτίων, -ον (morally) better 41
βία, -ας, ἡ force, strength 56
βιάζομαι force, constrain, act
    violently 56
βιβλίον, -ου, τό book 5
βίος, -ου, ὁ life 4
βιόω live, be alive 57
βιωτός, -ή, -όν worth living 59
βλάπτω harm, hurt 2
βοάω shout, call out 43
βουλεύω plan; (mid.) deliberate 11
βούλομαι want, prefer 25

γάρ for 6
γε at least; of course 48
γελάω laugh (at) 52
γένος, -ους, τό race, birth 24
γέρων, -οντος, ὁ old man 21
γέφυρα, -ας, ἡ bridge 18
γῆ, γῆς, ἡ earth, land, ground,
    country 29
γῆρας, γήρως, τό old age 59
γίγνομαι become; be; happen;
    prove to be; be born 14
γιγνώσκω know, perceive,
    recognize 46
γνώμη, -ης, ἡ thought, opinion,
    judgment 7
γράμμα, -ατος, τό letter; (pl.)
    letters, writings 53
γραφὴν γράφεσθαι (+ acc. of
    person) bring an indictment
    (against), indict 57
γράφω write 2
γυνή, γυναικός, ἡ woman, wife 21

δαιμόνιον, -ου, τό divine sign 58
δέ and; but 6
δέδοικα fear, be afraid (of) 37
δεῖ (+ acc. & infin.) it is necessary,
    must, ought 28
δείκνυμι show, point out 52
δειλός, -ή, -όν cowardly, miserable
    41
δεινός, -ή, -όν fearful, terrible,
    clever 9
δέκα ten 25
Δελφοί, -ῶν, οἱ Delphi 46
δέομαι (+ gen.) ask; need 29
δεσπότης, -ου, ὁ master, ruler 18
δεύτερος, -α, -ον second 53
δέχομαι receive, accept 12
δή in fact, actually 23
δῆλος, -η, -ον evident, clear 38
δηλόω make clear, reveal, show 51
δήπου obviously 52
δῆτα surely, indeed 49

διά (+ gen.) through
(+ acc.) on account of, because
of 8
διαβαίνω go across, cross 47
διαβολή, -ῆς, ἡ prejudice, slander
7
διαγίγνομαι go through, pass (of
time); go through life, live,
survive 58
διαλέγομαι (+ dat.) converse (with)
55
διανοέομαι think, have in mind,
intend 59
διατελέω (+ participle) continue 58
διαφθείρω corrupt, ruin 2 & 17
διδάσκω teach 14
δίδωμι give 52
διέξοδος, -ου, ἡ way out, escape,
escape route, passage 41
διηγέομαι describe 60
δίκαιος, -α, -ον just 9
δικαστής, -οῦ, ὁ judge; juror 18
δίκη, -ης, ἡ justice; court, case 7
διώκω pursue; prosecute 16
δοκέω think, imagine; seem, be
thought;(impers.) it seems best
32
δοκιμάζω test, put to the test,
approve 60
δόξα, -ης, ἡ reputation, opinion,
expectation 59
δουλεύω be a slave 51
δοῦλος, -ου, ὁ slave 41
δραχμή, -ῆς, ἡ drachma 59
δύναμαι be able, can 53
δῶρον, -ου, τό gift 5

ἐάν if 37
ἑαυτοῦ, -ῆς, -οῦ himself, herself,
itself 38
ἐάω allow; let go 33
ἐγκρατής, -ές self-controlled, self-
restrained 60
ἐγώ I; ἡμεῖς we 16

ἐθέλω wish, be willing 2
εἰ if 13 & 49
εἰ γάρ if only 44
εἶεν well then; very well 51
εἴθε if only 44
εἴκοσι twenty 55
εἰμί be 14
εἶμι go 47
εἰρήνη, -ης, ἡ peace 7
εἷς, μία, ἕν one 31
εἰς (+ acc.) into, to 4
εἴτε ... εἴτε either ... or, whether ...
or 56
ἐκ (ἐξ) (+ gen.) out of, from 13
ἕκαστος, -η, -ον each 35
ἐκεῖνος, -η, -ο that 12
ἐκκλησία, -ας, ἡ assembly 48
ἑκών, -οῦσα, -όν willing 32
ἐλάττων, -ον smaller, less, lesser
43
ἐλάχιστος, -η, -ον smallest, least
43
ἐλέγχω refute, cross-examine 42
ἐλευθερία, -ας, ἡ freedom 42
ἐλεύθερος, -α, -ον free 42
Ἑλλάς, -άδος, ἡ Greece 54
Ἕλλην, Ἕλληνος, ὁ a Greek 21
ἐλπίζω hope (for), expect 32
ἐλπίς, -ίδος, ἡ hope 47
ἐμαυτοῦ, -ῆς myself 38
ἐμός, -ή, -όν my, mine 52
ἔμπροσθεν (adverb or prep. + gen.)
before; οἱ ἔμπροσθεν
ancestors 57
ἐν (+ dat.) in on, among 4
ἐναντιόομαι (+ dat.) oppose,
forbid 58
ἐναντίος, -α, -ον opposite 38
ἐνταῦθα (adverb) there, in that
place, to that place; here; then
29
ἐντυγχάνω (+ dat.) meet 58
ἔξεστι(ν) (+ dat.) it is possible 16
ἐπαινέω praise, approve 24

ἔπαινος, -ου, ὁ praise, approval 55

ἐπεί, ἐπειδή when, since 12

ἐπί (+ gen.) on, upon; in the time of (+ dat.) at, by; for the purpose of (+ acc.) to, toward; against (in hostile sense) 19

ἐπιβουλεύω (+ dat.) plot against 29

ἐπιθυμέω (+ gen. or infin. or infin. & subj. acc.) desire 51

ἐπιλανθάνομαι (+ gen.) forget 29

ἐπιμελέομαι (+ gen.) take care (of), care for 35

ἐπιμελέομαι (+ gen.) take care (of), care for 35

ἐπινοέω have in mind, intend 47

ἐπίσταμαι know (as a fact), know how (+ infin.) 53

ἐπιστολή, -ῆς, ἡ letter 46

ἐπιτίθημι place upon, apply, impose 54

ἐπιτρέπω entrust, permit 51

ἐπιχειρέω put one's hand to, attempt 58

ἕπομαι (+ dat.) follow 12

ἐργάζομαι do (something to someone; + two accusatives), perform, make 49

ἔργον, -ου, τό work, deed 35

ἔρομαι ask 47

ἔρχομαι come; go 11

ἐρῶ say, tell, speak 34

ἐρωτάω ask 47

ἕτερος, -α, -ον (with art.) the other (of two); (without article) another, other 59

ἔτι still 35

ἕτοιμος, -η, -ον ready, prepared 42

ἔτος, -ους, τό year 25

εὖ well 14

εὐδαιμονία, -ας, ἡ good fortune, prosperity, happiness 49

εὐδαίμων, -ον fortunate, prosperous, happy 38

εὖ πράττειν (to) fare well 14

εὑρίσκω find 28

εὐσεβής, -ές pious, righteous 60

εὔχομαι pray (for), vow, boast 47

ἐφίστημι (+ dat.) place upon, set over 52

ἐχθρός, -οῦ, ὁ (personal) enemy 27

ἐχθρός, -ά, -όν hostile 27

ἔχειν χάριν thank, give thanks (to), feel grateful 21

ἔχω have 5; (+ infin.) be able, can; (+ adv.) be 16 & 42

ἕως as long as, until 12

ζάω live, be alive 57

Ζεύς, Διός, ὁ Zeus 33

ζητέω seek, search for 23

ἤ or, than 25

ἦ (sign of a question) 48

ἤ . . . ἤ either . . . or 25

ἡγέομαι (+ gen.) lead; be leader of; (dat.) be leader for; think, consider 32

ἤδη already, now 44

ἥδομαι (+ dat.) be pleased (with) 25

ἡδονή, -ῆς, ἡ pleasure, enjoyment 39

ἡδύς, -εῖα, -ύ sweet, pleasant 38

ἦθος, -ους, τό character 60

ἥκιστα least; not at all 56

ἥκω have come, come, arrive 43

ἡλικία, -ας, ἡ time of life, age, maturity 53

ἥλιος, -ου, ὁ sun 8

ἡμέρα, -ας, ἡ day 25

ἡμέτερος, -α, -ον our, ours 52

ἤν if 37

ἦ δ' ὅς he said 51

ἦν δ' ἐγώ I said 51

ἥττων, -ον inferior, weaker; ἧττον
less 56

θάλαττα, -ης, ἡ sea 18
θάνατος, -ου, ὁ death 3
θάπτω bury 13
θάττων, -ον swifter, faster 41
θαυμάζω admire, wonder (at), be
amazed 34
θεός, -οῦ, ὁ god 3
θυγάτηρ, -τρός, ἡ daughter 22
θύω sacrifice 24

ἰατρός, -οῦ, ὁ doctor 13
ἵημι let go, throw, send 52;
(mid.) hasten, rush; be eager (+
gen. or infin.) 53
ἱκανός, -ή, -όν sufficient,
enough, competent 48
ἵνα in order that 37
ἵππος, -ου, ὁ horse 3
ἴσος, -η, -ον equal 39
ἵστημι cause to stand, set (up), place
52;
(mid.) stand 53
ἴσως equally; perhaps 44

καί and; even, also 3
καί ... καί both ... and 49
καίπερ (+ part.) although 28
καίτοι and yet 48
κακός, -ή, -όν bad, evil 9
κακῶς badly 14
καλέω call, summon; (pass.) be
called (often with two
nominatives) 27
καλός, -ή, -όν beautiful, fine,
honorable, handsome 9
κατά (+ gen.) down from; down
under; against
(acc.) down along;
throughout; according to;
opposite; by (distrib.) 29

καταγιγνώσκω (+ gen. & acc.)
condemn 49
κατηγορέω (+ gen. & acc.) accuse
17
κατηγορία, -ας, ἡ accusation 17
κατήγορος, -ου, ὁ accuser 17
κελεύω order, command 6
κέρδος, -ους, τό gain, profit 22
κῆρυξ, -υκος, ὁ herald 20
κίνδυνος, -ου, ὁ danger 5
κλέος, _____, τό fame, glory 42
κλέπτω steal 2
κλώψ, κλωπός, ὁ thief 20
κοινός, -ή, -όν common 39
κρατέω (+ gen.) be strong, rule, be
master of 55
κράτος, -ους, τό power, might
55
κρείττων, -ον better, stronger 41
κρίνω judge 23
κτάομαι acquire 24
Κῦρος, -ου, ὁ Cyrus 46
κωλύω hinder, prevent 16

Λακεδαιμόνιος, -α, -ον
Lacedaemonian 46
λαμβάνω take, seize; receive 11
λανθάνω (+ part.) escape the notice
of 29
λέγω say, speak 4
λείπω leave 4
λίθος, -ου, ὁ stone 6
λόγος, -ου, ὁ word; speech; reason
3
λύω destroy, release, set free; (mid.)
ransom 8

μακρός, -ά, -όν long 41
μάλα very 43
μάλιστα most, certainly, very much,
especially 43
μανθάνω learn (by study);
understand 34
μαρτυρέω bear witness, testify 59

μάρτυς, -υρος, ὁ witness 59
μάχη, -ης, ἡ battle, fight 32
μάχομαι (+ dat.) fight (with) 33
μεγάλως loudly 43
μᾶλλον rather, more 25
μέγας, μεγάλη, μέγα large, great 9
μειράκιον, -ου, τό youth, boy, young man 55
μέλει it is a care 48
μελετάω attend to, study, practice 56
μέλλω (+ fut. infin.) be about (to), intend (to), be likely (to), be going (to) 6
μέμνημαι (+ gen.) remember 34
μέμφομαι blame, find fault with 16
μέντοι however; of course 46
μένω remain, stay, wait (for) 23
μέρος, -ους, τό part, portion 39
μετά (+ gen.) with; (+ acc.) after 8
μεταπέμπω (usually in mid.) summon, send for 46
μέχρι (+ gen.) as far as, until, up to 58
μή not 13, 16
μήν in fact 53
μήν, μηνός, ὁ month 57
μήτηρ, -τρός, ἡ mother 22
μικρός, -ά, -όν small, little, short 41
μισέω hate 35
μισθός, -οῦ, ὁ pay; reward 51
μνᾶ, -ᾶς, ἡ mina 59
μόγις hardly, scarcely, with difficulty 41
μοῖρα, -ας, ἡ fate, destiny, portion 18
μόνος, -η, -ον alone, only 48
μῶν (= μὴ οὖν) (sign of a question, expecting a negative answer) 48

ναῦς, νεώς, ἡ ship 22
νεανίας, -ου, ὁ young man, youth 18
νέμεσις, -εως, ἡ retribution, vengeance 39
νέος, -α, -ον young; new; strange 11
νῆσος, -ου, ἡ island 5
νικάω conquer, win 19
νίκη, -ης, ἡ victory 13
νομίζω regard as a custom; think, consider; believe in, believe 32
νόμος, -ου, ὁ law, custom 13
νόσος, -ου, ἡ disease 5
νοῦς, νοῦ, ὁ mind, intelligence, sense 54
νῦν now, at this time 37
νυν (connective; no temporal significance) now 48
νύξ, νυκτός, ἡ night 31

ξένος, -ου, ὁ guest-friend, stranger 13
Ξενοφῶν, -ῶντος, ὁ Xenophon 46

ὀβολός, -οῦ, ὁ obol 59
ὅδε, ἥδε, τόδε this 12
ὁδός, -οῦ, ἡ road 5
ὅθεν from where 49
οἷ where 49
οἱ τότε ... οἱ νῦν men of old ... men of today 43
οἶδα know (by reflection) 34
οἰκέω live (in), inhabit 33
οἰκία, -ας, ἡ house 7
οἶνος, -ου, ὁ wine 5
οἴομαι (οἶμαι) think, suppose 32
οἷος, -α, -ον of what sort, such as 56
οἷός, -ά, -όν τε εἶναι (+ infin.) be able, can 16
ὀλίγος, -η, -ον (a) little; (pl.) few 39

ὀλίγου almost 39

ὅλος, -η, -ον whole 25

ὅμοιος, -α, -ον like, similar 39

ὁμολογέω (+ dat.) agree (with) 57

ὄνομα, -ατος, τό name, reputation 24

ὄντι, τῷ in fact, really, actually 28

ὁπόθεν from where 49

ὅποι where 49

ὁπότε when 49

ὅπου where 49

ὅπως in order that 37
    that; how 48

ὁράω see 19

ὀρθός, -ή, -όν straight, upright; right, correct 54

ὅρος, ὅρου, ὁ boundary, standard 54

ὅς, ἥ, ὅ who, which, that 35

ὅσος, -η, -ον how great, as great as, how far; (pl.) how many, as many as 54

ὅστις, ἥτις, ὅ τι whoever, he who, anyone who, who, whatever, what 49

ὁστισοῦν, ὁτιοῦν anyone (anything) whatever, anyone (anything) at all 59

ὅτι that; because 34;
    (+ superl.) as ... as possible 41

οὐ (οὐκ, οὐχ) not 3

οὐ μόνον ... ἀλλὰ καί not only ... but also 52

οὗ where 49

οὐδέ (μηδέ) and not (and ... not), not even, not ... either 31

οὐδείς (μηδείς), οὐδεμία no one, no 31

οὐδέν (μηδέν) nothing; in no way, not at all 31

οὐκοῦν (sign of a question) 48

οὖν therefore, now, well, then 33

οὔποτε (μήποτε) never 23

οὐρανός, -οῦ, ὁ heaven, sky 4

οὔτε (μήτε) ... οὔτε (μήτε) neither ... nor 35

οὗτος, αὕτη, τοῦτο this 12

οὕτως (οὕτω) so, in such a way 19

ὀφθαλμός, -οῦ, ὁ eye 54

πάθος, -ους, τό experience, suffering 44

παιδεύω educate 2

παιδίον, -ου, τό (little) child 5

παῖς, παιδός, ὁ, ἡ child, boy, girl 23

πάλαι long ago, for a long time 44

πάλιν back, back again 47

πάνυ very; by all means 49

παρά (+ gen.) from (the side of)
    (+ dat.) at (the side of)
    (+ acc.) to (the side of); along (the side of); contrary to 14

παράδειγμα, -ατος, τό example, precedent 39

παρασκευάζω prepare; (mid. – intrans.) make preparations 29

πάρειμι be present 27

παρέχω provide, furnish 7

πᾶς, πᾶσα, πᾶν every, all 31

πάσχω suffer 11

πατήρ, -τρός, ὁ father 22

πατρίς, -ίδος, ἡ fatherland, country 21

παύω stop 8; (mid.) cease 11

πεδίον, -ου, τό plain 24

πείθω persuade 5; (mid. + dat.) obey 11

πειράομαι try, attempt 19

πέμπω send 4

πέντε five 25

πεντεκαίδεκα fifteen 55

περί (+ gen.) about, concerning
    (+ acc.) about, around 14

Περικλῆς, -έους, ὁ Pericles 55

πίπτω fall; fall out, turn out 39

πιστεύω (+ dat.) trust 7

πιστός, -ή, -όν faithful 38
πλεῖστος, -η, -ον most 41
πλείων, -ον more 41
πλέω sail 29
πλῆθος, -ους, τό largest part,
     multitude, majority, mob 44
πλήν (+ gen.) except 48
πλοῦτος, -ου, ὁ wealth 6
πόθεν from where 49
ποθεν from somewhere 49
ποῖ where, to what place 49
ποιεῖσθαι, περὶ πολλοῦ
     consider important 42
ποιέω make, do 17
ποῖος, -α, -ον what kind of 57
πολέμιοι, -ων, οἱ enemy 28
πολέμιος, -α, -ον hostile 28
πόλεμος, -ου, ὁ war 6
πόλις, -εως, ἡ city, city-state 22
πολίτης, -ου, ὁ citizen 18
πολλάκις often, many times 35
πολύς, πολλή, πολύ much, (pl.)
     many 9
πονηρός, -ά, -όν worthless, base,
     bad 49
πορεία, -ας, ἡ journey 46
πορεύομαι go, march, proceed,
     advance 14
πόσος, -η, -ον how much, how
     great, (pl.) how many 57
ποταμός, -οῦ, ὁ river 4
πότε when 49
ποτε at some (any) time, ever, once
     49
πότερον whether 49
πότερον ... ἤ (sign of a double
     question) 48
ποῦ where, in what place 49
που somewhere, anywhere;
     perhaps, I suppose 49
πρᾶγμα, -ατος, τό deed, act; (pl.)
     trouble 23
πράττω do; make; achieve 14
πρίν before; until 55

πρό (+ gen.) before; instead of, on
     behalf of 43
πρόθυμος, -ον willing, eager 46
πρός (+ gen.) in the presence of, in
     the sight of, in the name of,
     on the side of; like
     (characteristic of); by (agency)
     (+ dat.) near; in addition to
     (+ acc.) to , towards; with
     regard to; against 27
πρότερον formerly, before 38
πρῶτον first, at first, for the first
     time 33
πρῶτος, -η, -ον first 9
πύλαι, -ῶν, αἱ gates; mountain
     pass 43
πυνθάνομαι (+ gen. & acc.) learn
     (by hearsay or inquiry), inquire
     33
πω yet, up to this time 53
πώποτε ever 59
πῶς how 48
πως somehow 49

ῥᾴδιος, -α, -ον easy 41
ῥήτωρ, -ορος, ὁ speaker, orator
     21
ῥίπτω throw, throw away 43

σαφής, -ές clear, plain, distinct 49
σεαυτοῦ, -ῆς yourself 38
σιγάω be silent 48
σκοπέω consider, examine 57
σός, -ή, -όν your, yours (sg.) 52
σοφός, -ή, -όν wise 9
σπεύδω hasten, hurry 2
στάδιον, -ου, τό stade 25
στρατηγός, -οῦ, ὁ general 6
στρατιά, -ᾶς, ἡ army, expedition
     7
στρατιώτης, -ου, ὁ soldier 18
σύ you (sg.); ὑμεῖς you (pl.) 16
συγχωρέω (+ dat.) agree, concede
     54

συμβαίνω agree; happen 58

συμβουλεύω (+ dat.) advise; (mid.) consult (with), ask the advice of 29

σύμμαχος, -ου, ὁ ally 13

συμφορά, -ᾶς, ἡ misfortune, chance 37

σύν (+ dat.) with 19

σύνειμι (+ dat.) be with, associate with 49

σφάττω slay, kill 14

σφόδρα (adverb) very, very much 51

σῴζω save, bring safely 8

Σωκράτης, -ους, ὁ Socrates 22

σῶμα, -ατος, τό body 24

τάλαντον, -ου, τό talent 59

τάττω draw up, station, arrange, assign 24

ταχύς, -εῖα, -ύ swift, fast 38

τε ... καί both ... and 14

τεκμήριον, -ου, τό sign, proof, evidence 48

τελευτάω finish; die 58

τέλος, -ους, τό end, result, outcome 27

τέλος (adv.) finally, at last 27

τέτταρες, -α four 55

τηλικόσδε, -ήδε, -όνδε of such an age, so old, so young 56

τηλικοῦτος, -αύτη, -οῦτον of such an age, so old, so young 56

τίθημι put, place; make (with persons) 52

τιμάω honor 19

τιμή, -ῆς, ἡ honor 8

τιμωρέω avenge; (mid.) punish, take vengeance on 28

τινες, τινα certain, some, any 31

τίς who (?), τί what?, why? 31

τις, τι a, a certain, someone, anyone, certain, some, any, something, anything 31

τίς ποτε who in the world 49

τί ποτε what in the world 49

τοι you know, you see, I tell you 56

τοιόσδε, -άδε, -όνδε such as this, such as follows 55

τοιοῦτος, -αύτη, -οῦτο(ν) such 53

τολμάω dare 19

τοσοῦτος, -αύτη, -οῦτο(ν) so great, so much; (pl.) so many 53

τότε then, at that time 43

τράπεζα, -ης, ἡ table; bank 18

τρεῖς, τρία three 55

τρέπω turn 12

τρέφω nourish, raise, support 44

τρέχω run 42

τριάκοντα thirty 55

τριήρης, -ους, ἡ trireme 22

τρόπος, -ου, ὁ character, way, manner 24

τυγχάνω (+ part.) happen; (+ gen.) gain, hit, meet 29

τύπτω beat, strike 52

τύραννος, -ου, ὁ tyrant 39

τῷ ὄντι in fact, really, actually 28

ὕβρις, -εως, ἡ insolence, arrogance 44

υἱός, -οῦ, ὁ son 3

ὑμέτερος, -α, -ον your, yours (pl.) 52

ὑπέρ (+ gen.) over, above, on behalf of
    (+ acc.) beyond, in excess of 44

ὑπισχνέομαι promise 17

ὑπό (+ gen.) by, at the hands of; under
    (+ acc.) under (motion) 11

ὑπολαμβάνω take up; suppose, interrupt, reply 54

φαίνω show, reveal; (mid.) appear 17

φανερός, -ά, -όν evident, conspicuous, manifest 57

φάρμακον, -ου, τό remedy, medicine, drug 54

φείδομαι (+ gen.) spare 13

φέρω carry, bring, bear 44

φεύγω flee, escape, avoid 11

φημί say 32

φθόνος, -ου, ὁ jealousy, envy, hatred 17

φιλέω love 35

φίλιος, -α, -ον friendly 38

φίλος, -η, -ον dear 38

φίλος, -ου, ὁ friend 3

φόνος, -ου, ὁ murder 28

φρονέω have understanding, think, mean 54

φρόνιμος, -ον reasonable, prudent, sensible 60

φροντίζω (+ acc.) consider, ponder; (+ gen.) think about, take thought for 58

φύλαξ, -ακος, ὁ guard 31

φυλάττω guard 6

χαλεπός, -ή, -όν difficult 47

χάρις, -ιτος, ἡ favor, goodwill 21

χειμών, -ῶνος, ὁ storm, winter 21

χράομαι (+ dat.) use; enjoy; treat; consult (an oracle) 19

χρή it is necessary, must, ought 47

χρῆμα, -ατος, τό thing; (pl.) things, property, money 22

χρησμός, -οῦ, ὁ oracle, oracular response 41

χρηστός, -ή, -όν useful, good 49

χρόνος, -ου, ὁ time 4

χρυσίον, -ου, τό gold 8

χώρα, -ας, ἡ country, land 8

ψεύδω deceive; (mid.) lie 16

ψυχή, -ῆς, ἡ soul 8

ὦ (with voc.) O, oh 33

ὧδε thus, as follows, in the following manner 51

ὡς (+ fut. part.) as if, with the avowed purpose of 27 (+ part. except future) on the grounds that, as if 28 (+ ind. stat.) that 34 (+ indic.) as, since, when 37 (+ superl.) as . . . as possible 41 (+ adj. or adv.) how 60 (+ numerals) about 60 (+ noun) as 60

ὥσπερ just as, just as if (+ εἰ or part.); as it were 55

ὥστε that, so that; (+ infin.) as (to); so as (to); so that 19

ὠφελέω help, aid 42

ὠφέλιμος, -ον helpful, beneficial 60

able, be ἔχω 16
   οἷος τε 16
   δύναμαι 53
about (to), be μέλλω (+ fut. infin.) 6
about περί (+gen. or acc.) 14
   (with numerals) 60
abstain from ἀπέχομαι (+ gen) 25
accept δέχομαι 12
accompany ἀκολουθέω (+ dat.) 46
according to κατά (+ acc.) 29
account of, on διά (+ acc.) 8
accusation κατηγορία, -ας, ἡ 17
accuse κατηγορέω (+ acc. & gen.) 17
accuser κατήγορος, -ου, ὁ 17
achieve πράττω 14
acquire κτάομαι 24
actually 23
   τῷ ὄντι 28
act violently βιάζομαι 56
addition to, in πρός (+ dat.) 27
admire θαυμάζω 34
advance πορεύομαι 14
advise συμβουλεύω (+ dat.) 29
afraid (of), be δέδοικα 37
   φοβέομαι 37
after μετά (+ acc.) 8
against ἐπί (+ acc.) 19
   πρός (+ acc.) 27
   κατά (+ gen.) 29
agree (with) συγχωρέω (+ dat.) 54
   ὁμολογέω (+ dat.) 57
aid ὠφελέω 42
Alcibiades Ἀλκιβιάδης, -ου, ὁ 55
alive, be βιόω 57
   ζάω 57
all πᾶς, πᾶσα, πᾶν 31
   ἅπας, ἅπασα, ἅπαν 48
allow ἐάω 33
ally σύμμαχος, -ου, ὁ 13
almost ὀλίγου 39
along παρά (acc.) 14

already ἤδη 44
also καί 3
although καίπερ (+ part.) 28
always ἀεί 35
amazed, be θαυμάζω 34
among ἐν (+ dat.) 4
ancestors οἱ ἔμπροσθεν 57
ancient ἀρχαῖος, α, -ον 46
and καί 3
   δέ 6
and not οὐδέ 31
and yet καίτοι 48
announce ἀγγέλλω 27
another ἄλλος, -η, -ο 28
   ἕτερος, -α, -ον 59
answer ἀποκρίνομαι 34
any τις, τι 31
anyone τις 31
anyone whatever ὁστισοῦν 59
anyone who ὅστις 49
Apollo Ἀπόλλω, -ωνος, ὁ 33
appear φαίνομαι 17
apply ἐπιτίθημι 54
army στρατιά, -ᾶς, ἡ 7
around περί (+ acc.) 14
arrive (at) ἀφικνέομαι 24
   ἥκω 43
arrogance ὕβρις, -εως, ἡ 44
as ὡς (+ indic.) 37
   ὡς (+ noun) 60
as ... as possible ὅτι (+ superl.) 41
   ὡς (+ superl.) 41
as if (to) ὡς (+ part) 28
as it seems ἄρα 51
ask δέομαι (+ gen.) 29
   ἔρομαι 47
   ἐρωτάω 47
ask (for) αἰτέω 27
as long as ἕως 12
as many as ὅσοι, -αι, -α 54
assembly ἐκκλησία, -ας, ἡ 48
associate with (+ dat.) σύνειμι 49
at ἐπι (+ dat.) 19
   παρά (+ dat.) 14

Athenian Ἀθηναῖος, -α, -ον 13
Athens Ἀθῆναι, -ῶν, αἱ 14
at last τέλος 27
at least γε 48
at some time ποτε 49
attempt ἐπιχειρέω 58
at that time τότε 43
at the hands of ὑπό (+ gen.) 11
avenge τιμωρέω 28
avoid φεύγω 11
away, be ἀπέχω 25
away from ἀπό (+ gen.) 4

back πάλιν 47
bad κακός, -ή, -όν 9
    πονηρός, -ά, -όν 49
badly κακῶς 14
bank τράπεζα, -ης, ἡ 18
barbarians βάρβαροι, -ων, οἱ 33
base πονηρός, -ά, -όν 49
battle μάχη, -ης, ἡ 32
be γίγνομαι 14
    εἰμί 14
    ἔχω (+ adv.) 42
be with σύνειμι (+ dat.) 49
beat τύπτω 52
beautiful καλός, -ή, -όν 9
because ὅτι 34
because of διά (+ acc.) 8
become γίγνομαι 14
before πρό (+ conj.) 55
    πρίν (adv.) 57
    ἔμπροσθεν (adv.) 57
begin ἄρχομαι (+ gen.) 11
beginning ἀρχή, -ῆς, ἡ 44
behalf of, on πρό (+ gen.) 43
    ὑπέρ (+ gen) 44
believe ἀξιόω 51
believe in νομίζω 32
beneficial ὠφέλιμος, -ον 60
best ἄριστος, -η, -ον 41
    βέλτιστος, -η, -ον 41

better ἀμείνων, -ον 41
    βελτίων, -ον 41
    κρείττων, -ον 41
beyond ὑπέρ (+ acc.) 44
birth γένος, -ους, τό 24
blame μέμφομαι 16
    αἰτιάομαι 47
boast εὔχομαι 47
body σῶμα, -ατος, τό 24
book βιβλίον, -ου, τό 5
born, be γίγνομαι 14
both ... and τε ... καί 14
boy παῖς, παιδός, ὁ 23
    μειράκιον, -ου, τό 55
brave ἀγαθός, -ή, -όν 31
bravest ἄριστος, -η, -ον 41
bridge γέφυρα, -ας, ἡ 18
bring ἄγω 2
    φέρω 44
bring an indictment (against)
    γραφὴν γράφεσθαι (+ acc. of
    person) 57
bring safely σῴζω 8
brother ἀδελφός, -οῦ, ὁ 3
bury θάπτω 13
but ἀλλά 6
    δέ 6
by ὑπό (+ gen.) 11
    ἐπί (+ dat.) 19
by (distrib.) κατά (+ acc.) 29

call καλέω 27
call out βοάω 43
can ἔχω 16
    οἷός, -ά, -όν τε 16
    δύναμαι 53
capture αἱρέω 17
captured, be ἁλίσκομαι 46
care for ἐπιμελέομαι (+ gen.) 35
care, it is a μέλει 48
carry φέρω 44
case δίκη, -ης, ἡ 7
caught, be ἁλίσκομαι 46
cause αἴτιον, -ου, τό 53

cease παύομαι 11

character τρόπος, -ου, ὁ 24

 ἦθος, -κους, τό 60

chariot ἅρμα, -ατος, τό 51

child παῖς, παιδός, ὁ 23

child, little παιδίον, -ου, τό 5

choose αἱρέομαι 17

citizen πολίτης, -ου, ὁ 18

city πόλις, -εως, ἡ 22

clear δῆλος, -η, -ον 38

 σαφής, -ες 49

clever δεινός, -ή, -όν 9

collect ἀθροίζω 23

come ἔρχομαι 11

 ἥκω 43

come, have ἥκω 43

command κελεύω 6

common κοινός, -ή, -όν 39

compel ἀναγκάζω 56

concerning περί (+ gen.) 14

condemn καταγιγνώσκω (+ gen.
 of person, acc. of thing) 49

conquer νικάω 19

consider ἡγέομαι 32

 νομίζω 32

 σκοπέω 57

 φροντίζω 58

consider important περὶ πολλοῦ
 ποιεῖσθαι 42

constrain βιάζομαι 56

consult (an oracle) χράομαι (+ dat.)
 19

consult (with) συμβουλεύομαι (+
 dat.) 29

continue διατελέω (+ suppl. part.)
 58

contrary to παρά (+ acc.) 14

converse (with) διαλέγομαι (+ dat.)
 55

convicted, be ἁλίσκομαι 46

correct ὀρθός, -ή, -όν 54

corrupt διαφθείρω 2

country χώρα, -ας, ἡ 8

 πατρίς, -ίδος, ἡ 21

 γῆ, -ῆς, ἡ 29

court δίκη, -ης, ἡ 7

custom νόμος, -ου, ὁ 13

Cyrus Κῦρος, -ου, ὁ 46

danger κίνδυνος, -ου, ὁ 5

dare τολμάω 19

daughter θυγάτηρ, -ρός, ἡ 22

day ἡμέρα, -ας, ἡ 25

dear φίλος, -η, -ον 38

death θάνατος, -ου, ὁ 3

deceive ψεύδω 16

dedicate ἀνατίθημι 56

deed πρᾶγμα, -ατος, τό 23

 ἔργον, -ου, τό 35

defense ἀπολογία, -ας, ἡ 58

defend oneself ἀπολογέομαι 35

deliberate βουλεύομαι 11

Delphi Δελφοί, -ῶν, οἱ 46

demand αἰτέω 27

describe διηγέομαι 60

desire ἐπιθυμέω 51

destiny μοῖρα, -ας 51

destroy λύω 8

 ἀπόλλυμι 60

die ἀποθνῄσκω 17

 τελευτάω 58

 ἀπόλλυμι 60

different ἀλλοῖος, -α, -ον 57

difficult χαλεπός, -ή, -όν 47

disease νόσος, -ου, ἡ 5

disgraceful αἰσχρός, -ά, -όν 48

divine sign δαιμόνιον, -ου, τό
 58

do πράττω 14

 ποιέω 17

 ἐργάζομαι (+ 2 acc.) 49

do wrong (to) ἀδικέω 17

doctor ἰατρός, -οῦ, ὁ 13

down along κατά (+ acc.) 29

down from κατά (+ gen.) 29

down under κατά (+ gen.) 29
drachma δραχμή, -ῆς, ἡ 59
draw up τάττω 24

each ἕκαστος, -η, -ον 35
each other ἀλλήλων 43
eager, be ἵεμαι 53
eagerly προθύμως 46
earth γῆ, -ῆς, ἡ 29
easy ῥᾴδιος, -α, -ον 41
educate παιδεύω 2
either ... or ἤ ... ἤ 25
enemy πολέμιοι, -ων, οἱ 28
enemy (personal) ἐχθρός, -κοῦ, ὁ
    28
enjoy χράομαι (+ dat.) 19
entrust ἐπιτρέπω 51
envy φθόνος, -ου, ὁ 17
equal ἴσος, -κη, -κον 39
equally ἴσως 44
err ἁμαρτάνω (+ gen.) 41
escape φεύγω 11
escape the notice of λανθάνω (+
    part.) 29
escape-route διέξοδος, -ου, ἡ 41
even καί 3
ever πώποτε 59
every ἅπας, ἅπασα, ἅπαν 48
evidence τεκμήριον, -ου, τό 48
evident δῆλος, -η, -ον 38
    φανερός, -ά, -όν 57
evil κακός, -ή, -όν 9
example παράδειγμα, -ατος, τό
    39
excellence ἀρετή, -ῆς, ἡ 7
except (+ gen.) πλήν 48
expect ἐλπίζω 32
    ἀξιόω 51
expectation δόξα, -ης, ἡ 59
expedition στρατιά, -ᾶς, ἡ 7
experience πάθος, -ους, τό 44
explain φράζω 55
eye ὀφθαλμός, -οῦ, ὁ 54

fact, in δή 23
    τῷ ὄντι 28
    μήν 53
faithful πιστός, -ή, -όν 38
fall πίπτω 39
fame κλέος, _____, τό 42
fare badly κακῶς 14
fare well πράττειν εὖ 14
fast ταχύς, -εῖα, -ύ 38
faster θάττων, -ον 41
fate μοῖρα, -ας, ἡ 18
father πατήρ, -τρός, ὁ 22
fatherland πατρίς, -ίδος, ἡ 21
favor χάρις, -ιτος, ἡ 21
fear δέδοικα 37
fearful δεινός, -ή, -όν 9
feel grateful χάριν ἔχειν 21
fight (with) μάχομαι (+ dat.) 33
finally τέλος 27
find εὑρίσκω 28
fine καλός, -ή, -όν 9
first πρῶτος, -η, -ον 9
    πρῶτον (adv.) 33
five πέντε 25
flee φεύγω 11
follow ἕπομαι (+ dat.) 12
    ἀκολουθέω (+ dat.) 46
following manner, in the ὧδε (adv.)
    51
follows, as ὧδε (adv.) 51
follows, such as τοιόσδε 55
for γάρ 6
for the purpose of ἐπί (+ dat.) 19
forbid ἐναντιόομαι (+ dat.) 58
force ἀναγκάζω 56
    βιάζομαι 56
    βία, -ας, ἡ 56
foreign βάρβαρος, -ον 33
foreigners βάρβαροι, -ων, οἱ 33
forget ἐπιλανθάνομαι (+ gen.) 29
fortunate εὐδαίμων, -ον 38
four τέτταρες, -α 55
free ἐλεύθερος, -α, -ον 42

freedom ἐλευθερία, -ας, ἡ 42
friend φίλος, -ου, ὁ 3
friend (guest-friend) ξένος, -ου, ὁ 13
friendly φίλιος, -α, -ον 38
from ἀπό (+ gen.) 4
 ἐκ (+ gen.) 13
 παρά (+ gen.) 14
from where ὅθεν 49
 ὁπόθεν 49
furnish παρέχω 7

gain κέρδος, -ους, τό 22
 τυγχάνω (+ gen.) 29
gates πύλαι, -ῶν, αἱ 43
general στρατηγός, -οῦ, ὁ 6
gift δῶρον, -ου, τό 5
give δίδωμι 52
give thanks χάριν ἔχειν 21
glory κλέος, ____, τό 42
go ἔρχομαι 11
 εἶμι 47
go across διαβαίνω 47
god θεός, -οῦ, ὁ 3
going (to), be μέλλω 6
gold χρυσίον, -ου, τό 8
good ἀγαθός, -ή, -όν 31
go up ἀναβαίνω 46
government ἀρχή, -ῆς, ἡ 44
great μέγας, μεγάλη, μέγα 9
Greece Ἑλλάς, -άδος, ἡ 54
Greek Ἕλλην, -ος, ὁ 21
ground γῆ, -ῆς, ἡ 29
grounds that, on the ὡς (+ part.) 28
guard φυλάττω 6
 φύλαξ, -ακος, ὁ 31
guest-friend ξένος, -ου, ὁ 13

hands of, at the ὑπό (+ gen.) 11
handsome καλός, -ή, -όν 9
happen γίγνομαι 14
 τυγχάνω (+ part.) 29
 συμβαίνω 58

happiness εὐδαιμονία, -ας, ἡ 49
happy εὐδαίμων, -ον 38
harm βλάπτω 2
hasten σπεύδω 2
hate μισέω 35
hatred φθόνος, -ου, ὁ 17
have ἔχω 5
have in mind ἐπινοέω 47
 διανοέομαι 59
hear ἀκούω (+ gen.) 11
heaven οὐρανός, -οῦ, ὁ 4
help ὠφελέω 42
herald κῆρυξ, -υκος, ὁ 21
here ἐνταῦθα 29
himself ἑαυτοῦ 38
hinder κωλύω 16
hit βάλλω 23
 τυγχάνω (+ gen.) 29
honor τιμή, -ῆς, ἡ 8
 τιμάω 19
honorable καλός, -ή, -όν 9
hope ἐλπίς, -ίδος, ἡ 47
hope (for) ἐλπίζω 32
horse ἵππος, -ου, ὁ 3
hostile ἐχθρός, -ά, -όν 27
 πολέμιος, -α, -ον 28
house οἰκία, -ας, ἡ 7
how πῶς 48
 ὅπως 48
 ὡς 49
however μέντοι 46
how many πόσοι, -αι, -α 57
hurry σπεύδω 2
hurt βλάπτω 2
husband ἀνήρ, -δρός, ὁ 22

I ἐγώ 16
I tell you τοι 56
if εἰ 13
 ἐάν, ἤν, ἄν 37
if only εἰ γάρ 44
 εἴθε 44
illegal conduct ἀνομία, -ας, ἡ 56

imagine δοκέω 32
immortal ἀθάνατος, -ον 9
important, consider περὶ πολλοῦ
    ποιεῖσθαι 42
in ἐν (+ dat.) 27
in addition to πρός (+ dat.) 27
indeed δῆτα 49
independent αὐταρκής, -ές 60
indict γραφὴν γράφεσθαι (+ acc.
    of person) 57
in fact δή 23
    τῷ ὄντι 28
    μήν 53
inhabit οἰκέω 33
injure ἀδικέω 17
injury ἀδικία, -ας, ἡ 17
injustice ἀδικία, -ας, ἡ 17
in order (to/that) ἵνα 37
    ὅπως 37
    ὡς
inquire πυνθάνομαι (+ gen. & acc.)
    33
in return for ἀντί (+ gen.) 53
insolence ὕβρις, -εως, ἡ 44
instead of πρό (+ gen.) 43
    ἀντί (+ gen.) 53
intelligence νοῦς, -οῦ, ὁ 54
intend μέλλω 6
    ἐπινοέω 47
    διανοέομαι 59
in the following manner ὧδε (adv.)
    51
in the name of πρός (+ gen.) 27
in the time of ἐπί (+ gen.) 19
into εἰς (+ acc.) 4
island νῆσος, -ου, ἡ 5

jealousy φθόνος, -ου, ὁ 17
journey πορεία, -ας, ἡ 46
judge δικαστής, -οῦ, ὁ 18
    κρίνω 23
judgment γνώμη, -ης, ἡ 7
juror δικαστής, -οῦ, ὁ 18
just δίκαιος, -α, -ον 9

just as ὥσπερ 55
justice δίκη, -ης, ἡ 7
just now ἄρτι 53

keep away ἀπέχω 25
kill σφάττω 14
    ἀποκτείνω 17
killed, be ἀποθνήσκω 17
kind of, what ποῖος, -α, -ον 57
king βασιλεύς, -έως, ὁ 22
know (by reflection) οἶδα 34
know (by observation) γιγνώσκω
    46
know (as a fact) ἐπίσταμαι 53
know how ἐπίσταμαι (+ infin.) 53

Lacedaemonian Λακεδαινόνιος,
    -α, -ον 46
land χώρα, -ας, ἡ 8
    γῆ, γῆς, ἡ 29
large μέγας, μεγάλη, μέγα 9
last, at τέλος 27
law νόμος, -ου, ὁ 13
lawlessness ἀνομία, -ας, ἡ 56
lead ἄγω 2
    ἡγέομαι (+ gen. or dat.) 32
learn (by hearsay or inquiry)
    πυνθάνομαι (+ gen. & acc.)
    33
learn (by perception) αἰσθάνομαι
    (+ gen. & acc.) 34
learn (by study) μανθάνω 34
least ἐλάχιστος, -η, -ον 43
    ἥκιστα (adv.) 56
leave λείπω 4
lesser ἐλάττων, -ον 43
letter ἐπιστολή, -ῆς, ἡ 46
    γράμμα, -ατος, τό 53
letters γράμματα, -άτων, τά 53
lie ψεύδομαι 16
life βίος, -ου, ὁ 4
like ὁμοῖος, -α, -ον 39
likely (to), be μέλλω 6
listen to ἀκούω (+ gen.) 11

little, a ὀλίγος, -η, -ον 39
little child παιδίον, -ου, τό 5
live βιόω 57
    ζάω 57
    διαγίγνομαι 58
live (in) οἰκέω 33
living, worth βιωτός, -ή, -όν 59
long μακρός, -ά, -όν 41
long ago πάλαι 44
lose ἀπόλλυμι 60
loss, be at a ἀπορέω 42
loudly μεγάλως 43
love φιλέω 35

majority πλῆθος, -ους, τό 44
make πράττω 14
    ποιέω 17
make (with persons) τίθημι 52
make a defense ἀπολογέομαι 35
make clear δηλόω 51
make preparations
    παρασκευάζομαι 29
man ἄνθρωπος, -ου, ὁ 3
    ἀνήρ, -δρός, ὁ 22
man, young νεανίας, -ου, ὁ 18
many πολλοί, -αί, -ά 9
many, how πόσοι, -αι, -α 57
market-place ἀγορά, -ᾶς, ἡ 7
master δεσπότης, -ου, ὁ 18
maturity ἡλικία, -ας, ἡ 53
medicine φάρμακον, -ου, τό 54
meet τυγχάνω (+ gen.) 29
    ἐντυγνάνω (+ dat.) 58
men of old ... men of
    today οἱ τότε ... οἱ νῦν 43
messenger ἄγγελος, -ου, ὁ 32
mina μνᾶ, -ᾶς, ἡ 59
mind νοῦς, -οῦ, ὁ 54
miserable δειλός, -ή, -όν 41
misfortune συμφορά, -ᾶς, ἡ 37
miss ἁμαρτάνω (+ gen.) 41
money χρήματα, -άτων, τά 22
month μήν, -ός, ὁ 57

more μᾶλλον (adv.) 25
    πλείων, -ον 41
most πλεῖστος, -η, -ον 41
mother μήτηρ, -τρός, ἡ 22
much πολύς, πολλή, πολύ 9
much, very μάλιστα (adv.) 43
    σφόδρα (adv.) 51
murder φόνος, -ου, ὁ 28
must δεῖ (+ acc.) 28
    χρή (+ acc.) 47
my ἐμός, -ή, -όν 52
myself ἐμαυτοῦ 38

name ὄνομα, -ατος, τό 24
name of, in the πρός (+ gen.) 27
near πρός (+ dat.) 27
necessary, it is δεῖ (+ acc.) 28
    χρή (+ acc.) 47
necessity ἀνάγκη, -ης, ἡ
need δέομαι (+ gen.) 29
neither ... nor οὔτε (μήτε) ... οὔτε
    (μήτε) 35
never οὔποτε (μήποτε) 23
new νέος, -α, -ον 11
night νύξ, νυκτός, ἡ 31
no οὐδείς (μηδείς), οὐδεμία
    (μηδεμία), οὐδέν (μηδέν)
    31
no one οὐδείς (μηδείς) 31
nobly, more κάλλιον 41
not οὐ (οὐκ, οὐχ) 3
    μή 13, 16
not either οὐδέ (μηδέ) 31
not even οὐδέ (μηδέ) 31
not only ... but also οὐ (μή)
    μόνον ... ἀλλὰ καί 52
not yet οὔπω (μήπω) or
    οὐ (μή) ... πω 53
nothing οὐδέν (μηδέν) 31
notice of, escape the λανθάνω (+
    part.) 29
now νῦν 37
    ἤδη 44
    νυν 48

obey πείθομαι (+ dat.) 11
obol ὀβολός, -οῦ, ὁ 59
of another kind ἀλλοῖος, -α, -ον
    57
of course μέντοι 46
        γε 48
often πολλάκις 35
old ἀρχαῖος, -α, -ον 46
old age γῆρας, -ως, τό 59
old man γέρων, -οντος, ὁ 21
old, so τηλικόσδε, -ήδε, -όνδε
    56
        τηλικοῦτος, -αύτη,
        -οῦτον 56
on ἐν (+ dat.) 4
        ἐπί (+ gen.) 19
on account of διά (+ acc.) 8
on behalf of πρό (+ gen.) 43
                ὑπέρ (+ gen.) 44
once ποτε 49
one εἷς, μία, ἕν 31
one another ἀλλήλων 43
only μόνος, -η, -ον 48
on the grounds that ὡς (+ part.) 28
opinion γνώμη, -ης, ἡ 7
oppose ἐναντιόομαι (+ dat.) 29
opposite κατά (+ acc.) 29
            ἐναντίος, -α, -ον 38
or ἤ 25
oracle χρησμός, -οῦ, ὁ 41
orator ῥήτωρ, -ορος, ὁ 21
order κελεύω 6
other ἄλλος, -η, -ο 28
other (of two) ἕτερος, -α, -ον 59
ought δεῖ (+ acc.) 28
        χρή (+ acc.) 47
our ἡμέτερος, -α, -ον 52
outcome τέλος, -ους, τό 27
out of ἐκ (+ gen.) 13

pass (of time) διαγίγνομαι 58
pay μισθός, -οῦ, ὁ 51
peace εἰρήνη, -ης, ἡ 7

perceive αἰσθάνομαι 34
        γιγνώσκω 46
perhaps ἴσως 44
Pericles Περικλῆς, -έους, ὁ 55
perish ἀπόλλυμι (mid. & 2nd perf.
    act) 60
persuade πείθω 5
pious εὐσεβής, -ές 60
place τίθημι 52
plain πεδίον, -ου, τό 24
plan βουλεύω 11
pleasant ἡδύς, -εῖα, -ύ 38
pleased, be ἥδομαι (+ dat.) 25
pleasure ἡδονή, -ῆς, ἡ 39
plot against ἐπιβουλεύω (+ dat.)
    29
point out δείκνυμι 52
ponder φράζομαι 55
portion μοῖρα, -ας, ἡ 18
        μέρος, -ους, τό 39
possible, it is ἔξεστι (+ dat.) 16
power κράτος, -ους, τό 55
practice μελετάω 56
praise ἐπαινέω 24
        ἔπαινος, -ου, ὁ 55
pray εὔχομαι 47
prefer βούλομαι 25
prejudice διαβολή, -ῆς, ἡ 7
preparations, make
        παρασκευάζομαι 29
prepare παρασκευάζω 29
present, be πάρειμι 27
prevent κωλύω 16
proceed πορεύομαι 14
profit κέρδος, -ους, τό 22
promise ὑπισχνέομαι 17
proof τεκμήριον, -ου, τό 48
property χρήματα, -άτων, τά 22
prosecute διώκω 16
prosperity εὐδαιμονία, -ας, ἡ 49
prosperous εὐδαίμων, -ον 38
prove to be γίγνομαι 14
provide παρέχω 7
prudent φρόνιμος, -ον 60

punish τιμωρέομαι 28

purpose of, with the avowed ὡς (+ fut. part.) 27

pursue διώκω 16

put to the test δοκιμάζω 60

race γένος, -ους, τό 24

raise τρέφω 44

ransom λύομαι 8

rather μᾶλλον 25

reach ἀφικνέομαι 24

read ἀναγιγνώσκω 46

ready ἕτοιμος, -η, -ον 42

really τῷ ὄντι 28

reason λόγος, -ου, ὁ 3
    αἴτιον, -ου, τό 53

receive λαμβάνω 11
    δέχομαι 12

recently ἄρτι 53

recognize γιγνώσκω 46

refer ἀνατίθημι 56

refute ἐλέγχω 42

regard to, with πρός (+ acc.) 27

release λύω 8

remain μένω 23

remember μέμνημαι (+ gen.) 34

reply ἀποκρίνομαι 34
    ὑπολαμβάνω 54

report ἀγγέλλω 27

request ἀξιόω 51

responsible (for) αἴτιον, -α, -ον 41

retract (an opinion) ἀνατίθεμαι 56

retribution νέμεσις, -εως, ἡ 39

reveal φαίνω 17
    δηλόω 51

reward μισθός, -οῦ, ὁ 51

river ποταμός, -οῦ, ὁ 4

road ὁδός, -οῦ, ἡ 5

ruin διαφθείρω 2

rule ἄρχω (+ gen.) 11
    κρατέω (+ gen.) 55
    ἀρχή, -ῆς, ἡ 44

ruler δεσπότης, -ου, ὁ 18
    ἄρχων, -οντος, ὁ 27

run τρέχω 42

rush ἵεμαι 53

sacrifice θύω 24

safe ἀσφαλής, -ές 38

said, he ἦ δ' ὅς 51

said, I ἦν δ' ἐγώ 51

sail πλέω 29

same αὐτός, -ή, -ό 16

save σώζω 8

say λέγω 4
    φήμι 32
    ἐρῶ 34

scarcely μόγις 41

sea θάλαττα, -ης, ἡ 18

search for ζητέω 23

second δεύτερος, -α, -ον 53

secure ἀσφαλής, -ές 38

see ὁράω 19

seek ζητέω 23

seem δοκέω 32

seems best, it δοκεῖ 32

seize λαμβάνω 11
    αἱρέω 17
    ἁρπάζω 23

-self αὐτός, -ή, -ό 16

self-reliant αὐτάρκης, -ές 60

self-restrained ἐγκρατής, -κές 60

send πέμπω 4
    ἵημι 52

send for μεταπέμπομαι 46

set free λύω 8

set over ἐφίστημι (+ dat.) 52

set up ἵστημι 52

shameful αἰσχρός, -ά, -όν 48

shield ἀσπίς, -ίδος, ἡ 21

ship ναῦς, νεώς, ἡ 22

shout βοάω 43

show φαίνω 17
    δηλόω 51
    δείκνυμι 52

silent, be σιγάω 48
since ἐπεί, ἐπειδή 12
 ἅτε (+ part.) 28
 ὡς 37
sky οὐρανός, -οῦ, ὁ 4
slander διαβολή, -ῆς, ἡ 7
slave δοῦλος, -ου, ὁ 41
slay σφάττω 14
small μικρός, -ά, -όν 41
so οὕτως (οὕτω) 19
Socrates Σωκράτης, -ους, ὁ 22
soldier στρατιώτης, -ου, ὁ 18
some τις, τι 31
somehow πως 49
someone τις 31
something τι 31
son υἱός, -οῦ, ὁ 3
so old τηλικόσδε, -ήδε, -όνδε 56
 τηλικοῦτος, -αύτη, -οῦτον
 56
so that ὥστε 19
soul ψυχή, -ῆς, ἡ 8
spare φείδομαι (+ gen.) 13
speak λέγω 4
 ἐρῶ 34
speech λόγος, -ου, ὁ 3
speech in defense ἀπολογία,
 -ας, ἡ 58
stade στάδιον, -ου, τό 25
stand ἵσταμαι 53
station τάττω 24
stay μένω 23
steal κλέπτω 2
still ἔτι 35
stone λίθος, -ου, ὁ 6
stop παύω 8
storm χειμών, -ῶνος, ὁ 21
strange νέος, -α, -ον 11
stranger ξένος, -ου, ὁ 13
strength βία, -ας, ἡ 56
such τοιοῦτος, -αύτη, -οῦτο 53
 τοιόσδε, -άδε, -όνδε 55
such as οἷος, -α, -ον 56

such as follows τοιόσδε, -άδε,
 -όνδε 55
such a way, in οὕτως (οὕτω) 19
suffer πάσχω 11
suffering πάθος, -ους, τό 44
sufficient ἱκανός, -ή, -όν 48
summon μεταπέμπομαι 46
sun ἥλιος, -ου, ὁ 8
suppose οἴομαι (οἶμαι) 32
 ὑπολαμβάνω 54
surely δῆτα 49
survive διαγίγνομαι 58
swift ταχύς, -εῖα, -ύ 38

table τράπεζα, -ης, talent τάλαντον, -ου
take λαμβάνω 11
 αἱρέω 17
take care (of) ἐπιμελέομαι (+ gen.)
 35
taken, be ἁλίσκομαι 46
take part in politics τὰ πολιτικὰ
 59
talent τάλαντον, -ου, τό 59
teach διδάσκω 14
tell ἐρῶ 34
tell you, I τοι 56
ten δέκα 25
terrible δεινός, -ή, -όν 9
test δοκιμάζω 60
test, put to the δοκιμάζω 60
testify μαρτυρέω 59
than ἤ 25
thank χάριν ἔχειν 21
thanks, give χάριν ἔχειν 21
that ἐκεῖνος, -η, -ο 12
 ὥστε (conj.) 19
 ὅτι (conj.), ὡς (conj.) 34
 ὅς, ἥ, ὅ 35
 ὅπως 48
then ἐνταῦθα 29
 οὖν 33
 τότε 43
there ἐνταῦθα 29

therefore οὖν 33
 ἄρα 51
thief κλώψ, -πός, ὁ 21
thing χρῆμα, -ατος, τό 22
think δοκέω 32
 ἡγέομαι 32
 νομίζω 32
 οἴομαι (οἶμαι) 32
 διανοέομαι 59
think right ἀξιόω 51
think worthy ἀξιόω 51
thirty τριάκοντα 55
this ὅδε, ἥδε, τόδε 12
 οὗτος, αὕτη, τοῦτο 12
thought γνώμη, -ης, ἡ 7
thought, be δοκέω 32
three τρεῖς, τρία 55
through διά (+ gen.) 8
throughout ἀνά (+ acc.) 60
 κατά (+ acc.) 60
throw βάλλω 23
 ῥίπτω 43
time χρόνος, -ου, ὁ 4
time, at some ποτε 49
time, at that τότε 43
time of, in the ἐπί (+ gen.) 19
time, up to this πω 53
to εἰς (+ acc.) 4
 παρά (+ acc.) 14
 ἐπί (+ acc.) 19
 πρός (+ acc.) 27
touch ἅπτομαι (+ gen.) 52
toward ἐπί (+ acc.) 19
 πρός (+ acc.) 27
treat χράομαι (+ dat.) 19
trireme τριήρης, -ους, ἡ 22
trouble πράγματα, -άτων, τά 23
true ἀληθής, -ές 23
trust πιστεύω (+ dat.) 7
truth ἀλήθεια, -ας, ἡ 18
try πειράομαι 19
turn τρέπω 12
twenty εἴκοσι 55

tyrant τύραννος, -ου, ὁ 39
under ὑπό (+ gen. or acc.) 11
understand μανθάνω 34
unjust ἄδικος, -ον 9
until ἕως 12
 πρίν 55
unwilling ἄκων, -ουσα, -ον 32
up ἀνά (+ acc.) 60
upon ἐπί (+ gen.) 19
up to μέχρι (+ gen.) 58
up to this time πω 53
use χράομαι (+ dat.) 19

victory νίκη, -ης, ἡ 13
virtue ἀρετή, -ῆς, ἡ 7

wage ἵσταμαι 52
wait (for) μένω 23
want βούλομαι 25
war πόλεμος, -ου, ὁ 6
way, in such a οὕτως (οὕτω) 19
weak ἀσθενής, -ές 42
weaker ἥττων, -ον 56
wealth πλοῦτος, -ου, ὁ 6
well εὖ 14
well then εἶεν 54
what τί 31
 ὅ τι 49
whatever ὅ τι 49
what in the world τί ποτε 49
what kind of ποῖος, -α, -ον 57
when ἐπεί, ἐπειδή 12
 ὅτε, ὁπότε 49
 ὡς 37
 πότε 49
where, from ὅθεν, ὁπόθεν, πόθεν 49
where (in what place) ποῦ, ὅπου, οὗ 49
where (to what place) ποῖ, ὅποι 49
whether εἰ 49
 πότερον 49

whether ... or εἴτε ... εἴτε 56
which ὅς, ἥ, ὅ 35
who ὅς, ἥ, ὅ 35
    ὅστις 49
    τίς 31
whoever ὅστις 49
who in the world τίς ποτε 49
whole ὅλος, -η, -ον 25
why τί 31
    ἀντί τίνος 53
wife γυνή, γυναικός, ἡ 21
willing ἑκών, -οῦσα, -όν 32
willing, be ἐθέλω 2
win νικάω 19
wine οἶνος, -ου, ὁ 5
winter χειμών, -ῶνος, ὁ 21
wise σοφός, -ή, -όν 9
wish ἐθέλω 2
with μετά (+ gen.) 8
    σύν (+ dat.) 19
without ἄνευ (+ gen.) 60
with regard to πρός (+ acc.) 27
with the avowed purpose of ὡς
    (+ fut. part.) 27
witness μάρτυς, -υρος, ὁ 59
woman γυνή, γυναικός, ἡ 21
word λόγος, -ου, ὁ 3
world, what in the τί ποτε 49
world, who in the τίς ποτε 49

worse χείρων, -ον 41
worthless πονηρός, -ά, -όν 49
worth living βιωτός, -ή, -όν 59
worthy ἄξιος, -α, -ον (+ gen.) 9
write γράφω 2
writing γράμματα, -άτων, τά 53
wrong ἀδικέω 17
    ἀδικία, -ας, ἡ 17

Xenophon Ξενοφῶν, -ῶντος, ὁ
    46

year ἔτος, -ους, τό 25
yet πω 53
yet, not οὔπω (μήπω) or οὐ (μή)
    ... πω 53
you (sg.) σύ 16
you (pl.) ὑμεῖς 16
young νέος, -α, -ον 11
young man νεανίας, -ου, ὁ 18
    μειράκιον, -κου, τό 55
your (sg.) σός, -ή, -όν 52
your (pl.) ὑμέτερος, -α, -ον 52
yourself σεαυτοῦ 38
youth νεανίας, -ου, ὁ 18
    μειράκιον, -κου, τό 55

Zeus Ζεύς, Διός, ὁ 33

ἀγγέλλω, ἀγγελῶ, ἤγγειλα, ἤγγελκα, ἤγγελμαι, ἠγγέλθην *announce, report*
ἄγω, ἄξω, ἤγαγον, ἦχα, ἦγμαι, ἤχθην *lead, bring*
ἀδικέω, ἀδικήσω, ἠδίκησα, ἠδίκηκα, ἠδίκημαι, ἠδικήθην *injure, wrong, do
wrong (to)*
ἀθροίζω, ἀθροίσω, ἤθροισα, ἤθροικα, ἤθροισμαι, ἠθροίσθην *collect*
αἱρέω, αἱρήσω, εἷλον, ᾕρηκα, ᾕρημαι, ᾑρέθην *take, seize, capture*; (mid.) *choose*
αἰσθάνομαι, αἰσθήσομαι, ᾐσθόμην, ____, ᾔσθημαι, ____ (+ gen. of person,
acc. of thing) *perceive, learn* (by perception), *hear*
αἰτέω, αἰτήσω, ᾔτησα, ____, ᾔτημαι, ____ *ask (for), demand*
αἰτιάομαι, αἰτιάσομαι, ᾐτιασάμην, ____, ᾐτίαμαι, ____ *blame*
ἀκολουθέω, ἀκολουθήσω, ____, ____, ____, ____ (+dat.) *follow, accompany*
ἀκούω, ἀκούσομαι, ἤκουσα, ἀκήκοα, ____, ἠκούσθην (+ gen.) *hear, listen to*
ἁλίσκομαι, ἁλώσομαι, ἑάλων, ἑάλωκα ____, ____ (used as passive of αἱρέω)
be taken, be caught, be captured, be convicted
ἁμαρτάνω, ἁμαρτήσομαι, ἥμαρτον, ἡμάρτηκα, ἡμάρτημαι, ἡμαρτήθην
miss (+gen.); *err*
ἀναβαίνω, ἀναβήσομαι, ἀνέβην, ἀναβέβηκα ____, ____ *go up*
ἀναγιγνώσκω *read*
ἀναγκάζω, ἀναγκάσω, ἠνάγκασα, ἠνάγκακα, ἠνάγκασμαι, ἠναγκάσθην
force, compel
ἀνατίθημι *refer; dedicate*; (mid.) *retract* (an opinion)
ἀξιόω, ἀξιώσω, ἠξίωσα, ἠξίωκα, ἠξίωμαι, ἠξιώθην *think worthy, think right;
believe, expect, request* (+ acc. and infin.)
ἀπέχω, ἀφέξω (ἀποσχήσω), ἀπέσχον, ____, ____, ____ *keep away*; (+ gen.)
be away from; (mid.) (+ gen.) *abstain from*
ἀποθνήσκω, ἀποθανοῦμαι, ἀπέθανον, τέθνηκα, ____, ____ *die, be killed*
ἀποκρίνομαι, ἀποκρινοῦμαι, ἀπεκρινάμην, ____, ἀποκέκριμαι, ____
answer, reply
ἀποκτείνω, ἀποκτενῶ, ἀπέκτεινα, ἀπέκτονα, ____, ____ *kill*
ἀπόλλυμι, ἀπολῶ, ἀπώλεσα, ἀπολώλεκα, ____, ____ (act.) *destroy, lose; die,
perish*
ἀπολογέομαι, ἀπολογήσομαι, ἀπελογησάμην, ____, ἀπολελόγημαι, ____
defend oneself, make a defense
ἀπορέω, ἀπορήσω, ἠπόρησα, ἠπόρηκα, ἠπόρημαι, ἠπορήθην *be at a loss*
ἅπτομαι, ἅψομαι, ἡψάμην, ____, ἧμμαι, ____ (+ gen.) *touch*
ἁρπάζω, ἁρπάσομαι, ἥρπασα, ἥρπακα, ἥρπασμαι, ἡρπάσθην *seize*
ἄρχω, ἄρξω, ἦρξα, ἦρχα, ἦργμαι, ἤρχθην (+ gen.) *rule*; (mid.) *begin*
ἀφικνέομαι, ἀφίξομαι, ἀφικόμην, ____, ἀφῖγμαι ____ (with εἰς or ἐπί +
acc.) *arrive (in), arrive (at), reach*

βάλλω, βαλῶ, ἔβαλον, βέβληκα, βέβλημαι, ἐβλήθην *throw, hit*
βιάζομαι, βιασθήσομαι, ἐβιασάμην, ____, βεβίασμαι, ἐβιάσθην *force,
constrain, act violently*
βιόω, βιώσομαι, ἐβίων, βεβίωκα, βεβίωται, ____ *live, be alive*

βλάπτω, βλάψω, ἔβλαψα, βέβλαφα, βέβλαμμαι, ἐβλάφθην (ἐβλάβην) *harm, hurt*
βοαω, βοήσομαι, ἐβόησα, ____, ____, ____ *shout, call out*
βουλεύω, βουλεύσω, ἐβούλευσα, βεβούλευκα, βεβούλευμαι, ἐβουλεύθην *plan*; (mid.) *deliberate*
βούλομαι, βουλήσομαι, ____, ____, βεβούλημαι, ἐβουλήθην *want, prefer*

γελάω, γελάσομαι, ἐγέλασα, ____, ____, ἐγελάσθην *laugh (at)*
γίγνομαι, γενήσομαι, ἐγενόμην, γέγονα, γεγένημαι, ____ *become; be; happen; prove to be; be born*
γιγνώσκω, γνώσομαι, ἔγνων, ἔγνωκα, ἔγνωσμαι, ἐγνώσθην *know* (by observation), *perceive, recognize*
γράφω, γράψω, ἔγραψα, γέγραφα, γέγραμμαι, ἐγράφην *write*

____, ____ ἔδεισα, δέδοικα (δέδια) *fear, be afraid (of)*
δεῖ, δεήσει, δεήσει, ἐδέησε ____, ____ (+ acc. and infin.) *it is necessary, must, ought*
δείκνυμι, δείξω, ἔδειξα, δέδειχα, δέδειγμαι, ἐδείχθην *show, point out*
δέομαι, δεήσομαι, ____, ____, ____, ἐδεήθην (+ gen.) *ask; need*
δέχομαι, δέξομαι, ἐδεξάμην ____, δέδεγμαι, ἐδέχθην *receive, accept*
δηλόω, δηλώσω, ἐδήλωσα, δεδήλωκα, δεδήλωμαι, ἐδηλώθην *make clear, reveal, show*
διαβαίνω, διαβήσομαι, διέβην, διαβέβηκα, ____, ____ *go across, cross*
διαγίγνομαι *go through, pass* (of time); *go through life, live, survive*
διαλέγομαι, διαλέξομαι, διελεξάμην, ____, διείλεγμαι, διελέχθην (+ dat.) *converse (with)*
διανοέομαι, διανοήσομαι, διενοησάμην, ____, διανενόημαι, διενοήθην *think, have in mind, intend*
διατελέω, διατελέσω, διετέλεσα, διατετέλεκα, ____, ____ (+ participle) *continue*
διαφθείρω, διαφθερῶ, διέφθειρα, διέφθαρκα, διέφθαρμαι, διεφθάρην *corrupt, ruin*
διδάσκω, διδάξω, ἐδίδαξα, δεδίδαχα, δεδίδαγμαι, ἐδιδάχθην *teach*
δίδωμι, δώσω, ἔδωκα, δέδωκα, δέδομαι, ἐδόθην *give*
διηγέομαι, διηγήσομαι, διηγησάμην, ____, διήγημαι, ____ *describe*
διώκω, διώξω, ἐδίωξα, δεδίωκα, ____, ἐδιώχθην *pursue; prosecute*
δοκέω, δόξω, ἔδοξα, ____, δέδογμαι, ____ *think, imagine; seem, be thought;* (impers.) *it seems best*
δοκιμάζω, δοκιμάσω, ἐδοκίμασα, ____, δεδοκίμασμαι, ἐδοκιμάσθην *test, put to the test, approve*
δουλεύω, δουλεύσω, ἐδούλευσα *be a slave*
δύναμαι, δυνήσομαι, ____, ____, δεδύνημαι, ἐδυνήθην *be able, can*

ἐάω, ἐάσω, εἴασα, εἴακα, εἴαμαι, εἰάθην *allow; let go*

ἐθέλω, ἐθελήσω, ἠθέλησα, ἠθέληκα, ____, ____ *wish, be willing*
εἰμί, ἔσομαι, ____, ____, ____, ____ *be*
εἶμι *go*
ἐλέγχω, ἐλέγξω, ἤλεγξα, ____, ἐλήλεγμαι, ἠλέγχθην *refute, cross-examine*
ἐλπίζω, ____, ἤλπιϰα, ____, ____, ____ *hope, hope for, expect*
ἐναντιόομαι, ἐναντιώσομαι, ____, ____, ἠναντίωμαι, ἠναντιώθην (+ dat.)
    oppose, forbid
ἐντυγχάνω (+ dat.) *meet*
ἐπαινέω, ἐπαινέσομαι, ἐπῄνεσα, ἐπῄνεκα, ἐπῄνημαι, ἐπῃνέθην *praise,*
    approve
ἐπιβουλεύω, ἐπιβουλεύσω, ἐπεβούλευσα, ἐπιβεβούλευκα,
    (+ dat.) *plot against*
ἐπιθυμέω, ἐπιθυμήσω, ἐπεθύμησα *desire* (+ gen. or infin. or infin. and subj.
    acc.)
ἐπιλανθάνομαι, ἐπιλήσομαι, ἐπελαθόμην, ____, ἐπιλέλησμαι, ____ (+
    gen.) *forget*
ἐπιμελέομαι, ἐπιμελήσομαι, ἐπεμελησάμην, ____, ἐπιμεμέλημαι,
    (+ gen.) *take care (of), care for*
ἐπινοέω, ἐπινοήσω, ἐπενόησα, ____, ____, ____ *have in mind, intend*
ἐπίσταμαι, ἐπιστήσομαι, ____, ____, ____, ἠπιστήθην *know* (as a fact), *know*
    how (+ infin.)
ἐπιτίθημι (+ acc. and dat.) *place upon, apply, impose*
ἐπιτρέπω, ἐπιτρέψω, ἐπέτρεψα, ἐπιτέτροφα, ἐπιτέτραμμαι, ἐπετρέφθην
    entrust, permit
ἐπιχειρέω *put one's hand to, attempt*
ἕπομαι, ἕψομαι, ἑσπόμην, ____, ____, ____ (+ dat.) *follow*
ἐργάζομαι, ἐργάσομαι, εἰργασάμην, ____, εἴργασμαι, εἰργάσθην *do*
    (something to someone; + two accusatives), *perform, make*
ἔρομαι, ἐρήσομαι, ἠρόμην, ____, ____, ____ *ask*
ἔρχομαι, ἐλεύσομαι, ἦλθον, ἐλήλυθα ____, ____ *come; go*
____, ἐρῶ, εἶπον, εἴρηκα, εἴρημαι, ἐρρήθην *say, tell, speak*
ἐρωτάω, ἐρωτήσω, ἠρώτησα, ἠρώτηκα, ἠρώτημαι, ἠρωτήθην *ask*
εὑρίσκω, εὑρήσω, εὗρον (ηὗρον), εὕρηκα (ηὕρηκα), εὕρημαι, εὑρέθην *find*
εὔχομαι, εὔξομαι, ηὐξάμην, ____, ηὖγμαι, ____ *pray (for), vow, boast*
ἐφίστημι (+ acc. and dat.) *place upon, set over*
ἔχω, ἕξω (σχήσω), ἔσχον, ἔσχηκα, ____, ____ *have*

ζάω, ζήσω, ____, ____, ____, ____ *live, be alive*
ζητέω, ζητήσω, ἐζήτησα, ἐζήτηκα, ____, ____ *seek, search for*

ἡγέομαι, ἡγήσομαι, ἡγησάμην, ____, ἥγημαι, ____ *lead; be leader of* (+ gen.), *be*
    leader for (dat.); *think, consider*
ἥδομαι, ἡσθήσομαι, ____, ____, ____, ἥσθην (+ dat.) *be pleased (with)*
ἥκω, ἥξω ____, ____, ____, ____ *have come, come, arrive*

θάπτω, θάψω, ἔθαψα, _____, τέθαμμαι, ἐτάφην *bury*

θαυμάζω, θαυμάσομαι, ἐθαύμασα, τεθαύμακα, τεθαύμασμαι, *admire, wonder (at), be amazed*

θύω, θύσω, ἔθυσα, τέθυκα, τέθυμαι, ἐτύθην *sacrifice*

ἵημι, -ἥσω, -ἧκα, -εἷκα, -εἷμαι, -εἵθην *let go, throw, send;* (mid.) *hasten, rush; be eager* (+ gen. or infin.)

ἵστημι, στήσω, ἔστησα, ἔστηκα, ἔσταμαι, ἐστάθην *cause to stand, set, set up, place*

καλέω, καλῶ, ἐκάλεσα, κέκληκα, κέκλημαι, ἐκλήθην *call, summon;* (pass.) *be called*

καταγιγνώσκω (+ gen. of person, acc. of thing) *condemn*

κατηγορέω, κατηγορήσω, κατηγόρησα, κατηγόρηκα, κατηγόρημαι, (+ gen. of person, acc. of thing) *accuse*

κελεύω, κελεύσω, ἐκέλευσα, κεκέλευκα, κεκέλευσμαι, ἐκελεύσθην *order, command*

κλέπτω, κλέψω, ἔκλεψα, κέκλοφα, κέκλεμμαι, ἐκλάπην *steal*

κρατέω, κρατήσομαι, ἐκράτησα, κεκράτηκα, κεκράτημαι, ἐκρατήθην *be strong;* (+ gen.) *rule, be master of*

κρίνω, κρινῶ, ἔκρινα, κέκρικα, κέκριμαι, ἐκρίθην *judge*

κτάομαι, κτήσομαι, ἐκτησάμην, _____, κέκτημαι, ἐκτήθην *acquire*

κωλύω, κωλύσω, ἐκώλυσα, κεκώλυκα, κεκώλυμαι, ἐκωλύθην *hinder, prevent*

λαμβάνω, λήψομαι, ἔλαβον, εἴληφα, εἴλημμαι, ἐλήφθην *take, seize; receive*

λανθάνω, λήσω, ἔλαθον, λέληθα, λέλησμαι, _____ (+ participle) *escape the notice of*

λέγω, λέξω, ἔλεξα, _____, λέλεγμαι, ἐλέχθην *say, speak*

λείπω, λείψω, ἔλιπον, λέλοιπα, λέλειμμαι, ἐλείφθην *leave*

λύω, λύσω, ἔλυσα, λέλυκα, λέλυμαι, ἐλύθην *destroy, release, set free*

μανθάνω, μαθήσομαι, ἔμαθον, μεμάθηκα, _____, _____ *learn* (by study); *understand*

μαρτυρέω, μαρτυρήσω, _____, _____, μεμαρτύρημαι, ἐμαρτυρήθην *bear witness, testify*

μάχομαι, μαχοῦμαι, ἐμαχεσάμην, _____, μεμάχημαι, _____ (+ dat.) *fight (with)*

μέλει, μελήσει, ἐμέλησε, μεμέληκε, _____, _____ *care (it is a care)*

μελετάω, μελετήσω, ἐμελέτησα, μεμελέτηκα, μεμελέτημαι, ἐμελετήθην *attend to, study, practice*

μέλλω, μελλήσω, ἐμέλλησα, _____, _____, _____ (+ fut. infin.) *be about (to), intend (to), be likely (to), be going (to)*

μέμνημαι, μεμνήσομαι (μνησθήσομαι), ἐμνήσθην (+ gen.) *remember*

μέμφομαι, μέμψομαι, ἐμεμψάμην, _____, _____, ἐμέμφθην *blame, find fault with*

μένω, μενῶ, ἔμεινα, μεμένηκα, _____, _____ *remain, stay, wait (for)*

μεταπέμπω *summon, send for*
μισέω, ____, ἐμίσησα, μεμίσηκα, μεμίσημαι, ἐμισήθην *hate*

νικάω, νικήσω, ἐνίκησα, νενίκηκα, νενίκημαι, ἐνικήθην *conquer, win*
νομίζω, νομιῶ, ἐνόμισα, νενόμικα, νενόμισμαι, ἐνομίσθην *regard as a custom; think, consider; believe in, believe*

οἶδα, εἴσομαι *know* (by reflection)
οἰκέω, οἰκήσω, ᾤκησα, ᾤκηκα, ᾤκημαι, ᾠκήθην *live (in), inhabit*
οἴομαι (οἶμαι), οἰήσομαι, ____, ____, ____, ᾠήθην *think, suppose*
ὁμολογέω, ὁμολογήσω, ὡμολόγησα, ὡμολόγηκα, ὡμολόγημαι (+ dat.) *agree with, agree*
ὁράω, ὄψομαι, εἶδον, ἑώρακα, ἑώραμαι, ὤφθην *see*

παιδεύω, παιδεύσω, ἐπαίδευσα, πεπαίδευκα, πεπαίδευμαι, ἐπαιδεύθην *educate*
παρασκευάζω, παρασκευάσω, παρεσκεύασα, παρεσκεύακα, *prepare;* (mid.) *make preparations*
πάρειμι, παρέσομαι ____, ____, ____, ____ *be present*
παρέχω, παρέξω (παρασχήσω), παρέσχον, παρέσχηκα, ____, ____ *provide, furnish*
πάσχω, πείσομαι, ἔπαθον, πέπονθα, ____, ____ *suffer*
παύω, παύσω, ἔπαυσα, πέπαυκα, πέπαυμαι, ἐπαύθην *stop;* (mid.) *cease*
πείθω, πείσω, ἔπεισα, πέπεικα, πέπεισμαι, ἐπείσθην *persuade;* (mid.) *obey* (+ dat.)
πειράομαι, πειράσομαι, ἐπειρασάμην, ____, πεπείραμαι, ἐπειράθην *try, attempt*
πέμπω, πέμψω, ἔπεμψα, πέπομφα, πέπεμμαι, ἐπέμφθην *send*
πίπτω, πεσοῦμαι, ἔπεσον, πέπτωκα, ____, ____ *fall; fall out, turn out*
πιστεύω, πιστεύσω, ἐπίστευσα, πεπίστευκα, πεπίστευμαι, ἐπιστεύθην (+ dat.) *trust*
πλέω, πλεύσομαι, ἔπλευσα, πέπλευκα, πέπλευσμαι, ____ *sail*
ποίεω, ποιήσω, ἐποίησα, πεποίηκα, πεποίημαι, ἐποιήθην *make, do*
πορεύομαι, πορεύσομαι, ἐπορευσάμην, ____, πεπόρευμαι, ἐπορεύθην *go, march, proceed, advance*
πράττω, πράξω, ἔπραξα, πέπραχα, πέπραγμαι, ἐπράχθην *do; make; achieve*
πυνθάνομαι, πεύσομαι, ἐπυθόμην, ____, πέπυσμαι, ____ (+ gen. of person, acc. of thing) *learn* (by hearsay or inquiry), *inquire*

ῥίπτω, ῥίψω, ἔρριψα, ἔρριφα, ἔρριμμαι, ἐρρίφθην *throw, throw away*

σιγάω, σιγήσομαι, ἐσίγησα, σεσίγηκα, σεσίγημαι, ἐσιγήθην *be silent*
σκοπέω, σκέψομαι, ἐσκεψάμην, ____, ἔσκεμμαι, ____ *consider, examine*
σπεύδω, σπεύσω, ἔσπευσα, ____, ____, ____ *hasten, hurry*

συγχωρέω, συγχωρήσω, συνεχώρησα, συγκεχώρηκα, συγκεχώρημαι,
 (+ dat.) *agree, concede*
συμβαίνω *agree; happen*
συμβουλεύω, συμβουλεύσω, συνεβούλευσα, συμβεβούλευκα,
 (+ dat.) *advise*; (mid.) *consult (with), ask the advice of*
σύνειμι, συνέσομαι (+ dat.) *be with, associate with*
σφάττω, σφάξω, ἔσφαξα, _____, ἔσφαγμαι, ἐσφάγην *slay, kill*
σώζω, σώσω, ἔσωσα, σέσωκα, σέσωσμαι, ἐσώθην *save, bring safely*

τάττω, τάξω, ἔταξα, τέταχα, τέταγμαι, ἐτάχθην *draw up, station, arrange, assign*
τελευτάω, τελευτήσω, ἐτελεύτησα, τετελεύτηκα, _____, ἐτελευτήθην *finish;*
 die
τίθημι, θήσω, ἔθηκα, τέθηκα, _____, ἐτέθην *put, place; make* (with persons)
τιμάω, τιμήσω, ἐτίμησα, τετίμηκα, τετίμημαι, ἐτιμήθην *honor*
τιμωρέω, τιμωρήσω, ἐτιμωρησάμην, _____, τετιμώρημαι, ἐτιμωρήθην
 avenge; (mid.) *punish, take vengeance on*
τολμάω, τολμήσω, ἐτόλμησα, τετόλμηκα, τετόλμημαι, ἐτολμήθην *dare*
τρέπω, τρέψω, ἔτρεψα, τέτροφα, τέτραμμαι, ἐτράπην *turn*
τρέφω, θρέψω, ἔθρεψα, τέτροφα, τέθραμμαι, ἐτράφην *nourish, raise, support*
τρέχω, δραμοῦμαι, ἔδραμον, -δεδράμηκα, -δεδράμημαι, _____ *run*
τυγχάνω, τεύξομαι, ἔτυχον, τετύχηκα, _____, _____ (+ participle) *happen*; (+
 gen.) *gain, hit, meet*
τύπτω, τυπτήσω, ἔπαισα, πέπληγα, πέπληγμαι, ἐπλήγην *beat, strike*

ὑπισχνέομαι, ὑποσχήσομαι, ὑπεσχόμην, _____, ὑπέσχημαι, _____ (+ fut.
 infin.) *promise*
ὑπολαμβάνω *take up; suppose, interrupt, reply*

φαίνω, φανῶ, ἔφηνα, πέφηνα, πέφασμαι, ἐφάνην *show, reveal*; (mid.) *appear*
φείδομαι, φείσομαι, ἐφεισάμην, _____, _____, _____ (+ gen.) *spare*
φέρω, οἴσω, ἤνεγκα, ἐνήνοχα, ἐνήνεγμαι, ἠνέχθην *carry, bring, bear*
φεύγω, φεύξομαι, ἔφυγον, πέφευγα, _____, _____ *flee, escape, avoid*
φημί, φήσω, ἔφησα *say*
φιλέω, φιλήσω, ἐφίλησα, πεφίληκα, πεφίλημαι, ἐφιλήθην *love*
φοβέομαι, φοβήσομαι, _____, _____, πεφόβημαι, ἐφοβήθην *fear, be afraid*
φυλάττω, φυλάξω, ἐφύλαξα, πεφύλαχα, πεφύλαγμαι, ἐφυλάχθην *guard*
φράζω, φράσω, ἔφρασα, πέφρακα, πέφρασμαι, ἐφράσθην *tell, declare,*
 explain; (mid.) *ponder, contrive, perceive*
φρονέω, φρονήσω, ἐφρόνησα, πεφρόνηκα *have understanding, think, mean*
φροντίζω, φροντιῶ, ἐφρόντισα, πεφρόντικα, _____, _____ *consider, ponder* ;
 think about, take thought for (+ gen.)

χράομαι, χρήσομαι, ἐχρησάμην, _____, κέχρημαι, ἐχρήσθην (+ dat.) *use;*
 enjoy; treat; consult (an oracle)

χρή (impersonal verb, used with acc. and infin.) *it is necessary, must, ought*

ψεύδω, ψεύσω, ἔψευσα, _____, ἔψευσμαι, ἐψεύσθην deceive; (mid.) lie

ὠφελέω, ὠφελήσω, ὠφέλησα, ὠφέληκα, ὠφέλημαι, ὠφελήθην *help, aid*